Luther

Luther

The Life and Longing of Luther Vandross

Craig Seymour

 HarperEntertainment

An Imprint of HarperCollins*Publishers*

HarperCollins books may be purchased for educational, business, or sales promotional use. For information please write: Special Markets Department, HarperCollins Publishers Inc., 10 East 53rd Street, New York, NY 10022.

FIRST EDITION

Designed by Amy Hill

Printed on acid-free paper

Library of Congress Cataloging-in-Publication Data

Seymour, Craig.
  Luther : the life and longing of Luther Vandross / by Craig Seymour.
    p. cm.
  ISBN 0-06-059418-7 (hardcover)
    1. Vandross, Luther. 2. Rhythm and blues musicians—United States—Biography.
  I. Title.

  ML420.V272S49 2004
  782.421643'092—dc22
  [B]   2004047547

04 05 06 07 08 WBC/RRD 10 9 8 7 6 5 4 3 2 1

For Mom, Dad, Eric, and Seth

"There are vocalists, and then there's Luther. Luther's in a class by himself."

—SMOKEY ROBINSON

Contents

Acknowledgments

Thanks to everyone who has supported this book and my career.

To my agent, Caron K (thanks for taking a chance); my editor, Maureen O'Brien (for the subtle yet pitch-perfect guidance); and her assistant, Lindsey Moore.

To my miracle-working, life-saving photo editor, Diane Allford (www.allfordtrotman.com).

To everyone who talked with me about Luther for this book and previous projects: David Nathan (your devotion to Soul is an inspiration), Cissy Houston, Jaheim, Wayne Garfield, Delores Hall, Tony Silvester, Patrick Adams, Mike Garson, Michael Braver, David Sanborn, Christine Wiltshire, Phoebe Snow, Vince Aletti, and all of the others who wished to remain anonymous.

To supportive editors, colleagues, and friends (and those who cross the lines): DJ Mandrill, Jim Marks, Randy Schulman, Larry Villegas, Richard Harrington, Alona Wartofsky, Pam Strother, Eric Weisbard, Robert Christgau, Alan Light, Sia Michel, Michael Small, Mark Bautz, David Browne, Dulcy Israel, John McAlley, Tom Sinclair, Clarissa Cruz, Liane Bonin, Josh Wolk, Laura Morgan, Sue LoTempio, Toni Ruberto, Biff Warren, Mike Lupo, Eileen

Drennen (a frequent lifesaver), Sonia Murray, Shane Harrison, L Z Granderson, Jay Croft, and David Wahlberg (I think).

To the *VIBE* crew: Shani Saxon (I'm so happy for you), Emil Wilbekin (for believing), and Mimi Valdes (congrats on the well-deserved new gig).

To E. Lynn Harris and Michael Eric Dyson for the show of brotherhood.

To my favorite Toronto buddy for Wednesdays.

To Ria for keeping me company.

To Dr. Sheri Parks for always having faith in me and my crazy ideas.

To my oft-neglected friend Michael Dumas for still caring after all these years.

To Lucinda Moore (Sorry about Prince).

To my grandmothers (Vanilla Beane and Matilda Dawson) and the rest of my family, including those members who have gone home: Willie Beane, Louise Beane, William Dawson, and Joseph Shine.

Lastly, to a soul sista (in every sense): Valerie Boyd. (I couldn't even write these acknowledgments without you. To Hollywood and beyond.)

Luther

1

"Little Miracles (Happen Every Day)"

"Hang in there. God is able."

—ARETHA FRANKLIN TO LUTHER VANDROSS
FOLLOWING HIS STROKE-INDUCED COMA

April 16, 2003

It was morning as Max Szadek raced to his boss's apartment. Thoughts ran through his mind while he moved through the Manhattan streets. For ten years, Szadek had worked as personal assistant to R&B superstar Luther Vandross, and he was on his way to accompany the singer to the recording studio. It was a bright spring day, perfect for enjoying the eye-popping view from Luther's new condo overlooking the lush greenery of Central Park. But there was no time for that on this day. There was too much to do—way too much.

Like most entertainers, Luther maintained a full schedule, but the upcoming weeks promised to be especially taxing. The singer, who would turn fifty-two in four days, needed to finish recording his new album to be called *Dance with My Father*, review tapes for a future live album, and oversee extensive renovations on his apartment. Then there were the gowns he promised to design for Aretha Franklin's farewell tour, a stint as guest judge on the popular TV talent show *American Idol*, and preparation for a full slate of concert dates.

His itinerary also included an appearance at the April opening of the Stax Museum of American Soul Music in Memphis, a four-night gig at the Westbury Music Fair in May, and a headlining spot at the Essence Music Festival in July. More immediately, at the end of the week he had to leave for a lengthy promotional tour touting the new album. The commitments were stacking on top of each other like a house of cards, and Max was going to tell his boss that it had become too much for him, that things were getting out of hand.

This was Max's plan upon arriving at the apartment, but he soon discovered that nothing that day would go as expected. He tried entering the apartment, but the chain was locked from the inside. He knocked and yelled out to Luther. There was no response. At this point, Max began to worry. He called Luther's business manager, Carmen Romano, on his cell phone and described the situation.

"What should I do?" Max asked.

Carmen, who incidentally had just left Tiffany's where he'd bought Luther a birthday present, told him to break down the door. When Max finally entered the apartment, he found Luther collapsed on the floor. He couldn't move, but he was conscious and made two requests: one was for a glass of water, the other for someone to phone his mother.

"Call my momma," he said. "Get my momma."

An ambulance came and rushed him to the Weill Cornell Medical Center, which sits along the East River in Upper Manhattan. Upon arriving, Luther opened his eyes once. Then, just as suddenly, he closed them for what would be many weeks. Doctors examined Luther and determined that he had experienced a stroke, or what some clinicians call "a brain attack." However, where most strokes occur because a blood vessel becomes blocked, Luther suffered a more severe, less common kind in which a blood vessel ruptures, filling the brain with fluid, destroying tissue in its path. It's as if the normal blood flow goes haywire, traveling to places it shouldn't go and abandoning spots where it's needed. If this didn't make the situation dire enough, other factors deeply concerned Luther's doctors. For one, he had lost consciousness, an extremely rare occurrence for stroke victims. This made it nearly impossible to check for neurological damage. Second, there was the unfortunate way Luther was found. Chances for recovery dramatically increase if stroke victims receive treatment within three hours, but Luther was alone on his apartment floor for at least seven hours before Max arrived, placing him in increased jeopardy.

Soon after Luther's admittance to the hospital, word of his condition started to spread. Of course, this wasn't the first time there had been grim news about Luther's health. In 1986 there were false reports that Luther was near death with AIDS. In 2001 it was wrongly reported that he had died from the condition. Now, sadly, the bad news reports were true. His record company issued a tersely worded statement from his manager, Romano: "Luther Vandross suffered from a stroke on Wednesday, April 16th. He is under medical care and his family and friends are hopeful for a speedy recovery." Other accounts were more graphic. A source in the *New York Daily News* called the stroke "a major bleed," and added "he may never sing again."

A stroke is the worst kind of ailment for a vocalist, especially one with Luther's precision and sensitivity. If the stroke damaged the left side of his brain, it could wipe out his ability to speak. If it affected the right side of the brain, it could impact the way he experiences and perceives emotions.

In the days following the stroke, Luther showed few signs of what most would call life. A machine did his breathing, and he was fed by a tube. His birthday came and went on April 20, but still no response. By April 23, a spokeswoman said he was "battling for his life."

Luther's mother, Mary Ida Vandross, clocked many hours by her ailing son's bedside. It was a sadly familiar scene for her, helplessly watching a loved one struggle for life. In her seventy-nine years, she had buried her mother, her husband, and all three of her other children: Charles in 1992, Patricia in 1993, and Ann in 1999. The first two died from diabetes, the third from asthma. Now she faced the possibility of losing Luther, her youngest, the baby. It was almost too much to bear.

"He has to recover," she said. "He's all I have left. He's my last surviving child."

As more people learned about Luther's condition, many of his celebrity friends reached out to support him.

"It's upsetting to hear this news," said rocker David Bowie, who gave Luther his first big break as a background singer in 1974. "Still, we know he'll make it through this."

At the hospital, Luther's family received calls and get-well wishes from a host of celebrities: Aretha Franklin, Halle Berry, Patti La-Belle, Burt Bacharach, Star Jones, Gladys Knight, Dionne Warwick, and others. However, only relatives were allowed to see him.

"If he could have friends visit him in the hospital," said a spokeswoman, "it would be a who's who of show business."

Fans reached out as well. Cards and letters lined Luther's hospital room from floor to ceiling, and more than 10,000 well-wishers sent messages to a specially created e-mail address: tolutherwithlove@luthervandross.com.

This outpouring from fans spoke to the intense bond that Luther has formed with listeners throughout his more than two decade–long career. With his easy delivery and thoughtful phrasing, Luther singularly redefined R&B music. Before he hit the scene, male soul singing was rooted in the church. Think Teddy Pendergrass' spirit-shaking growls or the heavenly croons of Marvin Gaye or Al Green. Luther's musical reference point, however, wasn't gutbucket gospel but the smooth harmonic sounds of the vocal groups of the fifties and sixties. When Luther sang, he swapped sanctified testifying for poignant reflection, raw heat for fireside warmth.

This approach enabled him to sell over 20 million albums and fill up concert venues across the world; but more importantly, it helped him form an intimate connection with his followers, who incorporated his music into their everyday lives. Folks married to the exuberant "Here and Now," nursed heartaches with the haunting "Any Love," and sometimes reconciled through his yearning, nearly operatic take on Dionne Warwick's "A House Is Not a Home"—a performance so moving that even Warwick considers Luther's take to be the definitive version. Basketball legend Magic Johnson made sure that Luther was playing in the delivery room when his first child was born. People don't just listen to Luther. They *live* Luther.

On April 23, friends Aretha Franklin and Jesse Jackson tried to channel all of this love by calling for a national prayer vigil. They wanted people to stop whatever they were doing at noon and take a few moments to ask God to help Luther. What most of those praying didn't know at the time was that Luther's condition had worsened. He now battled meningitis, an infection of the membranes around the brain and spinal cord, and pneumonia, which caused his lungs to fill with fluid, blocking the passage of air.

To treat these problems, doctors injected Luther with a steady stream of antibiotics, then performed a tracheotomy—where an incision is made in the trachea, or windpipe—to help drain the lungs. This was risky to perform on a world-class singer since the trachea is so close to the larynx, which holds the vocal chords, but the surgery was done in such a way that his voice wouldn't be affected.

Throughout this invasive procedure, Luther was completely sedated. Everyone hoped that once the heavy anesthesia wore off, he would also emerge from his coma. Hours passed by, then days. Yet Luther's eyes remained closed. An anonymous source told the press that doctors feared he might be brain-dead. On April 30, his record label spokeswoman released a rather sullen statement: "There was a real feeling that he would've regained consciousness by now. I think it's a day-to-day analysis of the situation. No one really knows what to expect."

What made things even more frustrating was that there had been so many signs that something was wrong with Luther before the stroke—something he chose to ignore. One of the primary symptoms of an impending stroke is a persistent headache, and Luther had long been complaining that his head hurt.

"He called me the very same day [he had the stroke] and said, 'Momma, I've had a headache for six days,'" Mary Ida recalled. "He should have gone to the hospital the second or third day. Six days is too long to have a headache."

Yet, uncharacteristically, Luther ignored his body's warnings.

"I think he was afraid to go to the doctor," manager Romano explained, "because he had gained a lot of weight and he just didn't want to get a lecture about it."

Indeed, Luther's weight had gone up and down more than fourteen times since he was a teenager, from a waistband-stretching high of 340 pounds to a designer jean–wearing low of 140 pounds. His weight fluctuated so much that it became fodder for comedians. Eddie Murphy used to bring down the house in the 1980s when he'd refer to Luther, essentially, as that big, fat Kentucky Fried Chicken eater.

Luther sometimes made light of his weight. One time, he even brought a bunch of Kentucky Fried Chicken buckets onstage with him. It was funny for some. Yet the situation was critical. The extra pounds and soul food–loving eating habits had made him diabetic, meaning that his body failed to produce enough of the chemical insulin, placing him at dramatically increased risk for blindness, nerve damage, heart attacks, and strokes. The condition ran a tragic streak through his family history. His father, brother, and a sister all died from it. Luther wanted to live.

His recent weight gain disturbed his mother so much that she confronted him about it the weekend before the stroke. When Luther visited her home in Philadelphia, he seemed to be eating uncontrollably.

"Are you upset about something?" she asked him.

"I don't know," he said. "But when you go to your momma's house, you're supposed to eat."

"Why do you do this to yourself again?" she pleaded in frustration.

"I don't drink," he argued. "I've never drank. I've never smoked. I've never done drugs. . . ."

Then he stopped and simply said, "Momma, I just don't know what to do anymore."

It all seemed so unfair: how it took such enormous effort to make himself smaller.

Thinking back on the days preceding the stroke, as well as the tests and trials that came afterward, Mary Ida sometimes felt herself becoming overwhelmed. The idea of losing Luther scared her to the core, and for a moment this committed evangelist even questioned her faith.

"When you start losing your children, you look at your situation," she said. "And you say, 'What have I done in my life to deserve this?'"

Yet these questioning moments didn't last long.

"I know my grace is sufficient," she thought. "He's going to come through by the grace of God."

For support, she turned to the Scriptures, believing that even in her darkest time "there's nothing too hard for God." She found comfort in these familiar words: "The Lord is my shepherd / I shall not want."

Back at the hospital, efforts continued to revive Luther. Doctors suggested that the family play music for the singer, so the CD player in his room issued a steady stream of his own tunes and favorites from Aretha Franklin, Diana Ross and the Supremes, the Shirelles, and Dionne Warwick. His longtime background vocalists came to sing for him.

Friends tried hard to remain hopeful. Fellow singer Lionel Richie, who affectionately calls Luther "more of a diva than the divas" said: "As soon as he comes out of his coma and realizes his hair isn't in the proper place, and [thinks], 'How do you have me dressed' and 'Where is my Versace,' he'll be out of the hospital in five minutes."

Not all responses were kind, however. Popular New York City radio DJ Star speculated that Luther had the stroke because he was "stressed out" by a "special friend," a reference to rumors about the singer's sexual orientation that have followed him throughout his career. He has never been romantically linked with anyone, male or female, and when he spoke of relationships, he never mentions the gender of the other person involved.

Although Luther is that most conventional type of performer, a balladeer, these rumors give him a certain mystique. Some identify with his need to guard personal wants and desires, others feel protective of him.

When asked about his sexuality, Luther sometimes cracked jokes: "What do you want to know? Am I bicoastal? Yeah, I have a house in Beverly Hills and New York."

Other times these questions seemed to anger him. "I've always paid my own mortgage," he once said. "You know, there's nobody that can come to me and feel they're owed explanations to their suspicions about things. . . . I will neither deny nor confirm any such rumors about whether personal things like that are true or untrue."

Yet, guardedness took a toll.

"Does being so secretive make it hard to find a relationship?" he was once asked.

"Yeah, it does," he answered.

"So, is it worth it?"

"I wonder," he said. "You have come up with the question of recent days. I really wonder if it's worth it."

The irony of Luther's life is that he made a career out of singing love songs, yet he never truly knew love himself.

"I'm still waiting," he once said. "The time that I have spent being in love has never been reciprocated. Those are just the circumstances."

In many ways, this lack of love, this strong yearning for it, infused his singing with a truth and sincerity that only made fans love him more.

On May 19, thousands showed up at Detroit's Little Rock Baptist Church. They gathered to participate in a prayer vigil organized by Aretha Franklin to show renewed support for Luther. Outside, those who couldn't get in held candles that flickered against the night sky. Inside, the Queen of Soul went forth rousing the crowd.

"We're having church tonight," she said. "Can I hear the church say, '*Yeah*'?"

"Yeah," they roared back at her.

She then led them through a number of gospel staples, the kind she grew up singing in her daddy's church. By the time she began

"Amazing Grace," the entire congregation had caught the spirit. People were swaying back and forth in the pews and stomping their feet so hard the whole church shook. It was a joyful noise and a purposeful one.

"I felt [Luther] needed prayer," Aretha said. "And he needed it now."

As days passed by at the hospital, there were small signs that Luther was improving.

"The feeling that we're all getting is a very hopeful one," said a spokeswoman in May, "that he turned the corner in terms of being life or death."

Then one day Mary Ida entered the room and found his face turned to the window, his eyes closed.

She called out to him like she always did, "Your momma's here."

This time, he opened his eyes, smiled, and took a long look at her. Then she noticed his lips. He was trying to form the word "momma."

Within days, his level of alertness soared. He still couldn't speak because of the tracheotomy tube, but he began turning his head and nodding "yes" and "no."

"It was like a friend had come home," said manager Romano. By early June, doctors took Luther off the respirator, upgraded his condition to stable, and moved him from intensive care. Mary Ida felt that her faith had been rewarded: "The Lord is my shepherd / I shall not want."

"There have been some really sincere prayers sent up to heaven," Mary Ida said. "And, I do believe God has heard and he's answering. But you don't hurry God. He comes in His time."

One way family and friends knew Luther was getting better was that he started exhibiting some of his trademark testiness.

"He's being ornery, like the old Luther," said Patti LaBelle, who received daily updates on his recovery from Mary Ida. "His mother says that he's being as bad as he used to be."

One day when Dionne Warwick visited, a nurse asked Luther, "Are you well?" He snapped, "Absolutely not."

Another time, some family members noisily chatted away in his room. "They were just talking, talking, talking," Mary Ida recounted. "So after a minute he looked up and rolled his eyes and pointed toward the door. . . . And his assistant said, 'He means for you guys to get out of here.' We had to laugh."

By June 18, doctors allowed Luther to leave the hospital for a rehabilitation center. Luther's friend Oprah Winfrey was so excited that she announced it on her talk show: "Just this morning before I got out of the makeup chair, I was on the phone with Luther Vandross' manager, Carmen, and Luther is leaving the hospital today. . . . So Luther thanks you for all of your prayers, and keep praying because he starts rehab today."

The next several weeks brought rapid improvements. Ironically, Luther even managed to shed sixty pounds through his intense physical therapy regimen. For five hours a day, he stretched, did toning exercises, and practiced everyday skills like getting in and out of a car. Yet his loved ones felt most heartened when they heard him singing again.

One day he called his mother and said, "I want to sing you a song."

"What?" she asked.

He responded by telling her he was going to sing "So Amazing," one of his gorgeously hopeful love ballads. It was also one of Mary Ida's favorites.

"It has so much deep meaning to me, because he sang it at his niece's wedding," she said. "He [helped] raise this little girl, and the reason I think I love it so much is that when he sang the song, he said to his niece, 'I love you,' and she just broke down. We all hollered and cried."

Before Luther started singing, Mary Ida asked if he needed her help. Since he suffered memory loss, she wondered if he could recall all the lyrics. Luther cracked, "Momma, you're going to have to do a lot of rehearsing first." He then performed the song from beginning to end, and even remembered the year he recorded it: 1986.

One of the mysteries of the mind is how stroke victims can often vividly recall things that happened long ago, but have little short-term memory. On bad days, a disoriented Luther sometimes thought he was backstage at a concert, and when Clive Davis, the president of his current label, J Records, came to visit, Luther remembered him only from their dealings many years ago.

For a time, according to one source, Luther could only seem to remember things that happened ten years ago. If this is indeed true, then his thoughts were stuck in 1993, a turbulent year that brought the death of his sister Patricia, a well-publicized feud with the opening act on his tour that year, En Vogue (the girl group famously dubbed him "Lucifer"), and the painful dissolution of a romantic relationship. As he told the *Chicago Tribune* that year, "I've just been through a devastating breakup."

The process of recovering from a stroke requires Luther to hold onto these memories, however disturbing, less they slip away again. He has to slowly try to weave together the missing pieces of his life if he is ever to recapture or even come close to becoming the person he once was. It's a tediously slow process, for which he himself unconsciously determines the pace. It's as if a narrator in his head must be awakened, called onstage to part the dusty velvet curtains, then announce with grandeur: "Luther, this is your story. This is your life."

2
"Dance with My Father"

"All I know is that he was there one minute and gone the next."

—LUTHER VANDROSS,
ON LOSING HIS FATHER

When Luther started work on his twelfth album in 2002, he knew it had to be special. His previous album was a comeback smash, heralded as a masterful return to form. Luther needed to keep up the momentum. Of course, what every album needs in its early stages is one great song, something that will anchor it and provide the mood and direction for the rest of the recording.

Luther searched his mind for ideas. After decades in the business, it seemed that he had sung about nearly every form of love: good love ("So Amazing"), bad love ("Don't Want to Be a Fool"), matrimonial love ("Here and Now"), even hometown love ("Nights in Harlem"). There was one type, however, that Luther had never committed to song, but it would require him to delve into his personal life, a notoriously touchy place for the singer. Luther had never sung about the love between children and parents. He had always been branded the king of romantic baby-making music, but he had never touched on the relationships between these babies and the people who made them. This was a theme worthy of his twelfth album. This was something that might take his career to heights that he still longed to reach.

Luther worked on the song with his frequent collaborator of recent years, Richard Marx. Though known to most people as the shaggy-haired MTV pretty boy behind such soft-rock hits as "Hold On to the Night," Marx has long been a respected studio musician with pop/R&B chops. As Luther increasingly shot for pop success, Marx was exactly the type of person he wanted to work with.

The song the two composed would come to be known as "Dance with My Father." It starts with delicate, music box–like keyboards over a tippy-tap toy soldier beat. Then Luther's inimitable voice comes in and relays a touching story about his childhood, how he and his parents used to dance together. When Luther's father dies unexpectedly, Luther longs to have those dances back. It's a moving portrait and an unusual expression of paternal affection, especially from a male singer. The song's strength comes from Luther's plaintive, openhearted delivery as an adult soberly expressing the impossible dreams of a child.

When Luther finished recording the tune, he wanted everyone to know about it. He thought that "Dance" would be his "Tears in Heaven," the Grammy-winning, multimillion-selling song that Eric Clapton composed for his dead son. It would make him not only an established R&B rule maker but also a bona fide crossover phenomenon. Luther even sent rough copies of the cut to select radio stations, along with a note calling it "my career song."

However, the person he wanted to hear it the most wasn't part of the music industry. It was his mother.

"Momma, see what you think about this," he said before playing the song. The childlike melody began. She heard Luther's words start flowing over the simple track, and before long a whole host of feelings welled up inside of her.

"You could probably hear me crying all the way to your house when I heard it," she once joked with a reporter. "For him to have remembered everything as vividly as he did was shocking to me. . . . I never knew he was that deep with his father. [Luther] is a very serious person and a very private person."

Once released to the public, regrettably after Luther's stroke, the song quickly became a hit, moving people with its mix of memory and yearning. It was an all-too-rare peek into the singer's early years, a time that shaped the man he was to become and a time marked by a near tragedy that almost ended his life before it began.

When Mary Ida Vandross was carrying her fourth child in the wintry early months of 1951, she soon realized this wouldn't be like her other pregnancies. First there were the cravings that came over her in a rush. She hungered for the starchy taste of pasta, but it couldn't be just any kind. Only one brand would do: Ronzoni, which came in long, bright blue-and-yellow boxes bearing the slogan, "Ronzoni . . . sono buoni . . . Ronzoni is so good." Sometimes that was all she could keep down as months passed by, the baby growing steadily inside her.

Then there were other differences, the worst of which came to light one evening at Harlem's Audubon Ballroom when Mary Ida almost lost it all. With its sprawling dance floor and grand art nouveau design, the Audubon was a place for everyday black folks to dress up in their most hard-earned finery and celebrate all the joys that the segregated outside world hadn't stripped away: things like style, rhythm, melody, and love. Mary Ida was there on the arm of her husband, Luther. Though seven months pregnant, she wasn't concerned about how dancing might affect her condition.

"It never bothered me," she later explained, "because I danced with all of my children." However, this night wasn't like the others. One minute she was enjoying the music and all of the couples parading in their black and tan glory. The next minute, she said, "I passed out."

When she awoke, she was at Bellevue Hospital, where a doctor was giving her husband some terrifying news. "Your wife's appendix has ruptured," he told Mr. Vandross. "We might not be able to save both her and the baby. What should we do?" He thought it over for a moment, and then answered solemnly, "Just save my wife."

It was a heartbreaking decision, but ultimately an unnecessary one. "By the grace of God," as Mary Ida told the story, both she and her child pulled through, and on Friday, April 20, 1951—a warm spring day in Manhattan—she gave birth to a boy. He came out looking just like her, with deep earth-brown skin and big chocolate eyes, and he nearly had a full head of hair that shot up sideways in a big bushy tuft.

When it came time to name him, she chose to honor her husband, who had been such an unflinching source of strength. His name was Luther, his father had been Luther, and now his youngest son would be called Luther, too. For his middle name, Mary Ida paid her respects to something else that had supported her throughout the pregnancy, that brand of pasta that eased so many restless days and nights: Ronzoni. Thus, the baby's full name was Luther Ronzoni Vandross, but mostly everyone—including brother Charles and sisters Ann and Patricia—would call him Ronnie.

The year Luther was born, the country stood in the midst of a war against communist forces in North Korea. (Indeed, while Mary Ida was in the hospital giving birth to Luther, a group of 60,000—one of the largest assemblies ever in New York City—

showed up at City Hall to welcome General Douglas MacArthur, who had commanded the troops in Korea before being ousted due to a disagreement with President Harry Truman.) Also that year, a Jewish couple, Julius and Ethel Rosenberg, received death sentences for giving atomic secrets to the Russians; Senator Joseph McCarthy of Wisconsin waged a crusade to ferret out so-called anti-American forces in the government and media; and New York City schoolchildren were issued necklaces for identification in the event of a nuclear strike.

Not all of the year's news was so weighty, though. The cracklingly witty backstage drama *All About Eve* took the Oscar for Best Picture, J. D. Salinger wrote the primer on adolescent angst with his novel *The Catcher in the Rye*, and an uproarious redhead named Lucille Ball made her large-scale introduction to TV audiences in a show called *I Love Lucy*.

On the music scene, a song hit the R&B charts just one month after Luther's birth that would forever change how teenagers danced, how guitarists approached their instrument, and how youngsters with fantasies of pop stardom shaped their dreams. It was recorded by a group of young black men out of Clarksdale, Mississippi.

One day, when they were making the seventy-five-mile drive from Clarksdale to Memphis, Tennessee, in somebody's old run-down Buick, a tire blew, causing them to screech to a halt and making the bass amp fly from the top of the roof. By the time they got to the studio, all they could think about was how nice it would be to have a new car, especially one of those Rocket 88 Oldsmobiles that had just come out. The band then decided to put their thoughts on wax, and the single "Rocket 88" was soon issued on Chess Records. Though the group had been started by a slick, lean guitarist named Ike Turner (who would later marry a young singer named Anna Mae Bullock, whom he would rechristen Tina), the record was released under the name Jackie Brenston and the Delta Cats because the tune had initially been saxophonist Brenston's idea. Nevertheless, the cut went on to become not only a smash but what Sam Phillips—the man who helped discover and groom Elvis Presley—would call the very first rock-and-roll record.

The swinging beat, strumming guitars, and hellfire piano of "Rocket 88" were just a few examples of how rapidly the world was changing, particularly for black Americans. There were many signs that after years of painful segregation and discrimination, things were going to be different—better. Further integration of the armed forces was seen in 1951, as well as many "firsts": Janet Collins became the first black prima ballerina when she performed at the Metropolitan Opera House, and tennis player Althea Gibson made history as the first black American to play in the Wimbledon tournament in England. Nevertheless, even with these signs of progress, there were still reasons to be cautious. Every step forward seemed to be met by a stumble backward. For every law passed making it easier for somebody to go about their daily business, another mother's son seemed to be found swinging from a tree. It was also the year when Florida NAACP officials Harry Moure and his wife, two tireless antilynching advocates, were killed by a bomb in their home. No arrests were ever made. Yet even in the face of these horrors, it was still an undeniably hopeful time to be raising black children, knowing they would have opportunities that previous generations couldn't have imagined.

Soon after Luther's birth, Mary Ida brought her newborn home to the family's apartment at 180 South Street on the Lower East Side of Manhattan. The high-rise building was a part of the Alfred E. Smith Houses, a public housing project built just a few years earlier. The city had recently passed a law ending racial discrimination in public housing, and the Vandrosses took advantage of that by moving into one of the newer buildings for low-income families.

One of Luther's earliest memories was about the diversity of his neighborhood, which he once described as "60 percent Chinese [with] a little Italian and some Puerto Rican."

In those days, the projects weren't the blistering signs of urban decay and despair that they would one day become. Indeed, in many cases they exemplified hope, a way for a family whose finances had been stretched thin to slowly improve their lot.

"The projects back then were fabulous," Luther remembered, noting how adults looked out for children in the neighborhood. "If somebody saw you riding on the back of a bus, he'd tell your mother. When I was four, a bunch of us stole bubble gum from the candy store and ran like hell, and nothing happened right away. A few hours later when we got upstairs, we all got beatings, and learned that we were being monitored. I never did anything like that again."

The building where Luther's family lived overlooked the East River. Unlike many public housing compounds, it wasn't sequestered in some no-man's-land. To your right were the skyscrapers of Wall Street, and directly in front was the Brooklyn Bridge. Standing there, watching this metallic arm stretch across the lapping water, you could really imagine yourself going places.

Luther's father sometimes took Luther and his brother on late-night adventures beneath the bridge. "He used to wake my brother and me up at like three and four in the morning all the time," Luther recalled, "and take us out underneath the Brooklyn Bridge . . . and tell us ghost stories. Then my mother would start fussing at him because the teacher would call and ask, 'Why is Luther sleeping in class? He's falling asleep on his desk so many mornings.'"

Mary Ida, who soon put a stop to these early-morning excursions, was by all accounts the disciplinarian of the family. Sometimes when she would tell Luther to do something, he'd run to his father to try to get out of it. His father would indulge the boy for a bit by making him laugh, but soon coax him into abiding by his mother's wishes. One night, after intervening in a typical dispute between son and mother, Luther's father tried to comfort the boy by placing a dollar under his bedsheet as he slept. This remained one of Luther's most valued memories.

Another thing young Luther never forgot was how his parents used to dance. His mom would throw on some of her Dinah Washington records, bawdy boogie-woogie numbers like "Fat Daddy" and "TV Is the Thing This Year," and soon the two would be cutting the rug. They'd spin little Luther around in the air, then break into the Watusi or another popular dance of the day.

"My husband used to do a dance called the dip," Mary Ida remembered. "It would tickle the kids." Patricia, the eldest daughter, used to call her parents Fred Astaire and Ginger Rogers. Perhaps because of this love for dancing, music occupied a constant space in the Vandross household.

At age three, Luther started experimenting on the piano. "I don't know how I did it," he recalled. "But I just picked out the songs. My fingers were too small to play everything I wanted to." By the time Luther was five, his parents signed him up for piano lessons, but that didn't last long. "I mean, I used to hide from the piano teacher when he came," Luther said. "So we just discontinued that."

The first music star in the Vandross home wasn't Luther, but his big sister Patricia. In 1956, four neighborhood guys recruited her to join their group, the Crests. Led by an Italian kid from Brooklyn, John Mastrangelo, or, as he was known onstage, Johnny Maestro, the act embraced the swinging doo-wop sound that ruled the airwaves, dance halls, and street corners across the country, but they also had a touch of gospel in their harmonies.

"They used to rehearse in my living room when I was very

young," Luther once recollected. "I used to disturb the rehearsals and my sister would yell, 'Mama, would you come and get him, please, and make him stop.' "

The group got its big break the next year, when practicing their harmonies riding in a subway car. A woman heard them singing and brought them to the attention of an established agent who began booking the act around town. With the guys sporting checkered jackets and skinny ties and Patricia in a fluffy prom dress, they played anywhere that would have them—churches, schools, community centers. The agent soon got them a deal to cut a couple of records, and they quickly churned out some singles: "Sweetest One" / "My Juanita," and "No One to Love" / "Wish You Were Mine." The songs made no waves on the charts, but they did earn the group at least one royalty check for $17.50, which they had to split five ways.

Though they lacked a hit, there was a lot of interest in the Crests. A bigger record label wanted to sign them, and their manager felt that they could be more successful if they took their act on the road, beyond New York. It sounded like a good plan but Mary Ida wasn't having it. Though she was raising her family in New York City, she was originally from the tiny burg of Marion, South Carolina, and she still believed in the value of many of those small-town Southern ways. There was no way that she was going to let her fifteen-year-old daughter go gallivanting around the country with a bunch of older boys. Singing career or no singing career, it wasn't happening. So the four guys reluctantly said good-bye to Patricia and went on without her. Within a year, they scored a smash hit, ironically, with a song about a young woman just one year older than Patricia was when she left the group: "16 Candles."

Despite missing this shot at fame, the Vandrosses continued on as normal. During the summer, Luther's father would take the family to the beach as a break from his days toiling as an upholsterer and from Mary Ida's time working as a registered nurse. The soft sand, salty air, and cooling waves provided just the escape they needed from the incessant rush of city life and the many struggles that went with keeping a family of six fed and clothed. Like many others, the Vandrosses often brought a camera with them on those trips, providing a way to remember the good times in those inevitable moments when things turn bad.

Of the many photos, one shows Luther's mother and father together, personifying the saying "opposites attract." He's tall; she's short. He, of West Indian descent, appears oatmeal-tan next to her rich, dark-chocolate luster. He has the clean-cut look of someone in the military with close-cropped hair and a square jaw, while she seems straight out of the *Ebony* fashion fair with large movie star shades and hair perfectly parted down the middle. Despite these differences, however, two things unite them: his hand gently touching her shoulder, and their gaze focused on the same spot.

Another of the beach photos shows the trinity of Vandross men: Luther on the left, his father in the middle, and brother Anthony to the right. Grade school–aged Luther looks trim in his tight bathing trunks—all legs and butt. Charles, in a striped shirt and jeans, stands at least a head taller than his little brother. Their father, in the center, towers above them both. His head is bowed, eyes cast downward, and his arms are wrapped snuggly around his boys. If you look closely at Luther's face, you can see that his mouth is on the verge of a smile, as if he can't keep himself from grinning.

One evening in 1959, after a great day at the beach, the family arrived home and everything seemed normal, until Luther's father suddenly passed out and couldn't be revived. By the time they arrived at the hospital, the news was grim. He had slipped into a diabetic coma and he would never regain consciousness. Soon he died. The tragedy of the day seemed to be amplified by the simplicity with which it played out. They were at the beach, daddy was here, now he is gone.

Sometimes late at night, around when they used to sneak underneath the Brooklyn Bridge, Luther would pray for his father's return—if not forever, then just for one more ghost story, another dollar under the sheets, a last dance. It wasn't only for him that he said these prayers. He also hoped that if his father came back, maybe he would no longer hear his mother sobbing from behind her closed bedroom door. These thoughts remained with Luther throughout his life, serving as a reminder of his first lesson in how life could be unfair, senseless, and cruel. He had lost his father, the smell of his skin, the tone of his voice, the touch of his hand, but he would hold tight to the memory of their dances and how it felt to be wholly loved.

3

"There's Nothing Better Than Love"

"[Luther's] songs are always about love,
because that was taught very much
in my house."

—MARY IDA VANDROSS

Red plastic chips scattered across the table as twelve women watched intently. They held tight to their game boards and listened as someone either howled with happiness or sighed at sudden misfortune. It was Pokeno night, when a dozen neighborhood friends gathered for the game that, as the box boasted, joined "the thrill of poker with the suspense of Keno." It was one of Mary Ida Vandross' favorite pastimes, a chance to break up the sometimes draining routine of balancing work with raising four active kids on her own. Each month a different woman would host the game at her home. While others brought assorted treats, as well as a sampling of the latest gossip, Mary Ida often provided the entertainment in the guise of her youngest son, Luther, who she always called Ronnie.

"Ronnie, don't you want to perform?" she would ask the boy, who was on the cusp of becoming a teenager.

"If I sing, can I have some potato chips?" he'd answer.

"Sure."

"All right," he'd say somewhat reluctantly, before launching into a number like Baby Washington's snappy "That's How Heartaches Are Made" or the Shirelles' wistful "Will You Still Love Me Tomorrow." When finished, however, he'd rush right back out of the room, rarely smiling or stopping to enjoy the applause from his mother's impressed girlfriends.

"I was always embarrassed about singing around my family," Luther explained. "I never ever sang at home."

He and his mother continued to dance around the living room together doing the Watusi. Yet increasingly, music was something he experienced in private. Money was tight in the years after his father died, but Luther would spend whatever he could get on the latest 45's from the local record store. These tiny black discs seemed to hold a multitude of secrets, which they revealed slowly each time he played them.

One day, his mother gazed at his stacks of vinyl and asked, "Ronnie, why do you want records all the time?"

He answered, "I want records until they're as tall as me."

After his father died, Luther turned to music as a constant in a world that threatened to go haywire at any instant. If his father could be playing on the beach one minute and dead the next, what else could happen when he wasn't looking or when he dared to enjoy himself too much? It wasn't as if he thought about his father's death all the time, but it often crept up on him. Grief was like a shiftless relative: You didn't know when it would show up or how long it would stay.

"I still carry that pain with me," Luther said as recently as 2002.

"And whenever I see the relationship between a father and son depicted on television or in a film I am filled with sadness at what I have missed. There is a truly special bond there, which is about more than throwing a baseball around after school. It is about the comfort of a father's embrace. My mother never married again and throughout my childhood I felt there was a void where that male presence had been."

Losing his father left him with a sense that he was missing something everybody else seemed to have.

The household saw other changes, as well. Luther's siblings were growing up, moving out, and even having their own kids. "You know, I grew up in a house where my oldest niece was born when I was eleven," Luther remembered. "My mother taught us how to take care of babies. I helped my sisters raise those kids. They're like my own."

When Luther was thirteen, the family briefly moved outside of New York City, about an hour and a half down the East Coast to Philadelphia. They touched down in the northern part of the city in an area along the Schuylkill River, once renowned for its ritzy mansions. Settlers in the 1700s built these palatial estates as an expression of their wealth and good fortune, but—in an unlucky twist of fate—they filled them with Chippendale furniture made from imported mahogany that had the deadly larvae of yellow fever–carrying mosquitoes buried within its grain. Pretty soon, nearly the whole town was wiped out. By the time the Vandross family arrived, almost two hundred years later, the neighborhood was a haven for black folks trying to improve their living conditions by moving out of rented apartments into homes of their own.

As white folks fled the city of Philadelphia for the suburbs—92 percent left between 1950 and 1960—black folks were lured with newspapers ads like "Vacant! Move in right away! No Money

Down." Legendary jazz saxophonist John Coltrane even lived there for a bit in the 1950s after buying a three-story row house through the GI Bill.

For the Vandross family, it was a big change from cramped apartment living. Yet, Luther hated being in a house.

"I had grown up in small [apartments] with a single entrance through the front door," Luther explained. "But when we moved into the house, the various entrances and exits made me feel less secure."

Luther, now a teenager, also had other thoughts filling his mind. "I had a big crush on a teacher," he remembered, "which was possibly my first sexual stirring, although it was not clear to me at the time. I remember pushing back those feelings by receding into myself. Looking back on it now, I think the teacher was probably aware of how I felt."

The infatuation didn't last long, because the family soon moved from the house in Philadelphia back to New York City. Here Luther had a singular experience that forever altered his life.

It was 1964. Luther sat in the audience of Brooklyn's Fox Theatre for a concert organized by the city's top disc jockey, Murray the K. During the late 1950s and 1960s, Murray distinguished himself by playing an unexpected mix of music. He always started with a Frank Sinatra tune, but then he'd spin anything from a ballad by clean-cut Bronx crooner Bobby Darin to "Tutti Frutti" by that hootin' and hollerin' Georgia-born black dandy, Little Richard. Unlike many white DJs, Murray preferred playing original songs by black artists rather than the rerecorded cover versions by white acts. The live shows he sponsored reflected the same diverse mix, and Luther hated to miss them.

"I used to go to the Murray the K shows," Luther remembered. "And I used to see the Angels sing 'My Boyfriend's Back.' That was a white girl [singing]. And then the Shirelles would come on and sing 'Dedicated to the One I Love.' And that was a black girl [singing]. And then you'd have Frankie Avalon come on and do 'Dede Dinah,' then Ben E. King would sing 'Stand By Me.'"

What united the acts was a drive to work their way up the pop charts by chronicling the peppermint highs and punch-to-the-gut lows of teenage romance.

Murray's concerts also broke new acts, which is what happened on this particular night as darkness fell over the crowd and a single lit figure—a young woman—took the stage. With a red dress wrapped around her column-thin frame, she walked with a sophisticate's strut and held her head in the slightly upturned manner of princesses, shop mannequins, and women who've learned to survive in the street.

Music began playing: a spare, oddly lilting dirge. She turned toward the shadowed faces before her and sang, "Anyone who ever loved," then paused. Luther felt his breath stop. "Could look at me," she continued. "And know that I loved you."

It was like this woman, this newcomer named Dionne Warwick, was aiming her voice directly at him—not the words per se, but her spirit, the way she said them. It was as if she unlocked something within: feelings, desires, gummy notions that hadn't hardened into thoughts. Her tone, her style, her presence were like glimmers of uncharted worlds.

"You know those kind of movies where it's black-and-white and everyone is in a club," Luther once recalled. "And one spotlight goes on one person on one side of the room and another spotlight goes on the person on the other side of the room, indicating that they are the only two people in the world. That's what I felt like with Dionne Warwick that day. What she did to me just pierced me to the core, to the DNA, and I decided right then and there that that's what I wanted to do with my life. I wanted to do to somebody what she did to me."

The problem was he didn't know how to go about doing this, becoming a performer who could make people catch their breath. He also wasn't prepared to share his new passion. He kept it to himself, the way some teens hide an early sexual awakening.

Like most parents, Mary Ida sometimes asked, "What do you want to be when you grow up?"

Luther would shrug and say, "I don't know."

Yet, behind closed doors, he practiced intently. He went into the bathroom, locked the door, stood in front of the mirror, and sang to an audience of his own reflection. The songs he sang to himself largely came from Dionne or his beloved Shirelles. Soon, however, he discovered another act to idolize, another love that stayed with him for life.

It came in the form of a trio from Detroit. They started as just another of the era's popular girl groups but quickly distinguished themselves as something special. One of the young women was a full-figured honey blond named Florence. While elegant in a gown, she looked like she could hold her own in an alley fight. Another of the girls went by Mary. She was called "the beauty" because of her coy smile and late-night gaze. Then there was the lead singer, Diana, the one you couldn't stop staring at. She had eyes that popped as wide as a doll-baby's and a smile that was ferocious in its glee.

Together, the women were called the Supremes. They came courtesy of Detroit's black-owned record label Motown, helmed by the enterprising Berry Gordy. The label produced hits the way Cadillac manufactured luxury cars. Starting in 1964, the Supremes became the definitive girl group with a train of successive number ones: "Where Did Our Love Go," "Baby Love," "Come See About

Me," "Stop! In the Name of Love," and "Back in My Arms Again." Luther was enthralled by the sound of Diana's hungry coos gliding across the music's hammering beats. It sounded like confectioner's sugar sprinkled over a pound cake.

Luther never missed a chance to see them perform on television, on Ed Sullivan's Sunday night show. Whenever the Supremes were scheduled to appear, he planned to watch way in advance, drawing pictures of the group on his school notebooks in anticipation and hurrying himself to eat dinner and clear the dishes before the show began at eight P.M.

Watching the Supremes on Ed Sullivan was so important to Luther that sometimes Mary Ida had to use the show as her parental trump card. One day she had expressly asked Luther to clean the house while she went out, but she returned to the same mess that she left.

A couple days went by and she never mentioned the cleaning incident. It was water under the bridge, thought Luther. Then Sunday came and, as was routine, he finished dinner quickly and dutifully helped with his dishes before making his way toward the television.

"What are you doing?" Mary Ida asked.

"I'm getting ready to watch the Supremes on *Ed Sullivan*," he answered.

"But I told you earlier this week that I wanted the house cleaned," she reminded him. Then she issued his sentence. "You're not going to watch that tonight."

"But please, Momma," he argued. "The punishment has to fit the crime. I did not murder anybody."

Mary Ida remained unmoved, and Luther learned his lesson.

"She knew what she was doing," he later said.

Mary Ida recognized how important music was to her son, and for the most part—when he wasn't being bad—she supported his interest, giving him some extra money for records and letting him spend hours tangled in the wires of his headphones. Music was Luther's life. He hadn't made many new friends since moving back to New York City and settling in the Bronx. At parties, he sat in a corner and quietly listened to the tunes coming from the record player while everybody else danced and partied around him. It was lonely in a sense, but all he had to do was play one of his records and he was in a world much richer than the one around him. It was a world where people wore beautiful clothes, made lovely sounds, and seemed to understand about feeling different and alone. He could listen to Diana sing "Nothing but Heartaches" or hear Dionne chime about "The Last One to Be Loved." Songs like these played through his head all day like a personal hit parade. Without knowing it, he'd sometimes hum or sing out loud.

At sixteen, he started working after school in the stockroom at Alexander's, a discount department store in midtown Manhattan at the corner of East Fifty-eighth Street and Lexington Avenue. One day a coworker, another high school student, confronted him about his stealthy vocalizing.

"Do you sing," asked the round-faced, honey-complexioned young woman. "You always seem to be singing to yourself."

"Yeah," Luther answered.

She said, "Well, I sing, too."

Her name was Robin Clark, and she quickly became one of Luther's best friends. They started singing together, passing time in the stockroom, and soon their clique broadened with some of Luther's classmates from the Bronx's William H. Taft High School. The gang included the ambitious Diane Sumler, who longed to be a glamorous headliner like the women Luther admired; Anthony Hinton, a smooth tenor with lean lady-killer looks; Carlos Alomar, a Puerto Rican guitar whiz; and Fonzi Thornton, the youngest of the bunch, who in photos gazes at Luther with wide, inquisitive eyes.

Suddenly, Luther wasn't a loner anymore. He now had friends, people he could talk to, others who shared his musical secret.

They formed a group called Shades of Jade. With Luther as the leader, they practiced their harmonies everywhere—in the subway, in somebody's apartment building, so they could get that good "project echo," and even in the halls of the high school.

"You know how teachers usually say, 'Cut off that noise and go to class,'" Luther remembered. "We didn't have that. Our teachers used to listen and close their eyes and just groove because we really sounded good. And when the song was over, they'd clap and then say, 'Hurry up and go to class before the bell rings.' So we kind of knew we were good even back then."

They'd walk through the streets of the Bronx laughing and talking. Luther would be lugging his notebook filled with songs he'd written. Then someone would start to sing, another would strike a harmony, and the rest would chime in, making such a sweet sound. They might not have been able to pull together five dollars collectively, but like the fairy-tale gnome who spun straw into gold, they could create music simply from the air they breathed.

Emboldened by the reception they received from schoolmates, teachers, and friends, Shades of Jade entered several talent contests. Sometimes they won; sometimes they didn't. Luther, however, had his mind fixed on testing his skills in the most challenging arena of all, Amateur Night at Harlem's Apollo Theatre. The Wednesday night tradition, held at the most important venue in black music, was known to tax the nerves of even the most talented novice performer. For every Pearl Bailey, Sarah Vaughn, or James Brown who won over the demanding crowd, there were countless others who—if they were lucky—were pulled offstage by MC Porto Rico before the disapproving audience would shower them with pennies, chicken bones, or whatever else they could find to throw.

Yet Luther felt ready for the Apollo. After all, his group had fans all across the street corners, project hallways, subway stations, and classrooms of the Bronx. And he was the one who coordinated their harmonies, the one who got them sounding so good. So, flying solo, he showed up one Wednesday and gave it his best.

He lost.

He tried again and lost.

Once more: another loss.

Finally, he went back and did his best job yet. He could really feel that the judgmental audience was with him. Then his competition came out. They were a slick quintet that styled themselves after those suave musical exemplars of black male grace, the Temptations, another Motown act like the Supremes. The amateur group performed the Temptations' rendition of "Old Man River." It looked like it would be a close battle. Then one of their singers, a baritone, dug down real deep and hit a bottom-of-the-well bass note like the Temptations' Melvin Franklin. The whole audience went crazy, yelling, screaming, and stomping their feet like they were at a revival meeting. The group walked home with a cash prize. For Luther, it was yet another loss.

These multiple losses led to later rumors that Luther was booed off the Apollo stage, which he insisted never happened. However, the disappointment of it offered an important if painful lesson.

"The experience taught me that I was dedicated," Luther later said. "It showed me that winning at things like that were not the only considerations. It taught me that show business and these careers are really a process of rejection until you get to someone who might want to champion your cause."

For Luther, that wait would last a lot longer than he ever expected.

"Nights in Harlem"

"I didn't care about whatever stuff was going on in the playground. I couldn't have cared less about everybody playing basketball, and kickball, and stickball, and football and all of that. No, I cared about the Shirelles, the Sweet Inspirations, and the Temptations. That was my world."

—LUTHER VANDROSS

In 1967, twenty-six-year-old singer Aretha Franklin released the single "I Never Loved a Man (The Way I Love You)." She had put out records before, but never like this, never with so much emotion. Almost from her opening notes, this middle daughter of the esteemed Reverend C. L. Franklin erupted with a symphony of whoops and cries, wails and hollers, moans and breathless sighs. In less than three minutes, she summed up all there is to say about a love that rises and falls like a country road, swings like a wrecking ball, intoxicates like bootleg liquor, and pains like a phantom limb.

When Luther first heard this record, it stunned him. Again, a world of possibilities opened with just one song. He immediately added another favorite singer to his very short list. There was Dionne, whom he loved for her cool; Diana, whom he loved for her sweet tone; and now Aretha, who was unequaled in conveying emotion.

"Can you imagine a more heartbreaking journey than Aretha's [on "I Never Loved a Man"], going from bitchy to hurt and, at the end, rising triumphantly above it all," Luther said. "[That song] was the high point in my street education. Her technique felt so involuntary. She must have felt like Amelia Earhart flying over the desolate ocean. It was a powerful mission."

There was another reason Luther likely related to the song. He was sixteen and in love. This wasn't a simple crush like the one he had on his teacher in Philadelphia. This time it was for real, involving someone his own age. Typical for Luther, he never revealed his loved one's name—or gender—but he made no secret about the effect this person had on him.

He privately nursed the feelings for a while. Then he slowly mustered the courage to reveal them to the person who was making his heart beat as fast as the rhythms that came from his record player. The conversation didn't go the way it had played out in daydreams, though.

"The person was almost like, 'Thank you, but I'm not interested,'" Luther recalled. "It was very painful and unrequited and alienating, very alienating."

To cope with this disappointment, Luther turned to the thing that always provided comfort when life didn't go his way: food. It could be his momma's home cooking or something he picked up on the go, but the effect was the same. Somehow—he didn't even know why—it just made him feel better, made the world seem less sharp.

"The first thing I would do if I was depressed or dejected, whatever, is eat," he explained.

The strategy worked for a while, but increasingly it was creating its own set of problems. His shirts wrapped too tight around the middle. His pants rubbed in the thighs. Sometimes at school, the desks seemed too small. It was like he didn't fit in the world.

During gym class, he could never pull himself up the athletic rope that hung high from the ceiling. The instructor kept marking him down as if he was defiantly failing a test that he could've easily passed. What's worse is that a crowd would gather underneath the rope to watch his slow, defeated tries. When he jumped down, there was laughter all around him, but he never understood what was so funny.

Fortunately, he still had his music. He still had his voice. He still had his friends. They knew that there was more to him than someone who couldn't pass gym. They knew how he could hear any song on the radio, then arrange their voices so that they sounded just like the record. This was more important than what he ate, the things he couldn't do, or who didn't love him back.

Besides, soon Luther and his gang had a bigger outlet for their talents than the streets of the Bronx and the halls of Taft High School. Though he failed at amateur night at the Apollo, Luther and friends tried out for and were picked to join the Apollo's performing youth group called Listen, My Brother. It was a sixteen-piece outfit that wrote and performed its own songs and dramatic material with the goal of uplifting other urban youth.

"That was at the height of the civil rights conflict," explains renowned dance music producer Patrick Adams, who, as a teenager, was in Listen, My Brother with Luther. "The group's general message was, 'Stay in school, try to learn something, and embrace your fellow man, not to be hostile and negative.' It was a very positive, wonderful thing."

It also wasn't entirely altruistic. The Apollo was owned by the Jewish Schiffman family, and at the time neighborhood activists were heatedly raising questions about the large number of white-owned businesses in Harlem. One way to answer these charges was to offer programs, services, and support to the community, a task given largely to public relations director Peter Long.

At a time when being black in show business generally meant performing onstage rather than cutting deals behind the scenes, Long had a hard-won reputation for putting the right people together and making things happen. He engineered many of the great collaborations between jazz trumpeter Miles Davis and arranger Gil Evans; helped coordinate entertainment for the 1964 Democratic National Convention, which featured Paul Newman and Barbra Streisand; and staged the last Carnegie Hall concerts by searing vocalist Billie Holiday before heart disease, drug addiction, and despair took her life.

Now his duties included making performers out of a motley collection of local teens, a task he undertook with militaristic seriousness. He knew that if these kids really wanted to make a living in this business, they needed to be tough. For that matter, he knew that if these kids—these black sons and daughters who epitomized the dreams that everyone was fighting for—wanted to make it in this *world*, they needed to be tough. He knew that his position as head of Listen, My Brother was one of the most important tasks that he'd ever take on, and he was committed to doing it right.

Adams remembers the first time he came across Long, during his Listen, My Brother audition. About one hundred kids milled throughout the Apollo, but things were running behind because the piano player was a no-show. Long stepped out into the audience and asked, "Is there anyone who can play the piano?" Adams mostly focused on guitar, but he could do a little something on the keyboard, and his friend knew it. So the friend raised his hand, pointed to Adams, and said, "He plays piano." Adams stayed silent and still. He didn't think his piano skills were good enough, not to play in front of all these people, not at the Apollo. Long, however, didn't seem to take the hint.

"He walks down the aisle and grabs me physically by the collar," Adams recalled, "and yanked me up out of my chair."

In front of everyone, Long then said in a bellowing voice, "If you believe you can do something, say 'yes!' The worst that can happen is that you mess up, but you never know what you can do until you try." Soon, Adams was onstage playing the piano.

Luther remembered how Long would call each group member onstage and fire off questions to them like a drill sergeant.

"Why are you here?" he'd ask.

"Because I want to be in show business," most of the kids would answer.

"Why do you want to be in show business?"

Occasionally someone would make the mistake of saying something like, "Because it looks good."

Long would explode: "When you see Nancy Wilson up there onstage looking fabulous, do you think it's *easy*?"

"He really was teaching us certain values," Luther said. "You learned to defend yourself artistically."

Luther soon distinguished himself in the group with both his singing and his knack for arranging vocals.

"He was a shining talent from the first moment," Adams recalled. "He just had something special." Luther enjoyed Listen, My Brother and even found himself feeling less shy. Maybe it was Long's exercises, or maybe it was because his high school buddies Robin, Carlos, Diane, Anthony, and Fonzi were also in the group. Whatever the case, he was finally doing exactly what he wanted to do, making good music and performing it in front of cheering crowds. He had made it at the Apollo.

He even cut his first record with the group, a 45 like all those he had bought through the years. The A side was the troupe's snappy theme song "Listen, My Brother," a youthful call for emancipation. "Freedom, freedom," they sang, "let's shout to the world."

The B side was a singsongy ballad called "Only Love Can Make a Better World," written and produced by a D.C.-bred talent named Van McCoy. (In the mid 1970s, this man would seduce the whole music world into doing "The Hustle.") The single failed to even make the charts, and Luther's voice doesn't stand out on either song. Yet it didn't matter. Luther had a record out.

Listen, My Brother also provided the opportunity for Luther's TV debut. Peter Long's wife, actress Loretta Long, an experienced Broadway hoofer with roles in *Guys and Dolls* and *Sweet Charity*, had just been cast in an experimental public television show targeting inner-city kids. She played Susan, a mild-tempered homemaker who lived with her husband, George, in a humble brownstone on a bustling sunlit city block. Her neighbors included a shopkeeper, two cohabitating bachelors named Bert and Ernie, a gigantic bird, and a bunch of other furry creatures dubbed "muppets," since they combined features of marionettes and puppets.

In several of the initial programs, Listen, My Brother came on singing educational songs with the snap and edge of current radio hits. One time Luther, Fonzi, Robin, and the rest sat in a circle, singing about how "chil-dren are *beau-ti-ful*." Another time, they sashayed from side to side, sporting bright colors and smiles, listing the parts of the body "right on the beat."

"It was really an incredible thing," Fonzi remembered, "because we were getting the chance to be performers."

The show, which started airing in late 1969, was called *Sesame Street*.

Perhaps the most long-lasting benefit of being in Listen, My Brother, though, came from all the free shows Luther saw at the Apollo. Sometimes the teenagers opened for such acts as the interracial Bay Area funk-rockers Sly and the Family Stone or soul man Isaac Hayes, who cut a striking figure with his bald head and vest of chains symbolizing black oppression. Then there were all the groups—girl groups, predictably—that Luther loved to watch, loved to hear as they piled their voices on top of each other, sometimes sounding bold and aggressive like cacophonous Amazons, other times like a suite of angels.

"We could go in anytime we wanted and see all these shows," Luther recalled. "Do you know what a learning experience that is?"

One of his favorite acts was the quartet Patti LaBelle and the Bluebelles. They weren't the product of a hit-making machine like Motown. Bonded purely by friendship and a love for music, the Bluebelles seemed more grounded and less prissy than the other girl groups. Instead of gowns, they sported simple shop dresses or suits picked up from Woolworth's or Lerner's. Plus, when they sang, they didn't try to be coy or cute. Their signature move was taking mainstream show tunes and standards and delivering them as if the lyrics came from the fiery hand of the Almighty himself. Their marquee-rattling renditions of "Danny Boy," "Over the Rainbow," and "You'll Never Walk Alone" earned them the tag "Sweethearts of the Apollo."

"Their harmonies were so tight," Luther recalled. "I remember, not knowing any better, we used to admire the fact that they made the microphones buzz because their harmonies were so strong."

The group included lead singer Patti, a mammoth-voiced wonder who belted with a force that threatened to loosen the planks of the Apollo's dusty oak stage; Cindy Birdsong, the older, big sister of the group who later defected to the Supremes; Sarah Dash, who loved singing so much that she defied her minister father by performing "the devil's music"; and Nona Hendryx, a born hell-raiser who grew up hungry, cold, and fighting on the streets of Newark, New Jersey.

"I had nothing," Nona once explained. "So I took it out on anybody."

Luther loved them so much that he rallied his friends to become the first members of their fan club and appointed himself president. He would often devise schemes to get closer to the group.

"It was little Luther who was always just running after Patti LaBelle and the Bluebelles," Patti remembered, "because he was a big fan."

He once lied to Peter Long, saying that he had to interview the quartet for a school project or else he'd fail. Long couldn't have one of the kids flunking school on his watch, so he hastily set up the question-and-answer session. Much to Luther's disappointment, Patti was running an errand and he didn't get to talk with her.

When he later met with Patti, she was outside in her car with a Tootsie Pop stuck in her mouth.

He rushed over gushing, "Oh, Ms. LaBelle, I love you so much."

She smiled and popped the candy from her mouth. "Thank you, baby," she said, then put her lollipop back in, and rolled up the darkened window of her car.

Another act Luther never missed were the Sweet Inspirations, fronted by gospel-trained soprano Cissy Houston. Incidentally, Houston was aunt to one of Luther's other favorites, Dionne Warwick. Cissy made the Sweet Inspirations stand out, since she wasn't a teenager like the singers in many of the other female-fronted acts. She was a grown woman with a husband and three kids at home: sons Gary and Michael, and a baby girl named Whitney. When Cissy got behind a mike she was trying to be cutesy or coy. She sang with such a piercing, otherworldly quiver that it brought to mind strange natural wonders: rainbows, stalagmites, and desert sunsets. The Sweet Inspirations provided the background vocals for most of Aretha's biggest hits, which endeared them to Luther even more.

"When I listened to old Aretha Franklin albums, like *Lady*

Soul," he said, "I'd turn the balance knob on my stereo to the left to hear those girls sing—it was a total obsession."

Cissy was another of the stars Luther first met backstage at the Apollo. "Luther just came running up to me and said, 'Hi, I just love you. I love you,'" Cissy remembered. "And I said, 'Thank you, darling. I love you, too.'"

The young fan stood out to Cissy. "Luther was a jovial person," she remembered. "You know, he was nice and plump and I loved him like that. He didn't like that, but I loved him like that."

The Sweet Inspirations—or the Sweets, as fans called them—instilled Luther with a love for those singing behind the stars. "I would say Cissy Houston is the main reason that the field of background singing has grown so much," Luther once observed. "Backgrounds used to be just 'oohs' and 'aahs' . . . but then Aretha hit in the mid-sixties and suddenly background singers weren't so faceless. Aretha would sing, 'I take what I want, I'm a bad go-getter, yeah,' and the background singers didn't sing 'ooh' and 'aah' anymore. They'd sing, 'What you want, get what you want, now'— that call-and-response thing. Cissy pioneered those kinds of parts."

This wasn't just a musical innovation. It was another sign of a rapidly changing time that also saw the development of the Black Arts Movement with writers like Amiri Baraka and Nikki Giovanni, the founding of the Black Panther Party, and the appointment of Thurgood Marshall as the first black Supreme Court justice. All across the cultural and political map, black people were using their voices as never before. What Luther heard at the Apollo or in his headphones at night reflected a new spirit pervading the air.

"Soul music is a whole life's experience," he noted. "It's the way your mother fried chicken and sent you to the store for a *Jet* magazine. It's the whole thing. It's not having much money and seeing rich white kids on TV living in houses. That's what soul music is."

The music came out of the lives and experiences of a people, and the Apollo couldn't have provided a better training ground. Still, despite his happiness with what he was hearing and learning, certain things slowly began bothering him, things that felt sadly familiar.

"Remember, I was this sixteen-year-old, three-hundred-pound kid," Luther said. "So, when it came time for the lead vocals to be handed out, they didn't want me up there. I was the one, mind you, who always put the harmony together. I had the administrative role. I was real good at it. . . . I always had a good sense of who could do what, who sang top, who sang bottom. . . . But they didn't want me to front the group. I carried that with me for a long time."

It didn't help that Listen, My Brother director Long, who took on the role of father figure for many kids, wasn't always gentle in guiding his charges. After all, he was trying to prep them for the harsh world away from the footlights. Long could always be counted on for a rousing pep talk or an uplifting word, but he was sometimes short on praise. Luther's still-fragile self longed for more. For all of Long's undeniable support, he never told Luther the obvious: that he could sing. This bothered Luther for a long time, staying with him like a playground scar.

"What's done to you as a child can play a large part in your perception on things when, and if, you grow up," Luther said, reflecting on his experience with Long.

This wasn't the only thing bothering him then, either. In 1969, when Diana Ross bid farewell to the Supremes in order to launch a solo career, Luther's grades dropped from a B+ to a C–. It might have been a silly showbiz happening to some, but for him it was devastating, another thing that couldn't be counted on.

Adding to that, he was still alone. He still didn't have anyone to hold his hand or to serenade with all the beautiful love songs he'd committed to memory. This was during his senior year in high school, when everyone else was as coupled as the animals on Noah's Ark. He attended his prom, but later couldn't even recall his date.

"Maybe Robin," he said. "I think I took Robin to the prom."

Since he couldn't find what he was looking for in the world, he turned within. "I lived for the love of music," he explained in 1990. "Maybe that's why when everyone was forming couples and falling in love, when romance was all around me, I missed out. I was distracted. My life was in the headphones. It might have been lonely in there, but I had no choice. By then, music was an obsession. It still is."

"Searching"

"My career, you see, is my fantasy.
I'm living out the fantasy
I conceived in college. . . ."

—LUTHER VANDROSS

In spring 1969, Luther faced one of the biggest decisions of his young life: where to attend college. He had narrowed it to two choices. One was Bronx Community College, a relatively small institution housed in a refurbished high school. Founded eleven years earlier as a way to bring higher education to the boroughs, the school was only about two miles from where Luther lived with his mother.

His second choice, Western Michigan University in the city of Kalamazoo, might as well have been on the moon since Luther had never been that far from home. He pondered the choices thoroughly then made a decision that was rather uncharacteristic of the shy teenager who usually liked to stay close to his family and friends.

"I chose Michigan just to get away," he recalled. "I'd never been on a plane before."

He arrived on campus in fall 1969. Since he was undecided on exactly what he wanted to study, he enrolled as a liberal arts major. Like most incoming freshmen, Luther lived in the dorms, where his roommate was an aspiring medical student.

The semester began and typically things took off quickly. There was the rush of trying to meet new people, getting accustomed to college-level classes, and finding his way around the campus, which snaked across hundreds of acres. It was another world from life in the tightly packed Bronx, which is what he thought he wanted. Yet he soon started to miss things. There was no Apollo in Kalamazoo, no friends to sing with, no family. There were no subways that clanked overhead or grumbled underfoot, no skyscrapers that grew from the sidewalk like concrete beanstalks, and no masses of rainbow faces.

"I was so homesick and lonely," Luther said, " 'cause I didn't know anybody and I was the only black student in an all-white dormitory."

Race relations on Western Michigan's campus strained and simmered during this time, agitated by a 1967 riot in nearby Detroit and the assassination of Dr. Martin Luther King, Jr., one year later. Black students had recently formed the Black Action Movement to challenge the administration on racial issues. Throughout Luther's first semester there were whispers that the group was planning something big, an action to show the university's president—whom they dubbed "the flimflam man"—that they meant business.

Luther, however, was never very interested in politics. Instead of focusing his energies on fighting the system, he returned to the time-tested thing that always made bad times better.

"I just felt alienated and alone," he said, "and I found myself in the cafeteria all the time. I didn't even know what I was doing. All I knew is that every time I went and had something to eat, it calmed me down."

His other escape, of course, was music. Many in his dorm knew he loved music and admired his skills and accomplishments: the opening gigs at the Apollo, the way he played piano, and his voice, which was maturing to have a sweet, warm, soulful tone. His fellow students even thought they knew the reason for his considerably developed and refined talents—he was related to one of pop's biggest superstars.

"You know I'm Dionne Warwick's brother," he told his roommate one day.

Who knows why he first said it. Perhaps it was a way for him to be more than just "that black guy in the dorm." Whichever was the case, the story spread like a bout of mono.

"Wow, Dionne Warwick's brother is in our dorm," students would say.

The story worked well for Luther, and it squarely fit his musical fantasies. By being Dionne's brother, he was also, then, nephew to another of his favorite singers: the Sweet Inspirations' Cissy Houston. Away from his real family, Luther created a new one.

So imagine his shock and terror when one day his roommate burst in the room saying, "I won tickets and backstage passes to go see your sister's concert." Dionne was playing a show at nearby Michigan State University and Luther's roommate had scored tickets through a radio promotion.

The night of the concert came and Luther's roommate met Dionne backstage.

He said, "I know your brother Luther."

Dionne, who only has one brother, Michael, thought, "What? This man is nuts." She told the young medical student that she had no brother named Luther. He was stunned.

When the roommate returned with news of Dionne's denial, Luther, with a practiced cool, playfully laughed it off. "Oh, she's so crazy," he said.

Though he successfully defused the situation, Luther was shaken because he was nearly exposed as a fraud. It was another thing making him unhappy at school. As the fall semester ended and spring began, Luther kept returning to the thoughts he had the first time he saw Dionne sing at the Brooklyn Fox. He wanted to be a performer and he didn't see how Western Michigan University was helping toward that goal.

Instead of going to classes, he'd sit in his room writing songs and dreaming about the type of singer he wanted to be. He wouldn't just walk onstage and simply sing. No, he wanted to create extravaganzas. He wanted to be part of a group like those in the heyday of Motown, with guys and girls in glittering outfits strutting across the stage with elaborately choreographed movements, creating drama with every gorgeous step.

"When you're raised on the Supremes," he explained, "you never get over them."

Since he wasn't getting what he wanted in classes, he used the student lounge as his library and records as his textbooks. He meticulously studied the harmonies of the Sweet Inspirations and all things Aretha, dubbing himself an Arethacologist.

"That was 1970, when Aretha's *This Girl's in Love with You* album came out," Luther said. "Each morning, I'd listen to her while waiting for the cafeteria to open. In my loneliness, I put on at least sixty-five pounds."

This Girl's in Love with You, released in February, was Aretha's eighth album since breaking through with *I Never Loved a Man the Way I Love You*. It was recorded during a trying period in the queen's life, following the break-up of her marriage to husband/manager Ted White, who was known—as an infamous *Time* magazine article once chronicled—for "roughing her up in public." The album played like a document of one woman's battle with heartbreak and loneliness. Over the course of ten songs, she lamented affections that weren't returned ("Share Your Love with Me"), sought solace in the arms of a married man ("Dark End of the Street"), and lashed out at a life that had brought so much pain ("It Ain't Fair"). "Sometimes I wish I'd never been born," she cried.

The album featured a rendition of the Beatles' "Eleanor Rigby," about a woman who cleans up the church once all the wedding festivities are over. She has no love of her own, yet she must constantly wallow in the debris of someone else's happiness. At the end of the song, she dies alone, and as the priest wipes his hands of dirt from her gravesite, it's almost as if she never existed. This was one of Luther's favorites from the album. He found himself playing it over and over.

"I have often thought that Eleanor Rigby was a real person," he later said, "and that the graveyard was full of people who died lonely and didn't deserve to. I fear at times that I'm one of those people."

While Luther struggled with his loneliness, the campus threatened to explode. The Black Action Movement was finally ready to strike out at the administration. Among their demands was the establishment of a black student center, the discontinued use of the word "Negro" to refer to black students, and a 10 percent increase in black enrollment over the next three years. Their motto: "Open it up or shut it down."

On March 29, they seized the Student Union by barricading themselves inside. They told officials that no one could enter until their demands were met. In addition, the Movement tried to disrupt activities across the campus.

"We would gather each morning at the old administration

building," remembered Howard Lindsey, one of the participants in the protest, "and get the word from the 'generals' as to which building we would target for that day's protest. We would attempt either to disrupt classes in the building or to prevent students and others from entering the building by blocking the doorway."

The student activists knew that schools nationwide were increasingly taking a hard-line approach to campus protests, even calling in armed guards. Yet they were undaunted.

"I do not recall a fear of dying during our takeover in Kalamazoo, though the National Guard had been called and though there was talk of shooting and of guns," remembered Melba Joyce Boyd, another participant. "I recall our sense that we were right. This sense was not intellectual nor analytical. It was a feeling of four hundred years of disenfranchisement and the indignation of an American people who had helped to build a homeland for a racially hostile society. It was the blood of King and Malcolm and the fire deaths in Detroit that sustained our protest and our presence. It was not enough that a few of us would survive the racism of the system and the society. It was not enough at all."

The students stayed locked in the student center the entire night, as the media swarmed around Kalamazoo. Perhaps anticipating a public relations nightmare, the administration soon gave in to the students' demands. It was a victory with implications for black students across the campus.

Yet by this time, Luther's mind was elsewhere. He had made a decision. This would be his last semester at Western Michigan University. The time had come for him to try to realize his dreams, to at least see if there was a chance they could come true. If he stayed at school he'd always wonder, "What if."

After making the decision, the first thing he had to do was tell his mother about his plan to drop out of school and pursue a career as a performer. He worried about what she might say. She seemed so proud watching him go off to school. Nevertheless, he called her.

"You know what?" he said over the long-distance line. "College is not how I prepare for what I want to do with my life, so I'm kinda wasting time. Being in college is not for everyone."

He thought she'd be disappointed. After all, she had wanted him to study to become a cameraman. That way, Luther could be a part of the show business that he loved so much, but he'd also have a good trade, something you could count on—the kind of skills that she and her husband had raised their family on. However, to Luther's surprise, she simply said, "Sure." All that worrying to hear "sure."

"I think the reason she said 'sure,'" Luther said, "is because of what I didn't know [at the time], which is that my father was a brilliant singer. They always talked about how [he] could sing and how [he] could croon and the beauty of his voice."

Luther, unknowingly, was following in footsteps he never knew existed. Once that was settled, he continued making plans to leave, but his roommate confronted him.

"I can't believe you're bailing out," said the wanna-be medical student.

"Look," Luther shot back. "When you're a doctor and I get sick, I'll have my limo bring me to your office. I'm not bailing out. I'm following my vision."

In May, Luther returned home, and Mary Ida was overjoyed to see her son when she picked him up at the airport. Yet she was stunned—shocked by how much weight Ronnie had gained. He had always been a big boy, but his weight now seemed out of control. This was the first of many times that his weight would cause her worry.

6

"I've Been Working"

*"When I got back from college, it was rough.
I said, 'Momma, I want to sing,' and Momma
said, 'Fine.' But the gigs weren't there."*

—LUTHER VANDROSS

A woman just died young. She was a striking, long-haired brunette. She played classical piano like someone who graces concert stages, but she had put her career on hold for something even more promising: love. She was married to her college sweetheart, a thick blond bruiser of a guy with a ruddy baby face who was as at home knocking guys around on the hockey field as he was studying legal books in the library. After years of struggling, he had just gotten a job at a top Manhattan law firm, and he and his wife were trying to have a baby. That's when they got the bad news that she was dying, that " 'til death do us part" was going to come sooner than later.

In December 1970, millions turned out to watch this tale play out on the big screen. Luther was one of them. The movie was called *Love Story*, starring Ali McGraw as the tragic young beauty and Ryan O'Neal as the husband who is forced to go on without her. Although some panned the movie for being maudlin and overly sentimental, it hit with audiences, ultimately pulling in more than $100 million in ticket sales. Some critics speculated that crowds were drawn to this unapologetic weeper as a way to soothe psyches overwhelmed by the daily brutalities of the still-raging Vietnam War.

For Luther, however, seeing the film marked another defining moment, a flicker from a match that helped illuminate some truth about himself. Luther particularly remembered the final scene of the film, when the husband—now a widower—returns to the snow-covered park where his wife once watched him skate. The camera rises and recedes to reveal his lone figure against a stark background of white.

"When he went to the park and the camera pulled off and showed his back in the park, and there was this whole panoramic consideration of this alienated man who didn't have his other half—what can I tell you, that affected me," Luther said. "It was the first time I ever cried in a movie."

Once the film was over, Luther couldn't leave.

"I just sat there immobile," he said, "unable to consider anything else, and I think that penetrated my thinking. The sense of loss penetrated everything that I would begin to write and all of that. I think that's where it all began."

He stayed in the theater, replaying those final scenes in his mind. When he looked at his watch again, a half hour had passed.

In the most basic sense, *Love Story* simply chronicles "boy meets girl." Yet there is another reason Luther was likely taken by the film. As much as it deals with romance, *Love Story* is also about fathers. The tragedy-bound young woman enjoys an easy way with her modest baker dad, peppering their conversation with profanity and calling him by his first name. Her husband, on the other hand, is estranged from his father, a rather cold multimillionaire industrialist.

After his wife's death, the son reconciles with his father, using the film's signature and much-mocked catchphrase: "Love means never having to say you're sorry." Seeing these relationships on screen could've provided another reminder of Luther's early irreplaceable loss.

By the time Luther saw *Love Story*, several months had passed since he'd left school to pursue his dream of a singing career. But he wasn't any closer to his goal. Time was moving fast, and he felt like he was standing still.

Instead of singing, Luther worked a bunch of odd jobs. He served as a teacher's aide at a junior high school and also did a stint behind the counter at S & H Green Stamps. People would come in the store brandishing stamps they received while grocery shopping, and they'd trade in the sticky little green tickets for merchandise. If something didn't work right, that's when they'd go see Luther, who'd dutifully fill out a defective merchandise form. It was a fine way to pay the bills, but he might well have been back at Anderson's department store unpacking boxes with his old friend Robin. This was not why he left school, and the lack of movement toward his career was wearing at his resolve. There was a voice in his head that he couldn't seem to silence. It said, "You've made a huge mistake."

Luther tried to remain focused on music in his off-time, though. He still consistently studied the latest albums, singing along to the melodies and poring over the lyrics. In 1971, the year he turned twenty, two albums in particular received heavy play on Luther's turntable. One was *Exposed*, the spirited and still-underrated solo effort by Valerie Simpson, one half of the multitalented married duo Ashford and Simpson. The team met in 1964 at Harlem's

White Rock Baptist Church and soon began creating hits for Ray Charles and penning a slew of smashes for Motown acts, including such classics as "Your Precious Love" and "Ain't Nothing Like the Real Thing" by Marvin Gaye and Tammi Terrell.

Luther's other favorite that year was an album Ashford and Simpson wrote and produced: Diana Ross' second solo record, *Surrender*. He was especially taken with the title track, an unabashed plea for love, in which Diana breathily sings, "You've used me and abused me 'til I felt that I wanted to die / You've created a need in me that only you can satisfy." These lyrics crystallized Ashford and Simpson's status as Luther's favorite songwriters.

"I just said, 'Oh, nobody writes better than that,'" he recalled. "The things that they said and the way that they made their points from song to song just drained me. I'd wake up an hour later from having fainted from loving the songs so much. . . . They have emotional depth; they have street knowledge. I just think they're the greatest."

Inspired, he'd write his own tunes, steadfastly trying to commit to paper the melodies and emotions that went buzzing through his mind. He'd try them out with the reunited gang of high school friends, Fonzi, Robin, Diane, and Anthony. Carlos, their guitar-playing buddy, was now getting paid gigs, working in the Apollo's esteemed house band—where someone had to die for a slot to open up—and doing gigs with the lush soul trio, the Main Ingredient. Whenever Luther got discouraged, Carlos' success provided an example of someone who was on his way to really making it.

Although shy by nature, Luther aggressively tried to interest people in his music, talking to friends of friends and working old contacts he met at the Apollo. One day he finally got a break when he crossed paths with Ken Harper, a former radio DJ turned aspiring Broadway producer. Energetic with a flamboyant streak—an article once described him walking through New York in a full-length hooded raccoon coat—Harper was trying to develop a musical that would transform *The Wizard of Oz* into a funky urban fairy tale. He needed songs, and Luther was able to interest him in three, including the festive "Everybody Rejoice." Luther was ecstatic that he'd finally sold some songs, but he didn't really believe Harper's fledgling musical would ever make the Great White Way.

"Now, at that point it was a far-fetched idea," Luther remembered. "An all-black version for *The Wizard of Oz?*"

Luther also had other projects in the works. Through his contacts, he also met some producers who were working on the recording debut of one of Broadway's hottest black talents, a big-voiced, gospel-trained belter named Delores Hall. A former background singer for Harry Belafonte, Hall won raves for her appearances in *Hair*, *Inner City*, and *Godspell*, but she was ready to take her career in a different direction, tackling the pop music world. The producers of her album thought it would be a good idea to hook her up with an up-and-coming talent like Luther so that she'd have a fresh sound. Hall, however, wasn't interested.

"They said, 'Well, we have this new guy we want you to hear. He writes and does this, that, and the other, but let me tell you, he's a young guy—a young, young guy.'" Hall remembered. "And I'm thinking, 'Well, I don't have time to teach nobody nothing. I'm doing these shows; I'm trying to win myself a Tony Award; and I have an album I have to get out.'"

Nevertheless, Hall, then performing in *Godspell*, agreed to at least meet with Luther, telling the producers to bring him around on a matinee day and she'd talk to him between shows. So one day Luther showed up after an early performance with his mother in tow and made his way through the bustling backstage chaos to Hall's dressing room.

He came in, introduced himself and his mother, and told Hall that he was a big fan. Hall, for her part, looked him over and felt her reservations flare up again.

"He was this little chubby boy," she said, "and I'm going, 'Oh, no, what am I in for?'"

The meeting threatened to be a disaster, but then Luther sang for her and she was immediately charmed by his young earnest tenor.

"He was a baby," Hall said, "but he sang just as well then. Not as smooth as he came to be. He wasn't as experienced, but the talent was there. He was a diamond in the rough."

After the meeting, Hall chose to record two of Luther's tunes, "In This Lovely Hour" and "Who's Gonna Make It Easier for Me." What's more, she decided to duet with the young singer on the latter track, which seems modeled after the type of cuts Ashford and Simpson penned for Marvin Gaye and Tammi Terrell. To record the song, Luther went to RCA Studios in midtown Manhattan, and it was like stepping into a new world.

"He had never seen the inside of a recording studio before, period," Hall recalled. "So I gave him his first chance. I just walked him around the studio, as I told him where we would be standing and what was what. He took a look at the recording board, and before you knew it, he was saying, 'Oh, if you push this, you get this, that, or the other.' He was sweet, as precious as could be."

Hall's album *Hall-Mark* was released in 1973, the year Luther turned twenty-one. Finally, it looked as if his dreams were taking shape.

Around the same time, Luther would often go hang out with his friend Carlos as he worked in the studio with R&B trio the Main Ingredient. Luther once asked group member and producer Tony Silvester if it was OK for him to be there. Silvester said it was fine, but he didn't pay much attention to Luther. He initially didn't even know the young man was interested in a music career.

"He would watch us and he would sit there and be so quiet we wouldn't know he was there," Silvester remembered. "He was a shy guy. He always tried to stay out of everybody's way. If it was a big room, instead of being in the middle, he'd be in the corner somewhere."

Silvester felt that Luther was self-conscious because of his weight. "It was obvious," Silvester said. "He was a big guy. He was young and he was weighing about 350 pounds. He always wore a long buttoned overcoat and he never took it off."

After a while, Luther would start running daily errands for the band. He'd step out for lunch at noon, and then for dinner at around six, coming back with shopping bags full of sandwiches, beer, and sodas. "That became his task," Silvester said. "He felt better about himself because he now had a purpose. He had a job."

Once, during a recording break, everyone had left the studio except for Luther. Minutes later, Silvester ran back in the room to get something when he heard Luther singing and playing the piano beautifully.

"Luther!" Silvester yelled.

The young man at the piano jumped up. "What, did I do something wrong," he said.

"You mean to tell me that all this time you could sing and play like that? Who wrote these songs?"

"I did," Luther responded.

"Get out of here," said Silvester.

The producer was so impressed that he wanted to produce a record for Luther, but he was already so busy doing albums for other acts. "I was overwhelmed with the projects that I had," Silvester said.

Even though Silvester couldn't find time to work with Luther, an executive with Avco Embassy Records heard about the young talent and decided to sign Luther, Robin, Diane, and Anthony as a group. However, as soon as they made the deal, they quickly found out that having a record contract didn't necessarily mean getting the chance to make a record. Without a strong advocate within the company, the project languished and they were let go.

"There were problems over the budget, to be honest," Luther once explained.

What he needed then was a mentor, someone with even more experience in the record business than Hall, someone who could show him the right way for things to be done and how to make things happen in a notoriously wishy-washy music industry. At the end of 1973, there was no one like this on the horizon. Luther, however, would soon happen upon a superstar whose influence and support would transform his life.

"Fascination"

"Luther's voice had a magic about it. It was very, very warm, and it was sincere, fresh, and soulful. It was a blessed voice."

—MIKE GARSON, BANDLEADER FOR DAVID BOWIE IN 1974

September 2, 1974: The Universal Amphitheatre in Los Angeles, California

With the night sky bearing witness, the band was killing this evening, sending out grooves like fire-lit sparklers that emitted streaks of light as far as the eye could follow. The outfit hadn't played together long, but the chemistry—this odd mix of rock, soul, and jazz musicians—was working. Horns danced bawdy ballets around prowling bass lines. Guitars roared, snaked, and strutted, and drums thumped with vigorous precision, like a lioness keeping charge of wild-eyed cubs.

At the front of this controlled chaos stood a tall, shockingly thin man in a tailored suit. His hair was the color of flaming oranges, his skin as white as cake icing. The man's name was David Bowie, and he was touring the United States to try to replicate the kind of megastar rock success he had at home in Britain. So far it seemed to be working. Though he hadn't scored any major hits, he was playing to dense crowds of fans that screamed his name, flailed their bodies in the aisles, and streaked colored makeup down their faces as Bowie had in earlier incarnations.

Standing to his side on a stainless-steel platform were his waling background singers. Two of them had traveled with him for a while: Geoff McCormack, Bowie's childhood friend who went by the decidedly Vietnam-era stage name Warren Peace, and Ava Cherry, a tall, black former model with shaved eyebrows and an eye-catching shock of close-cropped white-blond hair. (Yes, that was her real name, she'd tell you if you asked.)

Ava met Bowie years earlier at a New York nightclub, where he promised to make her a star along the lines of the legendary Josephine Baker. Shortly thereafter, she and the then-married rock star began cultivating a relationship that went far beyond the professional.

The other four background singers were newcomers. There were Diane Sumler and Anthony Hinton, two kids from the Bronx; Robin Clark, who was married to Bowie's new guitar player, Carlos Alomar; and lastly, the man who helped coordinate the harmonies and get all the other singers in sync: Luther Vandross.

This wide-eyed twenty-three-year-old stood onstage and marveled at how his life had changed. One year ago, he was helping people fill out defective merchandise forms for broken junk. Now patterns of colored lights skipped all around him. A tight band was kicking out music so good and so loud that he felt it on the inside. In front of him, crowds were cheering, screaming, and waving their arms toward the odd orange-haired man planted at center stage.

Luther scanned the audience, and what he saw made an already dream-fulfilling night even more magical. Celebrities dotted the first few rows: Elizabeth Taylor draped in orange chiffon; young actress Tatum O'Neal decked out in a man's tuxedo; and seated next to her husband in the front row in a glittering floor-length gown that sparkled whenever hit with stray light from the stage was a member of Luther's divine three: Diana Ross.

It was as if something magical and unearthly had been dropped into Luther's little world. Suddenly, all of the decisions he had made to get to that spot onstage—dropping out of college, slogging through assorted day jobs—seemed worth it.

"I said, 'Yeah, this is for me,'" he remembered. "'I'm liking this.'"

That night, the band debuted a new number, "Young Americans," which Bowie had recorded about a month earlier. Musically, it was a funky piano-driven romp, the kind that practically calls out for people to get up out of their chairs, snap their fingers, and shake from side to side. Lyrically, however, it offered a cutting indictment of the American scene: the bankrupt politics of the Watergate White House, the numbing effect of pop culture, and the racism that continued to divide the country years after thousands had marched, rallied, and even died to bridge this divide.

For Luther, the song carried a strong personal meaning since it played a pivotal role in him getting his first big break. It all started back in New York City, when Bowie was looking for a new guitarist. Someone suggested Carlos Alomar, Luther's old friend from high school and Listen, My Brother, who was now married to one of Luther's best friends, Robin Clark. Carlos and Bowie quickly bonded, largely due to the British singer's infatuation with all things hip, urban, and soulful.

"I was like most English who came over to America for the first time," Bowie said in 1978, "totally blown away by the fact that the blacks in America had their own culture, and it was positive and they were proud of it."

Carlos became Bowie's ambassador to a vibrant, new—largely

black—world, even though Bowie's odd appearance initially made him uncomfortable. "You've got to understand," Carlos once explained, "I'm a Puerto Rican man living in Harlem doing black music. When you see a man so pasty white with red hair, you think that's strange."

However, Carlos soon warmed to the inquisitive foreigner and even invited Bowie home for dinner.

"What you need is to come to my house and my wife can make you some nice chicken and rice and beans and put some meat on those bones," Carlos told Bowie.

The singer answered, "Sure," and within days there was a limousine parked outside of Carlos and Robin's Harlem apartment.

One of the things Bowie especially admired about Carlos was that he played in the Apollo's house band. The theater still held its position as a mythic black music Arcadia, and Bowie hungered to know more about it. He had always loved James Brown's *Live at the Apollo* album, but Bowie had never actually gone to the theater, had never rested in those seats that had witnessed so much musical history.

Once Carlos took Bowie to the legendary venue, he was hooked and returned to the Apollo many times. Bowie loved the way it felt mixing with all the sharply dressed black couples who had come to the theater for a night out. It wasn't that they didn't notice the stark-white man with the sunburned hair. They just didn't care. They were doing their thing, he was doing his.

One of the most extraordinary shows Bowie ever saw there was a double bill with the Spinners and the Temptations. He liked the Temptations, the slick vocal blends, the machinelike dance moves, but it was the Spinners who brought down the house that night. The group, which had roots in Detroit, had been making records for more than a decade, but they were enjoying a resurgence after getting a new lead singer, the stirring Philippe Wynne, and hooking up with a hungry Philadelphia-based producer named Thom Bell. That night at the Apollo, they brought their new hits thrillingly to life.

"They dominated the evening," Bowie remembered. "Philippe Wynne was pure dynamite, an ultimate front man. And, jeez, the augmented house band nailed those Thom Bell arrangements to a 'T.' The roof plain sailed away by the time they did 'Mighty Love.' [It was] the best night at the Apollo ever, and I went to plenty."

Perhaps inspired by the Spinners' Philadelphia-based sound, Bowie booked a few weeks at the city's Sigma Sound Studios and invited Carlos to come along. Sigma was where the Spinners recorded, as well as all of the other high-charting acts then coming out of the Philly scene: the O'Jays, the Three Degrees, and Harold Melvin and the Blue Notes, which had recently discovered a dashing, powerful lead vocalist in its drummer Teddy Pendergrass. Overseeing the city's musical blossoming were two old friends and former band mates—Kenny Gamble from South Philly and Leon Huff, who hailed from nearby South Camden, New Jersey. Together, they not only wrote and produced hit records, but fostered an environment for talent to shine, nurturing musicians like arranger Thom Bell, the force behind the Spinners' recent success.

The music they collectively created—what came to be known as the Philly Sound—took a different approach than the thundering teenage rhythms of Motown or the sweat-soaked passion coming out of the South. The Philly Sound was lush, elegant, sophisticated, urbane, and aware. It reflected a people who had survived the day-to-day traumas of the early civil rights movement and were beginning to ask different questions about the world, all while nurturing expanded new dreams. Writer Nikki Giovanni captured this essence in a poem about Philly's musical heyday: "That's when the possibility was possible."

Bowie and his entourage arrived at Sigma on Sunday, August 11, 1974. When Bowie initially had the idea to record there, he wanted to use Gamble and Huff's renowned backing band, the interracial collective of pop, soul, and classical musicians, MFSB, or Mother, Father, Sister, Brother. But since they were booked solid, he relied on an ad hoc group of other talented sidemen to approximate the Philly Sound, including guitarist Carlos; drummer Andy Newmark, once of Sly and the Family Stone; bassist Willie Weeks, who played with the Isley Brothers; and alto saxophonist David Sanborn, who had put in time with everyone from Chicago bluesman Albert King to blind soul genius Stevie Wonder.

That first day, Bowie booked the studio for four in the afternoon, but he failed to show until around midnight.

"He was very thin in those days and living sort of reversed hours," remembered producer Tony Visconti, who oversaw the sessions. "He was going to bed at about eleven in the morning and all of that."

Much of this was due to a cocaine habit that was growing increasingly ravenous. Nevertheless, from the first few moments in this legendary studio, they all felt something special was happening.

"There was such an electrifying atmosphere in the air," recalled Visconti. Basically, they were just jamming, getting used to the curves and contours of each other's artistry, and trying to shape that into a good groove.

"Bowie kinda gave us more or less a framework to play the chord changes and stuff," remembered saxophonist Sanborn, "and we worked up the arrangements of the songs." For instance, during that initial session they developed the funky strut that would become "Young Americans."

Carlos liked the way things were going, and he called his wife, Robin, to tell her all about it. He invited her to make the short ninety-minute hop down to Philly so that she could hear things for herself.

"Oh, and bring Luther Vandross," he told her.

Luther jumped at the opportunity to return to his old Philly stomping grounds, but it was more about accompanying his friend than wanting to be in the presence of a buzzed-about British rock star.

"I didn't know anything about Bowie, except how to spell his name," Luther said. "Not pronounce it, just spell it."

Luther was only familiar with one of Bowie's songs, his 1973 breakthrough single "Space Oddity," an airy ballad about an astronaut who's lost in space.

"That was the saddest thing," Luther remarked of the song, "that whole isolated, cold feeling of loss."

Bowie was nowhere in sight when Luther and Robin arrived at Sigma. Carlos greeted them in a nearly empty studio, with the recently recorded track for "Young Americans" playing over and over again. Luther liked what he heard. The tune had a nice swaying beat and an interesting melody, but it lacked something. There was too much empty space where Bowie wasn't singing, and nothing else was going on. What it needed was something like the quality that Cissy Houston and the Sweet Inspirations brought to all those Aretha Franklin records. It needed some background vocals that would talk back to Bowie and push the song along.

"You know, that sounds very good," he said to Robin, "but there's a big chunk missing. It needs a catchphrase." He thought for a moment, then said to her, "Sing with me in unison."

While Bowie's recorded vocals played in the background, Luther and Robin shouted back at him like he was a Pentecostal preacher and they were his testifying flock.

"*Alllll-right,*" they sang, "Young American / Young American / he wants the young A-mer-i-can."

They kept this going a few times, refining the harmonies with every pass, until a tall, pale, wispy figure came rushing in.

"I love it," Bowie said. "Who are you?"

Unbeknownst to Luther, Bowie had been sitting in the control booth, indulging in one of his favorite hobbies—drawing. When he heard Luther and Robin singing, he knew their harmonies were exactly what he needed to complete his foray into soul.

From that moment, Bowie charged Luther with helping him come up with background arrangements for all of the new material he was recording at Sigma. Luther couldn't believe it. Here was this rock star who wanted his input on how to arrange records. It was the chance he'd been pining for. He was determined to make it work. He invited his old friends Anthony and Diane to join him, and then dug into creating intricate vocal blends and melodies.

Working with Bowie provided his first peek at how superstars operate and all that comes with the rock-and-roll lifestyle. There were drugs—which contributed to the round-the-clock working conditions—and, of course, groupies. Outside of the studio camped a whole gang of Bowie devotees who were quickly dubbed the "Sigma Kids."

Luther, however, focused on the music. When he wasn't thinking up new ideas for Bowie, he rehearsed Diane, Anthony, and Robin with some of his own numbers. Once, Bowie overheard them singing "Funky Music (Is a Part of Me)," a song that Luther had been working on for some time. Bowie was impressed with the song's sinister hook.

"Would you let me record it?" he asked.

"What do you mean, let you record it," answered a shocked Luther. "I'm living in the Bronx in a building with an elevator that hardly works and you're asking me to 'let' you record one of my songs."

Bowie changed some of the lyrics around, giving the party tune a darker, more ominous spin, and "Funky Music" became "Fascination," cowritten by Luther Vandross.

Bowie was increasingly impressed by Luther's budding talents and rarely missed a chance to tell him so.

"It was the first time that I ever had someone of his stature be so encouraging," Luther recalled. "He was constantly, constantly, constantly telling me: 'You've got to stick with this. You're going to make it. Trust me, you've got what it takes.'"

Bowie's Sigma sessions lasted about two weeks and resulted in around a dozen songs. When it was over, Bowie and his team listened to the results, a strange mongrel of rock, R&B, and jazz influences that sounded like nothing anyone had ever heard before. It had a touch of the Philly Sound, of course, but at heart it was a hybrid that pulled against chains of genre and convention.

"There was no point doing a straightforward take on American soul music because that had been done already," Bowie later reflected. "You couldn't envision any American soul artist doing any of these songs. But they paid homage to the soul sound. . . . I got these pretty heavyweight American soul musicians working on it that gave some sort of a kind of fake authenticity to it. It really was a 'plastic soul' album."

Before Bowie left Philly, he invited the Sigma Kids into the studio to hear what the band had recorded. The rock star sat near the back of the room, nervously watching. After all, this marked a new sound for him, stretching his audience's expectations. The group of Bowie disciples listened to each track, and when it was over, no one uttered a word. There was a tense, potentially devastating silence. Then one fan said, "Play it again," and everyone got up and started dancing.

With recording sessions completed, Bowie returned to the road, where he'd been in the midst of the massive *Diamond Dogs* tour to promote his current album of the same name. This was one of those road shows of rock legend. The set cost $400,000, took thirty workers to construct, and three forty-five-foot trailers to transport. Once erected, the stage resembled a city in ruins with crumbling skyscrapers, columns, and drawbridges. When Bowie sang about his lost astronaut in "Space Oddity," a cherry picker lifted him seventy feet above the stage, as if drifting off into his own orbit.

After his Philadelphia soul excursion, however, Bowie was bored with all of this spectacle. He wanted to strip down the show and refashion it to focus on the soulful sound of his new music. This plan included inviting several of the musicians from the Philly sessions to come along on the tour.

"He abandoned that [*Diamond Dogs*] set," remembered pianist Mike Garson, "and just changed the band. I became music director, and had this sixteen-piece band."

Bowie wanted to ask Luther to join him, but according to one source, he nursed reservations about the young singer's weight. In the record industry, image is as important as the music itself. Bowie was concerned about how it would look for him to be backed up by a three-hundred-pound, young black man whose look was far from the hipster persona that Bowie cultivated and fans expected.

This situation presented a dilemma, but it was short-lived. A hefty baritone soul singer named Barry White had recently hit number one on the pop charts with a plush dance number called "Can't Get Enough of Your Love, Babe." Bowie loved the record by what some critics called "the walrus of love," and figured Luther's weight wouldn't be an issue.

Luther, who, with the exception of college, had never been far from the East Coast, felt uneasy about going on the road with this rock star known for his wild reputation. Sure, joining the tour would help his career, but it would mean venturing far beyond all the things that made him feel comfortable and safe. His last foray from home at Western Michigan proved disastrous. He didn't want to risk another mistake.

Being on tour with Bowie would expose him to things he'd never experienced before. Bowie wasn't only one of the most exciting rising stars of rock, he was also one of the most controversial, largely because of his sometimes cross-dressing style and well-documented bisexuality. Once he told the press: "I like boys and I like girls—they're smashing." Another time, he notoriously said, "If I ever get sent to prison, I'll know how to keep happy." All of this made the boy from the Bronx very concerned.

"I was real nervous," Luther remembered. He told Bowie, "I'm not going on the road unless you take my other friends from the Bronx with me—Diane and Anthony."

Bowie agreed, and soon the whole gang, including Robin and Carlos, were off. Friends who started together in the streets of the Bronx, then moved to the stage of the Apollo, were now on tour with one of rock's most electrifying stars. Carlos remembered these as happy times.

"I was finally on the road with my wife and friends, making money," he said.

The rejiggered tour's first stop was the show in Los Angeles, where Luther spotted Diana Ross. Yet even before this eventful sighting, even before taking the stage, Luther's California trip proved to be an adventure. A car picked him up at the Los Angeles International Airport and shuttled him to his hotel, the four-star Sunset Marquis, a notorious rock-star hangout tucked in the hills of West Hollywood. Since Luther seldom traveled—and almost never without his mother—he didn't even know how to check into his room.

At the hotel, Angela Bowie, the headlining rock star's wife, sunbathed around the pool proudly holding court among her husband's minions. Bowie's inimitable pal Iggy Pop, the stringy-haired rocker with a proto-punk attitude, scrounged the grounds for food and a place to crash, and a gang of Bowie's gay groupies checked in to a room, camped out, and searched for signs of their idol.

The whole experience, from the car to the Marquis, felt exciting yet bewildering.

"The first thing I remember was the idea of having your own car," Luther said. "Remember, I was living at home with my mother. [With Bowie] I had my own car and my own hotel room at the Sunset Marquis. I could go to the store with my own money. Just the idea of having my own salary, my own independence. I was coming into adulthood at this same time, but in a way that I wish for everybody . . . which is doing what you really want to do and getting paid for it."

When Bowie brought Luther onboard, it wasn't just to sing, but also to arrange all the background vocals. Bandleader Garson used to watch Luther work with the other singers to create their lovely harmonies.

"He'd sit at the piano and bang the tunes out," remembered Garson. "He was the leader, and they all blended unbelievably. He gave them all the right notes to sing. He was just so certain about what everyone should do. It's like a gift."

One day in Los Angeles, Elizabeth Taylor showed up while they practiced. "We were rehearsing, doing vocals, and she was just sitting there," recalled singer and Bowie's extramarital paramour, Ava Cherry.

The tour progressed, going from the seven-night stay in Los Angeles, down the coast to San Diego, then over to Tucson and Phoenix, and Bowie increasingly wanted more from Luther. He felt a responsibility to help develop the talents of the shy young singer, and he thought there was no better training ground than the stage. Bowie went to Luther and asked him to open the show with several of his own songs, tunes like the Bowie favorite "Funky Music." Luther took the offer in and was almost too terrified to be flattered.

By this point, he felt comfortable doing what he did, standing in the background, working with the other singers. He no longer wanted to be out front, not like he used to, when they would by-pass him for lead vocals in Listen, My Brother. He had made peace with his position in the shadows. Onstage, he loved singing, but he avoided doing anything to draw eyes toward him.

"He would just sort of stand there," Garson remembered. "He was not moving initially when he started to sing. He wasn't danc-ing around. You could feel that he knew what he was doing, but he took a backseat in a way."

Even the other musicians noticed Luther's discomfort. "He seemed to be very self-conscious," Sanborn recalled. "I guess his weight had something to do with it. Whatever it was, he seemed to not want to have the spotlight on him. He would've preferred to be behind a curtain."

Nevertheless, Bowie persisted, and soon Luther made his solo stage debut in front of a crowd of thousands. It proved disastrous. For his whole set, this throng of expectant rock fans jeered the chubby, unknown singer. Luther was devastated. He could barely hear himself sing. His ears were filled with incessant, raving chants of "Bowieeeee!!!"

When that show finished, Luther found Bowie and told him that he couldn't go out there and sing by himself anymore.

"Listen, man," he said, "if you want to kill me, just use cyanide, but don't send me out there again."

"Hey," Bowie responded, trying to calm him. "I'm giving you a chance to get in touch with who you are. Go on and develop what you know. If these people aren't right for you—so what? Their re-action isn't the point. What you do is the point."

Bowie knew this firsthand, as his own career had been a series of mishaps and false starts. Born David Robert Jones in 1947 in Brixton, England, he had been performing in various bands since age thirteen. He recorded a few art-rock records before hitting in 1971 with "Space Oddity." Since then, he had managed to score a couple of hit albums at home, some recorded using the flamboyant persona "Ziggy Stardust," and he amassed a sizable cult following in the States, as evidenced by the crowds who showed up to see him on tour. Through his own experience, he knew that success in the music business meant working hard, staying hopeful, and most of all remaining in the game.

Bowie convinced Luther to continue as his reluctant opening act, yet the crowd response failed to change despite Luther's most impassioned efforts. One October night in Philadelphia, a raw egg came flying through the theater directed straight at Luther. It just missed where he stood, splattering between him and the bandleader.

Then there were the reviewers who were sometimes as dismissive and cruel as the crowd. Influential—and often offensively offbeat—rock scribe Lester Bangs called Luther "fat and much given to Stepin Fetchit rolling and popping of eyes." For someone already insecure, these words, essentially accusing Luther of being a compromised traitor to his race, must have been devastating.

Outside criticism wasn't the only obstacle Luther faced. The back-to-back shows forced him to learn the limitations of his voice. On October 28, 1974, the tour pulled into Manhattan's Radio City Music Hall, a storied institution for any New Yorker. It marked a homecoming of sorts. Just two months earlier, Luther had left the city to visit a friend in Philadelphia, and now he was returning on tour with one of music's most talked about artists.

Luther could feel the energy as the show began and the sold-out crowd started cheering. The band commenced playing the opening strains of "Funky Music." The bass line throbbed throughout the plush hall. Luther stepped to the microphone, opened his mouth, and joyously sang, "Every time I hear funky music . . ." That's when it happened, what all singers fear. He tried to make his voice soar like a hat thrown into the wind, and instead it fissured like a sun-baked mud pie.

"Yeah, he cracked a few times," acknowledged bandleader Garson. "We're all human."

Despite these internal and external challenges, Luther's attitude began to shift. He still fretted about his performance and the audience's reaction, but he was also viewing this time on the road as an opportunity to learn.

"I was aghast at the production values of his show," Luther recalled. "I wanted a show just like it—not that I wanted to be [David Bowie], but I wanted to go that extra amount he did. It's like when you go to someone's house—it's obvious if your host prepared for your arrival by serving a TV dinner or a smorgasbord. With Bowie, it was a feast every night."

The rocker's showmanship impressed most who worked with him.

"Ultimately Bowie got there and did it every night," Sanborn remembered. "He was the quintessential performer, and I think that's what all of us learned from watching him, how he paid attention to every aspect of the presentation of his music on the stage. He wanted to give people something to look at and to involve them in the experience. I'm sure that Luther went to school on that a little bit."

The behind-the-scenes happenings on the tour also provided Luther a chance to learn and stretch himself.

"I discovered a lot during that experience," he reflected. "I discovered a lot about living alone and about independence and entering into young adulthood. It's a time I'll never forget. What I learned were things no one can learn while living at home. . . . I learned to provide for myself and I learned to be my own cheer-leader and my own provider and partner."

Part of what he was discovering was how to get along with a number of eccentric personalities and their odd, sometimes illicit, habits. One of the most long-lasting relationships he forged during this time was with the platinum-haired, honey-toned Ava Cherry. Though now firmly ensconced in the jet-set ways of the rock high life, Ava, like Luther, had humble beginnings.

A daughter of Chicago's depressed South Side, Ava seemed to be plotting her escape from the confines of the neighborhood al-most since birth. She graduated from the Academy of Our Lady High School, and quickly swapped her Catholic school uniform for a bunny suit in order to serve drinks and mingle at Chicago's taste-fully naughty Playboy Club. *Playboy* magazine even featured her in a spread on the "Bunnies of 1971."

Ava, however, wasn't content with Chicago. She knew that you haven't really made it in show business until you've tackled New York City. With little pocket money, the eighteen-year-old said good-bye to her mother and father and headed to Manhattan to become a model. This was in the early 1970s, when fashion insid-ers were slowly starting to acknowledge the beauty of black women.

Work came quick, and Ava also began making the nightlife scene. The disco explosion hadn't ignited yet, but there was a feel-ing in the smoky air of the city's top nightspots, the combustible energy of a burgeoning cultural phenomenon.

One night, Ava stepped out at a hot club called Genesis for a party thrown in honor of Stevie Wonder, and as she made her way through the thick, celebrity-filled crowd—Aretha Franklin and Bill Cosby were there—she spotted a pale white face, and thought, "Isn't that David Bowie?"

That night, they met, talked, took in the crazy scene at the club, then talked some more. Both felt a steady buzz anytime Bowie's slender alabaster fingers neared Ava's warm bronzed skin.

"There's something about David," Ava observed, "that hypnotizes and takes over."

As they talked and drew closer, Bowie surged with ideas, big thoughts about how Ava should go on tour with him and how he could make her a legend—Josephine Baker for a new generation. He told her that he was leaving New York shortly, but would call her later about the tour. That was all she needed to hear. She packed up her things, gave up her hard-earned New York apartment, and headed back home to stay with her parents until her rock star Prince Charming called to whisk her away on his white jet plane.

She waited, and waited, and waited. Then she got a call, not from Bowie but an associate. He told her the tour had been canceled and that she wouldn't be meeting Bowie in Europe. Her Prince Charming had turned into a frog.

"That was my first lesson that you shouldn't count on things unless you're absolutely sure they are going to happen," Cherry reflected. "I took all the money I had and decided to go to Europe anyway to find [Bowie] and tell him what he did was tacky and low."

She made her way to Europe and went about seeing all the cities she could: Milan, London, Paris. She donned "the most outrageous clothes I had," and soon got more fashion work, landing in the pages of French *Vogue* and *Elle* and spending time in the workshop of designer Yves Saint Laurent.

"I would walk down the street, and fashion designers would stop me and say, 'We need this girl, she is fabulous, *magnifique*,'" Cherry recalled. "But the whole time I was there, in the back of my mind, I kept thinking, 'I've *got* to find this guy David Bowie.'"

She finally tracked him down one night near Paris. Impressed by her persistence, Bowie decided to make good on his promises. He arranged for his management company to set her up in an apartment, as well as finance singing and dancing lessons. Things felt like they were paying off, all the sacrifice and uncertainty, those transatlantic miles. She might just become Josephine Baker yet.

By the time Ava met Luther in 1974, she was in the midst of a full-blown affair with Bowie, who was still with his blond American wife, Angela, with whom he had a toddler son. Although they both sometimes enjoyed extramarital relations, Angela felt betrayed by how devoted Bowie seemed to Ava.

Everyone around Bowie knew of his relationship with Ava. In Philadelphia, he wrote and recorded a song about his feelings called "Can You Hear Me." On tour, he'd perform it almost nightly, singing: "Once we were lovers, can they understand? / Closer than others, I was your man."

Watching the story of Ava and Bowie unfold, Luther indirectly learned new lessons about love and life.

At the same time, Luther was being schooled in other ways of the music industry, like drugs. It was the early 1970s, when cocaine flowed like the powder from a Pixie stick. Nobody thought it was addictive. Everyone felt like it made them funny, sexy, creative, and invincible. Many in the band were using some form of intoxicant, and it caused a divide between those who did and those who didn't.

"I don't really remember there being a lot of socializing going on in general with people who didn't have a common interest," recalled saxophonist David Sanborn, who did his share of partying. "Luther came from a different world entirely. He was a native New Yorker, but I always had the feeling that he lived a more or less sheltered life. He was clearly not into what we all were into. He had no interest, not even a bit of curiosity about that. I think he saw it as counterproductive, which on many levels it was, but it

just wasn't his scene. He was very focused on moving his music career forward. He was like, 'What's the job. Let me do it, and let me
do as good of a job as I can.'"

With all the drug use in the Bowie camp, Luther was once again
somewhat of an outsider. He was both a part of the scene and also
removed from it.

Bandleader Mike Garson felt similarly. "Luther and me did not
participate [in the drugs]," he remembered, "so we had that in
common. He was just clean that way and so was I. So that kinda
caused a little friction, because when people are on drugs, they
sorta want everybody else to be on drugs."

On November 2, 1974, the morning after a concert, Bowie and
the band taped an episode of NBC's *Wide World of Entertainment*,
and the difference between those who did drugs and those who
didn't was striking. While still proficient, Bowie and the bulk of
his backing players seemed a bit shaky and dazed, lumbering
through a rendition of "Young Americans." Luther, meanwhile, cut
a much different figure. Sporting a blue denim pants suit and a
white shirt with a shoulder-spanning collar, Luther heartily belted
out his background parts, smiled as wide as he had on *Sesame
Street*, and led the other singers in a quick-footed, shuffling, cha-
cha step. He looked like he was on fast-forward while others were
in slow motion.

"We had to tape that at ten in the morning or some ungodly
hour like that," Sanborn remembered, "and we were on the vam-
pire shift. I can't even remember if I'd gone to bed the night before.
I was in that place where it's almost like nausea because I was so
tired. [But] Luther was extremely straight. He'd probably gone to
bed after the show and gotten up, had breakfast. None of the rest
of us had probably eaten for days."

During the taping, Bowie gave an interview to the show's host,

Dick Cavett. Bowie loudly snorted and sniffed, and at one point mentioned something about coming down with the flu.

"And I'm thinking, 'Yeah, right,'" Sanborn recalled, "'I think I've got that flu, too.'"

Despite sizable differences in lifestyle, interests, and experience, the band had one thing uniting them. "It was as unlikely a group of people that you could ever imagine together," Sanborn remembered. "It was a group of people that you could barely imagine in the same room, much less on the same stage, but somehow it worked. I remember some nights when that band was just smoking. All these people from such different backgrounds were just locked in, bringing their individual talents to the moment. And that's what I remember the most, the ability of people to rise to the occasion."

Music was their bond, and whenever it became the topic of discussion on the tour bus, Luther had something to say. He'd pontificate on the merits of Dionne Warwick; share plans about the group he'd already formed with Robin, Anthony; and Diane; and talk about all the songs he was writing.

One day, while riding down some seemingly endless byway, Luther read that the all-black version of *The Wizard of Oz* was heading into production. Maybe one of his songs would make it to Broadway after all.

"I always got the impression at that point that Luther wanted to be a songwriter," Sanborn noted. "My impression was that Luther was not interested in the spotlight, but a life behind the scenes as a songwriter and producer."

Few people he worked with during this time ever thought that Luther would one day be filling venues, fronting his own band of musicians.

"That's nothing I ever would've called," Sanborn observed.

"Not only did I not think it was likely, I didn't think he really had an interest in being a solo artist."

"He was meant to sing," bandleader Garson acknowledged, "but I never would've imagined that he'd become what he became."

The only person who consistently believed Luther could be a star was Bowie. After the last concert of the tour, on December 1, 1974, in Atlanta, Bowie pulled Luther aside.

"You're going to make it," he told the young singer. "Next year is your year."

Luther always remembered these words, because they were some of the most encouraging he'd ever heard. However, Bowie's prediction was off by many years.

"Everybody Rejoice (Brand New Day)"

*"I learned a lot from the way I saw
other people handle their careers . . .
you cannot help but take things in."*

—LUTHER ON WORKING WITH
DAVID BOWIE AND BETTE MIDLER

Some years move in baby steps. Others soar like continent-jumping jet planes. You begin in one place, and before you know it—in a frenzied rush that erases all normal sense of time—you're somewhere you never imagined. You look back and your starting point is so far in the distance, you can't even see it on the horizon.

For Luther, 1974 was that kind of year. It rang in with him as a college dropout and one of a million wanna-be musicians. By the time it closed, he was a professional arranger and background singer who had recorded and toured with David Bowie, one of the most interesting acts in rock.

It had been an exhilarating ride, but now it was slowing down. Bowie planned to take his rock-laced soul revue to Brazil, then later to Britain and the rest of Europe, giving Luther and his friends their first trip overseas. However, he canceled these dates abruptly in order to take a starring role in the film *The Man Who Fell to Earth*.

It was a disappointment of sorts, because by now Luther had grown fond of show business. He had sampled the life he wanted to live. He knew the ins and outs of it: the warmth of a spotlight on his skin, the cheers and roars of the crowd, the shiny late-model cars that rushed you to and fro, the hotel rooms where the towels were always fresh and the bed neatly made. He wanted more but, at the time, there was no way of knowing if his stint with Bowie was a first move toward something bigger or if it would come to mark a career peak, a handful of glory days never to be matched.

These questions lingered, but Luther had plenty to celebrate as 1974 turned into 1975. On January 5, he experienced something he once thought would never be: *The Wiz*, that all-black take on *The Wizard of Oz*, was opening at the Majestic Theatre on Broadway. Two of Luther's song had been cut, but one powerful number, "Everybody Rejoice," remained. The song came toward the end of the fantastical show, when—on a mission from an all-powerful force called the Wiz—Dorothy, a pigtail-wearing Kansas girl played by a blisteringly talented teenager named Stephanie Mills, defeats the Evil Witch of the West. She and her friendly accomplices, the Lion, the Tin Man, and the Scarecrow, then free the Witch's long-suffering minions and they all start singing Luther's words: "Can you feel a brand-new day / Can you feel a brand-new day."

Sitting in the audience, flanked by his friends, Luther felt giddy watching this once far-fetched idea come to colorful, glorious life. "We were astounded," he remembered. "First of all, Stephanie Mills sang the chandelier off of the ceiling. I was so proud to be a part of that."

Behind the scenes, things weren't so idyllic. Even amid all of the opening-night grandeur and flash, a closing notice had been posted backstage. Costs were running high, but ticket sales were going slow. Reviews appeared, but did little to boost sales. There were some raves: "The show, with all new music and lyrics, is saucy with urban humor," opined *Time* magazine. "Its talk is jumping jivernacular, its walk is a big city strut, its dances have a blowtorch frenzy, and its songs range from a warm gospel glow to the rock beat of a riveter mining asphalt." However, others, including the stodgy *New York Times*, panned it.

The producers then did something nearly unprecedented for a new Broadway production. They ran a TV commercial touting the show. It reached folks whose tastes weren't set by the *New York Times*, those whose idea of a good show was simply some swift-footed dancing and roof-shaking singing. And, as anyone could tell even from the short TV spot, that little Stephanie Mills sure could sing.

Tickets started moving fast. The box office took in $46,000 one week, then $53,000, and not long afterward, $77,000. Soon a sold-out crowd, standing ovations, and multiple curtain calls were a nightly occurrence. There was even talk of turning the show into a film.

It was a wonderful way to start a year that would find Luther joining forces with yet another spectacular—and decidedly edgy—young talent. Unlike Bowie, this one talked dirty, sang everything from rock to bawdy blues, and had a curious link to a revered Hollywood legend.

Throughout the 1930s and 1940s, no movie actress proved fiercer, wilder, more irascible, and obstinate than redheaded firebrand Bette Davis. Playing such roles as a Southern plantation princess in *Jezebel* or a hardened grande dame in *All About Eve*,

Davis personified those women who woo catastrophe in order to feel more alive. Her personal life was as volatile as the ways of the characters she portrayed. She warred with studio heads over roles and money and seldom missed the chance to alienate a costar. Her motto was that, in order to succeed, "you have to have the guts to be hated."

This is the legacy that Chesty and Ruth Midler bequeathed their third daughter when they chose to name her after the impetuous movie star. They loved the glamour of "Bette," but Ruth thought it was pronounced "bet" instead of "Betty," thereby inadvertently giving her daughter a unique way of bearing a name someone else already made famous. Growing up as one of a handful of Jewish girls in a Filipino enclave in downtown Honolulu, Hawaii, young Bette soon began exhibiting some of the defining qualities of the woman she was named after. She had a knack for performing, doing local theater and singing in a folk trio that toured nearby army bases.

By the time she met Luther around 1975, Bette had become the kind of artist who made folks talk—you loved her, you hated her, you didn't know quite what to do with her. After leaving Hawaii in 1965, Bette made her way to New York City, where after short stints as a hatcheck girl, typist, and go go dancer, she won the role of the young bride Tzeital in Broadway's *Fiddler on the Roof.* Yet it wasn't on the Great White Way where Bette earned her celebrated—and notorious—reputation. It was in the white-tiled innards of the Continental Baths, a popular gay hangout on the corner of West Seventy-fourth Street and Broadway.

Located in the basement of the Astoria Hotel, the Continental Baths aspired to be a polished take on those establishments where gay men congregated for a bit of relaxation, conversation, and the exchange of fevered touches. It featured an ample dance floor, roomy saunas, a sundeck, a cabaret lounge, and a competition-sized swimming pool done in Olympia blue. The Baths also show-cased performers to entertain the crowds of lusty young men whose numbers, on weekends, could reach a thousand strong.

Bette was one of the earliest acts to perform at the Baths, which she called "the tubs." At first, her set, consisting of mostly well-known torch songs, show tunes, and a little banter, failed to impress the towel-clad men who had other matters on their minds. However, Bette soon won a loyal audience by peppering her act with bawdy borscht-belt humor, breakneck double entendres, and an eclectic musical mix that could accommodate everything from the Andrew Sisters' brightly chaste "Chattanooga Choo Choo" to the scantly veiled "Long John Blues," about a dentist who knows how to work his drill. Between songs and schtick, Bette would sound off about the ups and downs of her own life, charming the crowd with her endearing combination of vulnerability and bravado.

"I was an ugly fat little Jewish girl who had problems. I was miserable," Bette once reflected on her twenty-four-year-old self. "I kept trying to be like everyone else, but on me nothing worked. One day, I just decided to be myself. So, I became this freak who sings in the tubs."

What made the men at the Baths love Bette was that she was one of the first performers to meet them openly on their own terms. She knew they were gay, knew what was going on when they dispersed after the show, heading to rooms upstairs or to foggy corners of the steam room. Yet, unlike much of society at that time, she didn't care. She acknowledged that she was on their turf, an almost sacred space simply because it was one of the few places they could be themselves. She understood and even seemed to empathize with their ongoing struggle to be treated with humanity at a time when homosexuality was still viewed as a mental illness and being gay could cause people to lose jobs, lifelong friends, the love of those who raised them, and in the worse cases, life and limb. At the close of every show, she sang Bob Dylan's nearly prayerlike anthem of emancipation, "I Shall Be Released."

Critic Rex Reed captured Bette's inspiring effect on this core audience in a review. "Magic is in the air," he wrote. "Magic that removes the violence of the cold, dark streets. The insecurities, the hates, the fears, the prejudices outside vanish in a haze of camp. . . . And the Jewish Tinker Bell is right there in front of you. Twinkling, glittering and making soft musical chimes of peace."

The devotion she inspired made the Baths an ideal place for Bette to refine her talents. "I was able to take chances on that stage I could not have taken anywhere else," she remembered. "Ironically, I was freed from fear by people who, at the time, were ruled by fear. And for that I will always be grateful."

It wasn't long before word of Bette's dynamic shows spread, landing her as a guest on *The Tonight Show* with Johnny Carson and drawing a flock of straight men and women, hipsters, and celebrities to the Baths. Among those who caught Bette in her early days were white-haired artist/scenester Andy Warhol, Rolling Stones' front man Mick Jagger with his striking wife, Bianca, and one of Jagger's close rock-world pals, David Bowie, who loved Bette's act and talked it up to friends.

Shortly thereafter, Bowie met Bette and the two bonded over their love of contemporary R&B. It was the only "real" music, they thought. Bowie, of course, was enamored of the Philly Sound and Aretha Franklin, and Bette raved about the Jackson 5, saying they made the greatest records.

Later that year, when Bette caught one of Bowie's new R&B-styled concerts, she loved it. She was inspired by the way he infused his sound with the kind of black music they both adored, and—with her eye for talent and her affinity for those who seemed a little out of place—she was especially impressed with one of the background singers, the chubby fellow who Bowie said helped arrange the vocals. He'd be perfect to help out with what was going to be her biggest career move to date: a full-scale Broadway show to be called *Bette Midler's Clams on the Half-Shell Revue.*

"Bette," remembered Luther, "was always the kind to say, 'What, there's somebody new who's fabulous? Why isn't he singing for me? Who is he? Bring him down here now!'"

Luther found out about Bette's interest in him and went to audition for the woman the bare-chested guys at the Baths had dubbed "The Divine Miss M." Even though he worked on Bowie's album and had been touring with the rock star for months, Luther was still relatively new to the scene. He didn't know what to expect from this wild redhead about whom everyone seemed to have a strong opinion.

He walked into the rehearsal space and found it full of people. This was so different from the way he'd met Bowie. In that case, he hadn't even known Bowie was in the room when he started making up parts to "Young Americans." Now he was being asked to perform on the spot, to prove to someone why he was worthy of being hired. It was the kind of situation that could tax the nerves of the most seasoned players, much less a newcomer.

Yet, if his time with Bowie had taught him one thing, it was that he should have faith in his abilities. "[Working with Bowie] gave me the confidence that my musical ideas were good," Luther said. "He was always, always encouraging me, saying, 'Your voice is going to make it for you. Your voice is going to make you successful.'" It was hard, but he knew that in order to make it in this business, he'd have to trust his own talents. By the time Bette entered the room, he was ready for her.

"You must be Luther," Bette enthused upon spotting him. She

walked toward where he was standing, moved closer to him, then closer still. At five-foot-one, her head reached to about Luther's chest, and perhaps because of this proximity, she leaned over and proceeded to bite his nipple. Luther wasn't prepared for *that*. He felt outraged.

"Look," he said, "I know you're famous and I'm not, but I don't play that way. I don't need this gig that bad. Back off!"

Bette, far from being offended at this reprimand from the young singer, found the whole situation hilarious. "Look everybody, a momma's boy," she said to the gathered crowd, and the truth was that Luther still did live with his mother at the time.

The whole scene put Luther off. He loved singing, loved arranging vocals, loved the feeling of being onstage and seeing stars like Diana Ross grooving in the audience. Yet he refused to change who he was in order to make it in this strange new world. For all of his self-doubts and concerns about his weight, he was determined that no one—no matter how big a star—was going to change him from the boy that Mary Ida had worked so hard to raise. If Bette wanted him to work for her, she had to accept him the way he was.

Bette appreciated the newcomer's spunk. She'd been at enough auditions to know that many people would offer to do nearly anything, sacrifice all sorts of personal principles and dignity, to get a shot at working on Broadway. Luther, on the other hand, refused to be compromised. She respected that, and despite being a little— well, very—square, he was hired.

Besides, anyone who had shared a stage with Bette knew she courted a bit of tension in her personal and professional relationships. In many ways, she had two sides. She could, on the one hand, be extraordinarily nurturing.

"When you work with Bette, you become her friend," said Charlotte Crossley, a member of Bette's campy trio of female background singers dubbed the Harlettes. "She's interested in you.

She's sensitive to you because she wants you to be sensitive to her."

On the other hand, Bette's manner could take on a darker cast. "We would scream back and forth," Charlotte recalled. "That's her way of communicating. . . . She grew up in a family where there was constant fighting, and you couldn't get any results from being nice. And that, unfortunately, spilled over into her work. . . . It really pushed a lot of people over the edge and away from her."

Luther, however, remained largely unfazed by what was going on around him as he began working for Bette. He was developing a professional veneer, a shield of sorts that protected him from Bette's temper tantrums or the drugs in Bowie's camp. Unlike others on the scene, he wasn't trying to insinuate himself with the stars or attempt to become their best friends.

"I didn't really hang out with them," Luther remembered. "I didn't have that much in common with them as people go." He focused on the music.

Bette entrusted Luther with arranging the vocals for three numbers in her show: the yearning ballad "I Don't Want the Night to End," the strutting Bobby "Blue" Bland number "Ain't No Love in the Heart of the City," and a tune Luther was intimately familiar with—Bowie's "Young Americans." By this time, the *Young Americans* album had hit the streets, allowing people to weigh in on the British rocker's excursion into American R&B. Many critics trashed the record, some even exposing their own racism in the process. "I get a persistent picture of nigger patronization as Bowie flips through his soul take-offs . . . like some cocktail party liberal," one scribe wrote in the respected British music magazine *Melody Maker.* "He patently lacks any emotional commitment to his material."

Other critics misread what Bowie tried to accomplish with the album. He didn't want to do soul music as much as he wanted to see what soul music could do to his sound. What he created with

Luther and the rest of the band was a hybrid. Not an orange, but a tangerine.

The mainstream listening public seemed to get it, though. *Young Americans* quickly became Bowie's biggest-selling U.S. album, reflecting Americans' longtime love for blue-eyed takes on black music. The title track also climbed into *Billboard* magazine's Top 40 pop chart. Bowie had a smash on his hands, and Luther played no small part in helping him achieve it.

"*Young Americans* was a turning point for Bowie," observed saxophonist David Sanborn. "And Luther was certainly instrumental in the success of that record. There's almost as much of him on that record as there is of Bowie."

The album's success dramatically upped Bowie's profile. Within the next year, he made appearances on *The Cher Show, Soul Train,* and the annual Grammy Awards, where he presented Aretha Franklin with an award for Best Female Soul Singer. When Aretha arrived onstage to receive the golden statue from the pale, effeminate, streetlamp-thin British singer, she exclaimed, "I'm so happy, I could even kiss David Bowie." This comment offended him so much that he forbade girlfriend Ava Cherry from playing Aretha's records, lest he break them in two.

For Luther, the payoff from *Young Americans* was simply more work, such as the gig with Bette. Rehearsals for her Broadway revue largely went untroubled—that is, until the week before opening night. The tremendous scope of the show and the pressure to make it a success began weighing on Bette.

"I never imagined it would turn into this epic of death," Bette recalled, "the most mind-boggling, stupendous production ever conceived and built around one poor small five-foot-one-and-a-half-inch Jewish girl from Honolulu. All of a sudden, I'm a whole industry. People run, they fetch, they carry, they nail, they paint, they sew."

Bette flipped out, terrorizing the staff with her eruptions of doubt-fueled anger. "I had two or three days when I literally hit people," she said, "and called them horrendous names." At night, her sleep was disturbed by a recurring nightmare that David Bowie would open up a show directly across from hers, and that he'd have all the same sets and wear identical costumes.

Luther experienced an altogether different view of the show-business high life than what he saw on the road with Bowie. In many ways, each star offered case studies on the sometimes corrupting effects of fame. When Luther worked with Bowie, the rock star was descending into a drug-laden pit of self-destruction. Bette, on the other hand, often masked her fears and insecurities by lashing out at those around her and hoping that the force of her celebrity would ultimately excuse her behavior and serve as its own type of apology. His time spent with Bowie and Bette made him an accelerated student in a comprehensive immersion course: "How to be a Superstar 101."

On April 14, 1975, Bette's *Clams on the Half-Shell Revue* opened at Broadway's recently built Krinskoff Theatre, which had just played host to a two-person show with Lena Horne and Tony Bennett. Fans buzzed around the venue on opening night. As celebrities made their entrances, camera bulbs flashed and a spotlight lit up the Manhattan sky.

The curtain raised around eight, and one of the first things the audience saw was a giant clamshell being pulled onstage as the supporting cast launched into "Ol' Man River" from the Broadway classic *Showboat.* Then the clamshell slowly opened and Bette appeared, scantily clad and glowing like the love goddess from painter Botticelli's masterwork *The Birth of Venus.* Bette then proceeded to dance, sing, and joke her way through a nearly three-hour production, where she sent up Barbra Streisand, Liza Minnelli, and Tina Turner, spoofed Broadway shows *Oklahoma* and *South Pacific,* and sounded off about current events such as the 1974 kidnapping of newspaper heiress Patty Hearst.

"Oh, listen, you must all rush out to McDonald's," she joked. "They're featuring a new item on the menu. It's called the Hearst burger—there's no patty."

Critics raved about the show. "The revue is indeed a devastating delight: a play without a plot, a concert without the gaps," a reviewer wrote in *Portland Opera* magazine. "Clad in what looks like a combination of Liberace leftovers and a basement sale at Frederick's of Hollywood, Bette Midler and her Clams had one cracking Broadway open with Ziegfeldian zest in the stage extravaganza of the year."

Clive Barnes of the *New York Times* enthused: "Bette Midler, the tackiest girl in town had come home to roost. . . . She is a modern phenomenon, the low priestess of her own jukebox subculture, an explosion of energy and minutely calculated bad taste, a drizzle of dazzle, a lady both brash and vulnerable, a grinning waif singing with a strident plaintiveness of friendship and love. . . ."

In addition to these great notices, the show also broke a Broadway box-office record by moving more than $200,000 worth of tickets in one day. The initial four-week run was soon extended to ten weeks, making it a career pinnacle for Bette.

For the second time that year, Luther had been an essential part of someone else's success. It made him hungry for his own.

9

"It's Good for the Soul"

*"Luther [the group] was my Temptations,
my Gladys Knight and the Pips . . ."*

—LUTHER ON HIS EPONYMOUS
FIVE-PERSON ACT

In 1975, when walking down Manhattan's West Fifty-sixth Street, near the corner of Eighth Avenue, an observer might have noticed that one apartment building stood out among all the other squat, dull structures. This building, at 330 West Fifty-sixth, flaunted style, where the rest seemed penned in by function. Its body stretched long toward the sky, and its facade wasn't mauled by rusting fire escapes running down the front like jagged scars. It also didn't have boxy air-conditioning units jutting out of every other window like the neighboring buildings, 330 West Fifty-sixth Street had the smooth, cool look of central air.

To enter the building, you dashed up several steps from the sidewalk. Then you'd pass some curiously twisting bit of modern art, a mini-garden of assorted greenery and waifish trees, and a couple of bulbish lamps that resembled lighted white dandelions.

At the entrance, you'd see a doorman sitting on the other side of two giant glass doors, and as you moved closer, the doors opened automatically for you with a near-whispering *whoosh*. This was the site of Luther's first apartment.

Money was finally coming in. Bowie's *Young Americans* album was an undeniable hit, and since it included "Fascination," the song Luther cowrote, he was getting a cut of every copy sold. This was a pleasant surprise for the novice songwriter, who initially was just happy that Bowie was even interested in recording the tune. "I thought people gave away songs for the artistic gratification, until the checks began rolling in," Luther recalled. "I made a lot of money from that song." This upward turn in his financial situation allowed Luther to move from his mother's apartment in the crowded Bronx, where he spent most of his teenage years. For the first time since he went off to college, Luther was again on his own. This time, however, he was ready. He was twenty-four years old and he was closest to living his dreams than he'd ever been before.

Following his stint arranging songs for Bette's Broadway show, Luther got steady work. Bette introduced him to the prolific producer Arif Mardin, a Turkish émigré who had helmed recordings for everyone from the rock quartet the Young Rascals to—most impressively for Luther—Aretha Franklin. Mardin was behind the recording panels when Aretha sang that favorite of Luther's, "I Never Loved a Man (The Way I Love You)," as well as many of her other early hits. Mardin later referred to these years as his "apprenticeship at the Aretha Franklin School of Soul, Gospel and Funk and Supreme Artistry." For her part, Aretha called Arif "a musician's musician" and raved of his "magic touch" and "illustrious arrangements of depth and beauty."

Arif hired Luther to sing background on Bette's *Songs for the New Depression* album, and he was so pleased with the results that he soon began booking Luther for lots of other gigs. "He stole the show," Arif remembered. "This incredible sound—velvety, warm—came out of the man. The voice left an imprint on the studio session scene."

Luther quickly found himself shuttling from one recording studio to another, singing with a grab bag of different artists who all wanted him to give their songs some added soul. One day he'd work with someone like long-haired folkie Judy Collins, then the next he'd be belting on tracks by British glam rocker Gary Glitter or former Motown queen Martha Reeves.

He sang behind both established acts and newcomers. One vocalist he worked with that year was a promising male R&B talent named Peabo Bryson. Peabo and Luther were the same age—in fact, Peabo was born just seven days before Luther—but their careers were headed in different directions. Peabo—with his smooth caramel skin; dense, rounded Afro; and thick physique made firm from a youth working on his family's South Carolina farm—was being groomed as a lead singer. He looked and sounded like somebody's sweet Southern dream.

Luther, still holding on to the weight he'd picked up in college, was content to be behind the scenes. Nobody since Bowie had tried to push him out front and he was fine with that.

"I had questions about my value as a lead vocalist at that point," he remembered. Besides, he was finally doing something he adored, something that made all those youthful nights spent alone, embraced only by a pair of headphones, seem worthwhile.

"I love background vocals so much I can't breathe," Luther said. "So when I got the chance to do background vocals on a professional level, in my mind, I had made it. It was absolutely fine for me."

The jobs often came with nice perks, too. In late 1975, Luther, along with his childhood friend and singing buddy Anthony, took his first overseas trip to Europe touring with progressive rocker Todd Rundgren and his outfit Utopia. The world was opening up for Luther. He was seeing new places, meeting different people, learning new things—musical and otherwise—all because of the rich beauty of his voice.

Yet even with these considerable accomplishments, Luther still yearned for things that seemed just out of his grasp. He'd had success placing songs with Bowie and in *The Wiz*, but he was having trouble finding homes for his new tunes. People were willing to give them a listen, but no one wanted to put them down on wax. It became nearly a singular goal: He wanted people to hear his songs.

Patrick Adams, a former Listen, My Brother member who had become an executive at the fledgling Perception Today Records, remembered Luther trying to pitch his tunes. "Luther would come to the office periodically to shop his songs," Adams recalled. "And I was constantly turning them down. It was always good material. It just wasn't apropos for anything I was doing at the time."

Saxophonist David Sanborn also remembered how, after the Bowie tour wrapped, Luther invited him to hear some material. Sanborn listened carefully to the music and could sense potential, but felt the songs needed work. "I had great respect for him," Sanborn said, "but it didn't pan out. I was more impressed with his vocals than his songwriting."

In addition to these songs, there were other concerns on Luther's mind. He still vividly remembered that vision he had in college of finely dressed men and women on an elaborate stage, moving and singing in expertly crafted style. As a member of a group, he wouldn't be the sole focus, the target of so many judgmental eyes. He would be one of a team, and the group could provide an outlet for his arranging talents and, most importantly, a home for all of his songs.

The only problem was that his core group of friends, the buddies who followed him through high school in Listen, My Brother and then onstage with Bowie, were being pulled in different directions. Success was providing opportunities that threatened to separate them. Luther and Anthony, of course, had already been to Europe with Rundgren, and soft-rock singer/songwriter Cat Stevens had just asked Diane to accompany him on tour.

Luther decided that if he didn't act soon, he wouldn't have a group to pull together. So he contacted everyone and let them know that the idea for a group was back on. They would be like the Temptations meets the Supremes, and they would bear the name of their shy yet musically confident leader: Luther.

After hearing his plans, Anthony and Diane signed on. Robin, however, had other commitments and went on to sing background for jazz guitarist/vocalist George Benson and troubled blues and soul siren Esther Phillips. Luther replaced her with Christine Wiltshire, another popular session singer, and Theresa V. Reed, a vocalist who was barely eighteen.

When Christine started working with Luther she was struck at how different he was from most folks she knew in the music business. He didn't smoke, drink, or do drugs, and he never had sexual or romantic dalliances that she knew of. "I'm really sure he was a virgin when I met him," Christine remembered. "I really am sure. He was *that* straitlaced. I'm serious."

The new fivesome recorded demos in order to drum up record company interest. Luther played them for various music industry executives that he met through his backup work. But, as he explained, they "were turned down by everyone—every single record company."

Undaunted—and, by this point, growing accustomed to a certain level of rejection—Luther continued trying to nail down a recording contract. He told producer Arif Mardin about his group and gave him a copy of the demo. Mardin was impressed and arranged for Luther to have a meeting with Henry Allen, a top executive from Atlantic Records, then one of the biggest labels in the business. Atlantic was home to two of Luther's favorites, Aretha Franklin and the Sweet Inspirations. Signing with them would be more than simply getting a record deal, it would be like finally being invited to a party that he had long watched from the outside.

On the morning of Luther's meeting at Atlantic, there was a lot of bustling going on in the hallways and sleek conference rooms. The company was about to make a major announcement to the press. It would bring new opportunities for a lot of people, and folks were talking about what the changes might mean for the future direction of the esteemed label.

The news was that Atlantic was launching a boutique mini-label called Cotillion, which would focus on developing and nurturing new and innovative talent. The executive chosen to helm this new venture was the same person Luther had met: Henry Allen. The just-promoted honcho took one listen to the demo recording of Luther's thumping bass-driven number "It's Good for the Soul" and promptly made an executive decision: Luther, the group, would be the first act signed to Cotillion.

From there, things accelerated quickly. As 1975 turned into 1976, and as many people were in a patriotic frenzy getting prepped for the country's two hundredth birthday, Luther was clocking long hours in the studio with his group, trying to vividly capture his musical vision on tape. Most of the album was done at New York City's Atlantic Recording Studios, but Luther also cut a few tracks at Philadelphia's Sigma Sound, the place where he first met Bowie. The only difference was that he was now in charge. It was his show.

The group finished the album and delivered it to the record company in March 1976. Excited by what he heard, label president Allen quickly rush-released the funky "It's Good for the Soul" to clubs across the country. There was a new movement welling in these nightspots that was drawing people to the dance floor like never before. It was called disco, and it was both a style of music and a splashy way of being. The sound was birthed from the long, sashaying grooves of the Philly Sound. The scene was shaped by a whole host of groups who sat just on the margins of American culture: black people, Puerto Ricans, women, working-class folks who lived for the weekend, and all those randy young men who used to watch Bette at the Baths. Disco was a way for outsiders to create a colorful, rhythmic world of their own.

Once the mainstream got a taste of its addictive rhythms and cool, flagrant style, disco became a full-fledged pop culture phenomenon. The number of clubs soared. YMCAs gave disco dancing lessons in the suburbs, and the music industry raked in millions selling peppy extended dance tunes. Disco even introduced a whole new constellation of stars: the breathy, toffee-colored Venus, Donna Summer; Newark, New Jersey–born belter Gloria Gaynor; and that thick-set baritone from Galveston, Texas, Barry White. The folks at Cotillion earnestly hoped their newly signed group, Luther, would be added to that list.

The strategy of first releasing the record to the clubs paid off. It created a buzz, which led to radio airplay, and on May 8, just over two weeks after Luther's twenty-fifth birthday, "It's Good for the Soul" debuted on the R&B charts.

The song was a capable introduction for the group. Backed by a spare bass line, the song plays like a libertine anthem with its message that "if its good for the body / it's good for the soul." The single continued picking up momentum through the spring of 1976. It reached the Top 40 on the R&B charts—and even made a showing on the pop chart.

With the single becoming a hit, the group started doing press for the album. The first article, which appeared in Britain's *Blues and Soul* magazine and was written by journalist David Nathan, related the act's beginnings: how Luther, Diane, and Anthony met in high school; then joined Listen, My Brother; toured with Bowie; and worked with Bette. It recounted how the group was initially rejected by every record company in the book, and then the almost fairy-tale story of how they were ultimately signed.

True to the astrologically obsessed times, the article included each member's zodiac sign. Luther, a Taurus, was called "the group's main man . . . who wrote and produced the album." Anthony Hinton was described as a Gemini who "would like to continue to sing with the group and maybe one day make it out there on my own." Diane, a Pisces, said that she wants to be a singing-acting-dancing-modeling legend. Christine, another Gemini, struck a pragmatic tone. In the future, she primarily saw herself writing music and collaborating with other artists. "I don't want to always depend entirely on singing," she said. Lastly, Theresa, a married Libra, seemed ambivalent about the choices that stardom might force her to make in life. She loved music, but noted, "I always want a family."

The enthusiastic article concluded by predicting big things for the group: "Together, Luther seem well equipped to deal with the exciting future they have ahead of them. All the indications are that 'It's Good for the Soul' is going to establish the group and their debut album should set the seal."

A press release sent out by the record company predictably took an even more optimistic tone: "the time to start living . . . the dream begins now."

The album reached stores in June 1976, sharing the racks with Harold Melvin and the Bluenotes' moving Philly Soul classic "Wake Up Everybody," Motown superstar Marvin Gaye's sensual epic "I Want You," and the self-titled album by the multiracial act Rufus featuring Chaka Khan, which included a slow-burning ballad that Luther loved, "Sweet Thing."

When record shoppers saw the Luther album in stores, they might've been surprised by the cover. It lacked any picture of the group, simply depicting an empty spotlight-illuminated stage with a closed black curtain in the background. On the curtain—in shiny platinum letters that, strangely, had a sharply cut gothic look most associated with hard-rock bands—was the group's name: Luther.

The back cover found the five members standing on the stage. Luther, Diane, and Anthony hang together, all dressed in sky-blue suits. Luther donned a thick gold rope chain around his collar, and his belly strained against a tightly buttoned vest. Diane accented her suit with a striped peppermint scarf and red patent leather shoes, and Anthony posed himself sideways, his hand resting fashionably in his pocket. Theresa and Christine seemed set off from the others by their placement and dress. Theresa wore a pastel yellow suit; Christine was dressed in black from head to toe with a red rose pinned to her lapel. Her long hair was pulled into a thickly coiled braid that stuck straight up from the top of her head.

"I looked like I had a fucking Mohawk," Christine recalled. "Lord, have mercy. We looked so tacky. We didn't have no clothes. We didn't have no look."

Underneath the picture were the album's acknowledgments, thanking Henry Allen, the label president; Arif Mardin, the producer who helped them get their deal; and Cissy Houston, "for inspiration." Luther sent Cissy a copy of the album with a note stating that he hoped they would one day sing together.

The album opened with the charging "Funky Music (Is a Part of Me)," the song Bowie liked so much that he retooled it as "Fascination." This was one of the album's three up-tempo cuts, including a version of "Everybody Rejoice" from *The Wiz*. The album's ballads found Luther in recovery from a broken heart. On the yearning yet hopeful "Second Time Around," he sang, "To get over the first love is kinda hard / but don't let it get you down."

One of the album's most interesting cuts was the slow number "This Strange Feeling," notable—and rather unconventional—because it was a romantic duet between two men, Luther and Anthony. Listening to the lyrics, about the transforming rush of newfound love, it was unclear whether they are singing to the same person, different people, or each other. The song started with the two singers trading verses: first Luther in his caramel-like tenor, then Anthony, whose soft caressing falsetto recalled the Temptations' Eddie Kendricks. The song slowly and steadily built until Luther and Anthony started singing together, "This strange feeling takes me over."

With the album in stores, the group did some live shows to support it. They were backed by a six-piece band that included a hungry young guitarist named Nile Rodgers and his friend and ace bass player Bernard Edwards. The group opened for some of the top acts on the charts: the Godfather of Soul James Brown, the funky six-piece Average White Band, popular R&B/jazz saxophonist Grover Washington, Jr., and Marvin Gaye, who was then the R&B male vocalist to beat. The group performed as an opening act for Marvin at New York City's Radio City Music Hall, but—even though it was a hometown show—Luther's mother didn't attend. Despite all of his success, Luther still felt nervous performing in front of his family.

These concerts raised the group's profile but did little to spur sales. Their album never even debuted on the charts. Pretty soon the label stopped financially supporting the group's touring efforts, and there wasn't enough interest from promoters to justify staying out on the road.

This turn of events devastated Luther. He felt responsible. The group had been his vision. He produced the album. They sang his songs. He was their leader. But after nearly a year of hard work, they were nowhere.

The stress of being responsible for four other people hung on Luther like a weighted chain. It affected his health. His weight was up, and his blood pressure ran so high that each night before he went to bed, he took four aspirin so that he wouldn't wake up feeling like his head was going to explode.

The group was also being pulled apart from the inside. Christine and Theresa complained that they weren't making enough money and were being paid less like group members than hired hands. Besides, they had other stuff going on. Christine was pregnant, and Theresa wanted to spend more time with her husband. They both bid "Luther" good-bye.

When the group's second album, *This Close to You,* appeared the following spring, it was clear that there had been a lot of changes. The group was now downsized to a trio: Luther and his old friends and road dogs, Diane and Anthony. The cover of the album clearly reflected these shifts. Luther—in a black suit set off by a sparkling blue-sequined shirt—was the sole figure on the front. He leaned against a green wall where there's a billboard bearing a giant blowup of his smiling face.

To find Diane and Anthony, you had to flip the cover over. There, they stood against the same green wall. Anthony, dressed just like Luther and looking like one of the handsome Jackson 5 brothers, held his hand out, waving hi. Diane smiled widely, lifting one foot up and throwing her hands exuberantly in the air. Under the picture, their names were listed not as group members, but "featured soloists." It seemed that Luther, the group, had become a one-man show.

This Close to You had the same sound as the first album since many of the songs were written around the same time. One of the highlights was the earnestly apologetic "This Is for Real," where Luther tries to convince his wronged partner "that love ain't playing this time." Another interesting inclusion was "I'm Not Satisfied," one of the first songs Luther ever wrote, right after leaving college. In the tune, he somewhat clumsily reprimanded a friend he has a crush on: "Don't give me 'like' when it's love I need."

The more recently written songs were moodier, seeming to reflect Luther's recurring troubles and preoccupations. On the sweeping "Don't Want to Be a Fool" he chose to be alone rather than with a lover who's "playing around." "Come Back to Love" included the line "life without love is scaring me to death," and "Follow My Love" simply reported "I am a sunshine person / but it's been raining."

Commercially, *This Close to You* fared even worse than the first album. Luther later joked that the two records "sold fourteen copies combined." The record company soon let the group go, and Luther was once again without a musical home, an outlet for his voice and his songs. (Before leaving the label, he bought the rights to the albums back from the company, which is why they weren't rereleased in the wake of Luther's later success.)

Luther soon returned to what he knew could pay the bills, what had already bought him that fancy apartment in midtown Manhattan. He became a background singer again, using his talent to boost others. His dream, that recurring image of being onstage surrounded by well-dressed singing and dancing men and women, had been deferred.

"Everybody Dance"

"I haven't been able to turn on a pop AM radio station for more than an hour and not hear myself in some capacity."

—LUTHER, ON HIS POPULARITY
DOING BACKGROUND VOCALS AND
SINGING JINGLES

"Dance, dance, dance, dance," they sang together, so loud and strong, over the pulsing rhythm. "Keep on daaaa-n-cinnn!"

"Dance, dance, dance, dance," they continued, "keep on, keep on."

The words came out sharp and punchy at first, then they stretched out like two finely dressed steppers doing a slow slide across a ballroom floor. The words spoke power. They weren't just lyrics. This was a mandate, a call to action. For some, reason for one more day of being. These were get-happy words, bring-people-together words, and everybody-is-a-star words. All they were talking about was dancing, but the joyous way the singers belted out the words made them sound like freedom.

The voices behind this edict, this rhythmic command, were a

host of New York's most acclaimed background singers, the folks you went to if you knew you needed a soulful sound. Their names were Norma Jean, David Lasley, Alfa Anderson, Diva Gray, Robin Clark, and her old high school running buddy Luther Vandross.

Luther's self-titled group had folded and he was back to helping make other folks sound better. The loss of the group was crushing in one sense, the sidelining of a longtime dream, yet in some respects it was liberating.

"I always felt the product was good," Luther reflected shortly after the group folded, "but with the benefit of hindsight, maybe it's better this way. I think I am better off without the responsibility of having a whole group behind me. I feel much better without that kind of pressure."

Singing background brought hardly any stress at all. Luther simply showed up, learned the lyrics, and infused them with life, making them sound like something someone just had to say. It was what he wanted. It was simple, stable, and didn't involve the headaches and scrutiny that came with fronting a group or performing on his own.

"I didn't have my sights set on a solo career or my own musicality," he said. "It was fine for me to help someone else do their musical trip."

At this particular session, he was helping out two guys who were briefly in Luther's backing band when his group performed their few live shows. One was Nile Rodgers, a classically trained guitar player who grew up in New York City. Nile's friend and musical partner, Bernard Edwards, came from down South, raised by his mother and grandparents in Greenville, North Carolina. For most of the early seventies, Nile and Bernard were two struggling black men nursing big musical dreams.

Their hearts were in rock music. Yet they found those doors closed to them. "When I first started, all I played was heavy-duty rock and roll," Nile once said. "To be a guitarist in a heavy glitter band was the whole thing. To be Hendrix or Jimmy Page was success to me. Life became more real when I tried to get a record deal. There's a hell of a lot of racism in rock and roll. As a black man playing lead guitar, I could never get a record deal."

Enter disco. "It was like a gift from heaven," Nile said. "Discos gave us the perfect opportunity to realize a concept, because it wasn't about being black, white, male, or female. Further, it would give us a chance to get into the mainstream. We wanted millions of dollars, Ferraris, and planes—and this seemed like the way to get them."

Let the others have rock, they felt. Instead, they would transform the look, sound, and feel of a type of music that had people rushing out and buying records in numbers that rock hadn't inspired for years. Disco was something new, something they could still make their own. Nile and Bernard called their new outfit Chic because it evoked everything they wanted the group to be.

"Chic is about good vibes, good grooves, good clothes," Nile explained. "That's what we talked about: the fantasy life."

The concept for Chic was that it wasn't so much a formal group as it was a case of Nile and Bernard surrounding themselves with some of the best musicians and singers they could hire. Almost from the start, they wanted Luther to be part of their vision, because they knew what others in the industry were slowly beginning to recognize: Luther Vandross was one of the baddest male vocalists in town.

"Dance, Dance, Dance" was one of the first songs they recorded, and they could feel its power and pull even in the studio. The singers gleefully wailed as the background music offered a compelling blend of disparate sounds: glitzy washes of strings, bouncy guitar licks, smooth tugging beats, and a thunderously rolling bass. Then Luther put the defining accent on the song by chanting "yowsah, yowsah, yowsah," a reference to the 1969 film about the feverish dance competitions of the Depression era, *They Shoot Horses, Don't They?*

When "Dance, Dance, Dance" hit the streets, discos, and airwaves in October 1977, it became an instant hit, peaking near the top of both the pop and R&B charts. An album followed two months later, and you could hear Luther's voice all over it. Yet in what would become a disco convention, none of the people performing on the album were pictured on the cover. Instead it showed two glamorous, gold-dusted young women—one black, one white—with silver whistles in their mouths. For some singers, this would have been an insult, but it didn't bother Luther. After more than a year of being the center of attention as the leader of his group, he was ready to slip back into the background.

As a session singer, he didn't have to worry about how he looked. He could come in with his hair uncombed and shirt hanging out and no one cared. It was all about his voice. He didn't have to be "chic" as long as he could sound "chic," and from the response to the record, he was successful at it. The album soon sold over one million copies. Luther had contributed to yet another smash.

When it was time to record the second Chic album, dubbed *C'est Chic*, Nile and Bernard called Luther onboard for another go. The new songs were even more polished and fully formed than the tunes on the first album. Holed up at New York's state-of-the-art Power Station studios for weeks, the group cut numbers like the lush paean to unrequited affection "I Want Your Love" and the funky ingratiating stomp "Le Freak." The album reached record stores in 1978, and Luther was once again missing from the cover. However, the album's credits showed that his status in the industry was changing. Under the heading "Vocals," the album listed Alfa Anderson, Bernard Edwards, Diva Gray, Luci Martin, David Lasley, and "special guest artist" Luther Vandross.

It seemed nearly everyone wanted Luther on their record. He was soon tapped for two projects by no less an industry force than Quincy Jones, the jazz trumpeter turned multimedia Renaissance man. Quincy was working on the music for the film adaptation of *The Wiz*. The surprise-hit Broadway show, which had provided Luther one of his first breaks, was finally headed for the big screen. For the most part, Quincy felt unimpressed by the show's musical numbers, despite their widespread success, and planned to tweak them for the film, but he always loved the celebratory jump of "Everybody Rejoice." When recording the tune for the movie, he decided to let Luther sing the first line of the song. In the film, the lyric was mouthed by a grotesque hooded creature, a denizen of the Wicked Witch's lair, but the smooth, warm voice was unmistakably Luther's.

At the same time Quincy was working on *The Wiz*, he was also trying to finish up a new album, *Sounds—And Stuff Like That*, and planned to feature both new and established talent. Luther was asked to take part in the sessions, and he quickly accepted. This, however, wasn't going to be like Luther's other background singing gigs. He was even a little nervous and uncomfortable about it. Quincy was one of the biggest artist that he'd ever worked with. Bowie and Bette Midler were huge stars in their own right, but Luther wasn't that familiar with them before he was hired to back them up. The situation with Quincy was entirely different. This was a man who'd worked with people whose faces he used to see on the walls of the Apollo Theatre: Billie Holiday, Dinah Washington, Ray Charles. He had even produced Aretha.

Luther also felt uneasy because it had been a while since he had worked with a whole new group of people. Luther, the group, and even Chic had been composed largely of his friends, but now he was set to work with folks he didn't personally know. This wasn't just any old bunch of musicians either. These were people whose experience far outweighed his own. He didn't know what to expect, and there was always that nagging fear that someone would take one look at him—much heavier than he wanted to be—and tell him that he didn't belong.

His fears quickly proved unfounded. One of the album's arrangers, Leon Pendavis, perhaps sensing Luther's discomfort, decided to shepherd Luther through the recording process. "[He] helped me get used to the studio more," Luther remembered. "I was quite a bit heavier then and a little paranoid around strangers in a studio situation, but Leon put me at ease and helped me overcome being afraid of the microphone."

Recording for the album only lasted a couple of days, but Luther would later consider it a defining moment in his career. "I got more experience from that session than all of the rest of them put together," he said. "There was such a great atmosphere to that album. . . . [It was] the super session of all time for me."

Quincy chose Luther to sing two duets on the album. One was a cover of the Doobie Brother's rousing "Taking It to the Streets," which paired Luther with Gwen Guthrie, a shining Newark, New Jersey–born protégée of Cissy Houston herself. Gwen had sung backup on Aretha Franklin's number-one hit "I'm in Love," so naturally Luther gravitated toward her. "Anybody whose name was on an Aretha album was always of interest to me," Luther said.

Luther's other song was a deceptively smooth ballad about an illicit affair, "I'm Gonna Miss You in the Morning," which he sang with one of Quincy's favorite and most used singers, Patti Austin. Luther quickly bonded with Patti. Like him, she was on the heavy side yet she was still successful, always in demand.

Since age five, Patti had been making money with her cool breeze of a voice, performing with entertainers like Sammy Davis, Jr., and Dinah Washington. She cut her first single—a gutsy tune about interracial romance called "The Family Tree"—as a teenager. Since then, she'd diversified and was no longer relying solely on concerts and record sales for income. Like a lucky handful of artists, she'd broken into the lucrative world of commercial jingles. She'd use her pipes to shill for any number of products. This meant a real payday because jingle singers received a flat fee for recording an ad, then residual payments each time it aired. Where other singers were worried about their next gig, Patti's thoughts ran to the value of her real estate properties and how her business investments were faring.

"The thing is," Patti once explained, "no one is a star forever."

One day, while recording the *Stuff* album, a jingle arranger stopped by to see Patti and she introduced him to Luther. The idea of singing jingles greatly appealed to Luther. It was good money, low effort, and again, it didn't matter what you looked like. As long as you could make a product sound like something everyone had to have, that's all that mattered. Luther was quickly snapped up for a Welch's Grape Soda commercial, and after that, more work came quick and easy.

Luther found jingles to be quite different from background vocals. He often couldn't stretch out as much as he was used to. "I did have a slight conflict at first," Luther remembered, "because I'd come up with hip vocal lines for a chewing gum jingle, say, and the ad agency or client in the control room just wouldn't want to hear about it. I had to learn that there's a certain way some clients and jingle producers want their music done. Ultimately, it wasn't that big of an adjustment because I like being able to do as the Romans do. And as I cooled out, I found that once you show some of the more open-minded jingle writers that you can do exactly what they want you to do, then they can appreciate your ideas."

There was the time he was in the studio doing a spot for NBC-TV, where his line was simply, "We're proud to be NBC." The first time he sang it, he delivered the line as straightforwardly as possible, but then he started to get into it. He made the notes quiver, working them into an Aretha-like gospel frenzy. In many cases, the jingle producer would've asked Luther to tone it down, but this time the producer was in the booth encouraging Luther along, yelling, "More, more, go!"

This enthusiastic producer wasn't the only one who allowed Luther to experiment. It was while singing jingles that he created what would become one of his trademark techniques. He was recording an ad for Geno's pizza, singing the line "Geno's—you'll go for the food we've got / Geno's—you'll go for it sizzling hot." The producer of the spot listened to him run through the line and was mostly pleased, but felt it could use just a tad more punch.

"Can you give me just something to make me feel it hot," she called from the control room. "Make me feel it sizzling hot."

Luther thought about it for a moment, then opened his mouth again. "Geno's—you'll go for the food we've got," he sang just as before. Then, he changed it: "Geno's—you'll go for it si-i-i-i-i-zzling hot."

He turned the word "sizzling" into an extended, stuttering bass rumble, and when he looked out from the recording booth he saw the whole room going nuts. "I could see people just jumping up and clapping and stuff," Luther remembered, "and I said to myself, 'I guess when I make a record I'm gonna throw that on there.' So I didn't do it on any more jingles. I saved it for my own records."

Luther was slowly—tentatively—beginning to think about making his own records again. After the setbacks of the group's albums, his dreams were starting to resurface. Part of the reason he was thinking about making his own records again was that Quincy had expressed interest in working with him. But Quincy had to first finish recording the adult solo debut of nineteen-year-old Michael Jackson, the once precocious lead singer of the Jackson 5 whom Quincy had worked with on the set of *The Wiz*.

In the meantime, Luther continued getting jobs from all over. Singer Roberta Flack had heard about him from a number of friends and associates, and she felt that she wanted him for her new album and tour. After several years of success, Roberta had entered a slump of sorts. She hadn't released a record for years, and it had been almost as long since she stepped onto a concert stage. It was as if she'd vanished. The impact of all her accomplishments—Grammy's, number-one hits—were fading with time. This extended hiatus surprised friends and critics because her career had once held so much promise.

Roberta's arrival in 1968 was the kind of event that made music lovers of almost any ilk take notice. As skilled on the piano as she was using her supple voice, Roberta could play and sing a dizzying range of styles: jazz, classical, soul, blues, and Broadway. Adding to her mystique and appeal, she came with a compelling back story.

She grew up in Black Mountain, North Carolina, the daughter of a draftsman father who sometimes played a mean jazz piano and a mother who graced the organ at church each Sunday in the name of the Lord. A quick study, Roberta learned her way around a keyboard by sitting on the piano bench by her mother's side, and by age fifteen she was a college student studying music at Howard University. There, she met a man who would become one of her dearest friends and musical soul mates, the shy and extraordinarily gifted Donny Hathaway. He could play piano like God himself was guiding his hands, and his voice could make you holler or break out in tears, the way he'd take a note and make it ripple like a warm, rushing stream.

After graduation, Roberta spent several years teaching high school, twice the only black instructor at all-white schools. Yet she always felt the pull of performing. She finally got a regular gig playing for the Sunday brunch crowd at Mr. Henry's, a bar that sat near the U.S. Capitol in Washington. Her smart and agile blend of songs and styles quickly drew a crowd, including such visiting A-listers as comedian Bill Cosby, crooner Johnny Mathis, big-screen funny man Woody Allen, and that bejewled, piano-playing dandy Liberace.

"People were coming by the hundreds," Flack recalled. "No kidding, all of a sudden they were lining up on the sidewalk like I was some kind of movie star." They congregated in the bar's upstairs lounge, which had been furnished with church pews and stained-glass windows especially for Roberta.

It wasn't long before she had a record deal. By 1971, she had scored her first hit, a duet with her old college buddy Donny on a song that exemplified the bond between them: "You've Got a Friend." A number of records followed: the crystalline "The First Time Ever I Saw Your Face" and the swaying "Killing Me Softly with His Song." Audiences seemed to be as taken with her gentle tones and slow, smart phrasing as they were with her image, which was perfectly suited for an era in which all things black were indisputably beautiful.

Once in concert Roberta told the crowd about how she grew up as a little girl wearing her thick hair pressed and slathered back with nearly "half a jar" of Royal Crown grease. Then, she shook the curling, fully-bloomed Afro that crowned her head, saying, "Times have changed, haven't they?"

By 1978, however, Roberta had experienced a tough run of bad luck: flop records, poorly reviewed concerts, a divorce, miscarriages, and a $1 million unpaid tax bill. It was clearly time to take inventory and make changes. Partly, she needed to reinvigorate her music.

Roberta aggressively sought out Luther because of his surefire reputation. She knew that getting him for her records and upcoming tour wouldn't be easy because he was in such demand, but she had a secret weapon. "I seduced Luther by inviting him to my house for rehearsal," explained Roberta, who had a beautiful New York apartment in the tony Dakota building, where her neighbors included actress Lauren Bacall and former Beatle John Lennon. Anyone entering the apartment couldn't help but be impressed by the beautiful view and striking living room, where the white carpet matched the walls.

That first meeting proved fruitful. She quickly fell in love with Luther's light and buoyant tenor. In fact, he reminded her of a friend. "When I heard his voice," she recalled, "I immediately thought of Donny, not in terms of the actual sound, but the attitude and the way he uses his voice." Luther was thrilled because he finally had a mentor, someone who, unlike Bowie or Bette, was actually doing the kind of music that he loved and dreamed of one day making himself.

During the tour, Luther got close to other members of Roberta's musical crew, including a young bassist named Marcus Miller. Luther and Miller would spend hours laughing while listening to tapes of comedian Pigmeat Markhum, known for his uproarious "Here Comes the Judge" skits. However, most rewarding for Luther were his interactions with Roberta.

One day during rehearsal, he was sitting at the piano working out an idea he had about taking Dionne Warwick's lonesome ballad "A House Is Not a Home" and really stretching it out, transforming it into a full-blown soul epic. It was a deceptively complex song. It took him a lot of time to work it out, to make the notes and his voice sound the way he heard it in his head, but he thought he had finally gotten it down. Roberta passed by and he stopped her.

"Roberta, listen to this," Luther said. "One day I'm gonna *sing* this song." Luther put his hands on the piano keys, starting slowly and building the song, layer by layer, piling on the emotion until it became a perfect musical picture of loneliness.

"Ooo, you're gonna sing that song to death," Roberta exclaimed excitedly. Yet, ever the teacher, she had some notes for him: "Let me show you two chords you got wrong."

Once Luther returned from touring with Roberta, other work kept coming his way. He now ranked among New York's elite core of behind-the-scenes vocalists, including folks like Patti Austin, Gwen Guthrie, Brenda White, Ullanda McCullough, and Tawatha Agee. Quincy Jones dubbed this talented group "the New York Super Singers." The funk group Mtume called the harmonizing bunch, including Luther, "the Grand Divas."

What made the singers stand out was their versatility, how they could go from backing up a superstar to infusing a jingle with that extra selling edge. It was a rare talent and a heavily valued one. "It's a small clique of people who do all the jingle work," Luther said. "There're a few people who make half a million or eight hundred thousand dollars a year, as opposed to lots of people making sixty thousand dollars a year."

Throughout much of 1979, Luther spent his days shuttling from studio to studio, session to session. "I would go from Carly Simon to Chaka Khan and come home exhausted," Luther recalled. "Then I'd wake up the next morning and be off to the Army, to Chic, Bette Midler . . ."

Jingles paid the bills and kept Luther living in fine style, lavishly decorating his apartment in his favorite color, pink. "I don't think I could remember them all if I tried," he said. "[There was] Kentucky Fried Chicken, Miller Beer, that AT&T 'Reach Out and Touch Someone' commercial." He also pitched for Revlon, Bell telephone, Burger King, Schaeffer Beer, Mountain Dew, and Steak and Ale restaurants. He told folks that NBC-TV was "proud as a peacock," that "there's nothing like the flavor of Juicy Fruit gum," and "when it's time to relax, Miller stands clear . . . Miller Beer."

Someone once likened singing jingles to musical prostitution, and Luther scoffed: "Oh please, the fickle finger of fate to anybody who thinks that. We are all out here for a career. What is that selling out to? You will be amazed at the stars who anonymously go and sing jingles. The money is fierce. Listen, on the way to the airport you stop and make a jingle and earn thirty grand. You leave an hour early, that's all."

Yet there were downsides to doing jingles. He saw some of his friends, other jingle singers, get so seduced by the quick money that they lost themselves, indulging in drugs and other illicit pleasures. "They got caught up in the scene's whirlwind of sophistication and money," he explained.

Luther remained grounded by keeping to the same routine. He was still like that chubby teenager growing up dreamy and lonely in the Bronx. He kept to himself and his close ring of friends. On most nights, he'd still find himself alone in his apartment while everyone else was on dates, at parties, or just connecting with others amid the exhilarating lights and expectant shadows of the big city.

"I would leave those jingle sessions and come home and listen to the Sweet Inspirations," Luther said.

It was important for him to stay focused, because he saw other dangers in the jingle scene, as well. It wasn't just the money that changed people, but also the grind of doing commercials day after day. Constantly aiming for a slick, homogenized sound could make even the most promising vocalist forget why she or he started singing in the first place.

"I have lots of friends who also sang jingles right along with me in the beginning, and some of them got robbed of that zeal," Luther observed. "They lost the passion for singing by always singing something that was required of them instead of singing things that were totally maybe without reason. I never bought into the whole idea that chance-taking was no good. I don't care [what it was], I was going to try. And if I was told, 'Hell, that sounds really good, but it's got a little bit too much emotion and passion for a gum commercial, you've gotta straighten out a little,' then I would. But my first instinct was going to be to give you what I got."

This attitude made Luther so popular that his voice was all over the airwaves. You could barely turn on the radio without hearing his warm, roasted tenor trying to seduce you into a store to buy something or other. Luther loved this part of the work, hearing his voice all around him, coming out of stores and windows. Sometimes his voice would rub against those of his favorite singers like Dionne, Diana, or Aretha, whenever his ads were played near one of their hit songs.

He would even hear people singing his jingles while walking down bustling streets, not knowing they were passing the person who voiced the words. This was the biggest problem with jingles, the thing that nagged him sometimes. "Everyone had heard my voice," he explained, "but no one knew my name."

Still, the money was good and, for the time being, he had few complaints. He was too busy. As his jingle career took off, he continued doing background vocals for a staggering array of projects. His longtime supporter, producer Arif Mardin, continued to hire him. He worked on sessions for singer/songwriter Carly Simon, ex-Beatles drummer Ringo Starr, Scottish funksters the Average White Band, and, of course, more tunes for Bette.

The demand for Luther didn't end with these gigs. He soon added a host of other names to the list of people he worked with: teenage disco prodigy Evelyn "Champagne" King, Stephanie Mills from *The Wiz*, soft rock singer/songwriter Cat Stevens, rising Hollywood actress Irene Cara, and a group of four female siblings from Philadelphia, Sister Sledge.

Nile Rodgers and Bernard Edwards of Chic were working on the Sisters' new album and they called Luther to help out. Two of the songs they recorded became era-defining anthems: that universal theme of togetherness "We Are Family" and the playfully lush "He's the Greatest Dancer." Luther remembered that he loved the latter song from the moment he heard it: " 'Oh, what, wow—he's the greatest dancer.' Well, you know I loved *that*."

Indeed, Luther's voice seemed especially prominent on the track. "I kept saying to them, 'You know what, I'm too loud,' " Luther explained, "and they kept saying, 'Man, just move closer to the microphone.' And I said, 'Move in? I'm too loud. I can't even hear [lead singer] Kathy. What are you talking about?' But that's the sound they wanted."

It seemed that wherever there was a major project in the making, Luther was called on to contribute his talents. "See, I was adored by the people I sang for," Luther explained. "That's because I came to the studio for a session or to a live gig with vocal ideas. I was wanted for my brain as much as for my voice. I felt very much appreciated."

Luther often placed more demands on himself than his employers did. One time in the studio, he was in the middle of singing when he stopped abruptly.

"Why'd you quit?" the producer asked, a tad perplexed.

"That last F [note] sounded weird to me," Luther answered.

This uncompromised musicianship made him the person to go to if an album was in trouble. When the Delfonics, those seventies soul masters of sweet falsetto harmony, disbanded while making one of their last albums, producers called Luther in to help complete the vocals. The same thing happened with albums by his old friends the Main Ingredient and the disco trio Odyssey, which had a hit with the urbane "Native New Yorker." Whenever group members were missing or vocals needed to be beefed up, Luther was the person to get. However, to maintain a facade of group solidarity, his contributions were often uncredited.

Frequently, Luther had the chance to work with people he'd admired while growing up. He sang on an Average White Band album featuring Ben E. King, whom he used to watch at those Murray the K shows at the Brooklyn Fox. Later, Patrick Adams, Luther's old friend from Listen, My Brother, who was now a successful producer, invited him to sing on a session with former Temptation Eddie Kendricks.

The Temptations had been one of the few male acts that interested Luther as a teen. He would stand in the mirror pretending that he could sound like them, move like them, look the way they looked in their sharp lean suits. He jumped at the chance to sing with this legend.

Adams explained: "You call somebody up and say, 'I'm producing one of our childhood idols' and they're fighting to get in on the session."

Luther did have one stipulation, however. "Just bring me a pound of macadamia nuts," Luther told Adams, "and I'll be there."

The Eddie Kendricks session lasted several hours as they ripped through songs like the kicky disco number "I Never Used to Dance" and the gently pleading "I Just Want to Be the One in Your Life," on which you can hear Luther prominently. "The backgrounds on that song are just so magnificent," Adams remembered.

Before long, those macadamia nuts were history. "He *ate* those macadamia nuts," Adams recalled, chuckling. "He was finished before the session was over, but that was fine because this was during the height of the drug experience in the industry. I've seen a lot of bad things in the studio, so to have a singer come in and all they wanted was some macadamia nuts, well, that was fine with me."

Luther also got the opportunity to record with four of the top—and most intriguing—female artists in the business. These weren't just singers, they were stars: women with histories, myths, scars they shared with fans and those they kept hidden. For a few moments in 1979, Luther crossed their paths.

One of them was Cher, the long, tan California-born singer who often styled herself as a sleek, dark-tressed Native American princess. Cher rose to fame making records and doing TV shows as a part of a duo with her husband Sonny Bono, but by the mid-seventies, she was a newly divorced independent woman. She had her own TV show now and her own record: the plush and pulsing disco stormer *Take Me Home.* Her next release was an album called *Prisoner*, on which she appears nearly nude and draped in chains. One of the quirkiest tunes on the album is the Broadway show tune–like "Shoppin'," about using credit cards and new clothes to chase blues away. The background vocalists on the song were called "the Consumers," and Luther was one of them.

That same year, Luther was asked to arrange background vocals for a potentially explosive musical pairing with two of the four female superstars. Donna Summer, the shimmering, newly crowned queen of disco, was going to duet with Barbra Streisand, the reigning maven of pop balladry, on an up-tempo dance number called "No More Tears (Enough Is Enough)." The match-up meant new school would grapple with old school, frisky disco would bump against mannered pop. For Donna, the song, if successful, would mean that the twirling newcomer could hold her own with one of the industry's most celebrated—and thoroughly establishment—talents. For Barbra, it was the chance to show that she was more than a pedestal-perched chanteuse. It would prove that she could be hip, and when called upon, could "get down" with the best of them.

Weeks before it happened, the duet was the talk of the industry. What was going to happen in the studio? Would the two of them fight? Who would be left standing when it was over?

Recording was scheduled to begin in early August, but problems arose from the start. They went through four separate studios before laying down a single note. The track's songwriter and producer, Paul Jabara, hated the first studio. Donna disliked the second. Barbra felt the third was all wrong. And nobody thought the fourth would work. Finally, recording commenced on August 14, with Donna, Barbra, and all the musicians working at Crimson Studios in Santa Monica, California. Still, there were more problems with the dueting megastars.

"Those first vocals were terrible," remembered Jabara. "The girls were screaming. Donna sounded horrible, and Barbra sounded horrible. And I said so."

They regrouped a few days later, and the vocals sounded better, but tragedy almost befell one of the two marquee talents. There was a friendly but decidedly competitive atmosphere as the singers sat together on stools carefully positioned in front of a microphone. At one point, Donna and Barbra had to sing a very high note and then hold it for as long as possible. Barbra started the note off. Donna chimed in, but for some reason, had trouble getting air. She suddenly felt faint. Everything seemed woozy, with the whole scene growing dark. The next thing Donna knew, she was off her stool, passed out on the floor.

"Here's the best part," Donna recounted. "When I came to and opened my eyes a few seconds later, Barbra was still holding her note! I could have died. It was so long! It was only when she finished that she turned and asked me, 'Donna, are you all right?' in a way only Barbra speaks. I said I was, got up, cleared my throat, and finished the session."

When it was all over, both stars were surprisingly and uncharacteristically cagey about the whole experience. "Working with Barbra," Donna reflected. "It was, let's say, a *different* experience."

When Barbra was later asked about the cut, she said: "The song with Donna Summer? What song? Oh yeah, the disco thing. It was cute."

Nevertheless, the song, on which Luther sang and arranged the background vocals, became an instant hit, quickly reaching number one on the pop charts and staying there for a couple weeks. Luther had contributed to yet another top-of-the-charts smash. Yet while Donna and Barbra's careers moved forward, Luther's stayed in the same place.

Still, the background work kept coming, including what would be one of the most memorable recording sessions of his career. Not only would he be supporting Chaka Khan, one of the most dynamic—if erratic—singers around, he'd also be working with his idol Cissy Houston and her teenage daughter, Whitney.

The session, produced by Arif Mardin, was for Chaka's second solo album, titillatingly called *Naughty*. Though Chaka started out with the funk/rock combo Rufus, she'd recently embarked on a solo career. One of her first concerts without the group was held at Manhattan's Avery Fisher Hall and drew the most luminous talents of the New York City music scene. Nile and Bernard of Chic were there, along with Roberta Flack and Luther.

Chaka, wearing high-heeled black boots and a loose-fitting red shirt hanging over her rounded, then-pregnant body, delivered a fiery set that, one critic wrote, left fans "unhinged." Chaka—whose name means "woman of fire" in Yoruba—was the person people either wanted to work with, gossip about, or just hear wailing freely over a record.

Part of her appeal was that her reputation was as wild as her long, thick mane of honey-tinted hair. "I've never seen six A.M. unless I stayed up 'til then," she once told a *Rolling Stone* reporter, "even pregnant." She was known to alienate other vocalists ("Bitch, I never did think you could sing," she'd say), as well as longtime fans hoping to make a connection ("Hell, no, I don't remember you," she'd tell even the most steadfast follower). Then there were the concert appearances, which were often far less sharp than the Avery Fisher Hall gig. Throughout the seventies, it wasn't uncommon for Chaka to appear on stage, eyes glazed, barely mouthing the lyrics, and knocking over her mic stand again and again.

When she recorded *Naughty*, Chaka was going through particularly strange and trying times: a divorce that was preceded by a violent gunfight, an ongoing drug habit that threatened her life and career, and a deep belief that her California home was being haunted by the ghosts of fourteen slaughtered Native American virgins. Yet little of this mattered to those who worked with her. Whatever problems anyone had with Chaka often disappeared as soon as she opened her mouth to sing.

Luther was ecstatic over getting the chance to sing for Chaka. He'd adored her voice ever since her hit 1975 ballad with Rufus, "Sweet Thing." He knew that working with her would allow him to stretch in ways he wasn't able to with jingles and more pop-oriented acts like Cher, Donna, and Barbra.

"When you're singing for [Chaka], you're going to give it all up emotionally," he explained, "because she's so honest and giving herself."

What made the session extra special was Cissy Houston. He'd always longed to work with her, and now he was getting his chance. Cissy, who had long since left the Sweet Inspirations, brought her daughter with her to the session.

"I took Whitney with me everywhere," Cissy remembered. "She would watch me at various recording sessions. I could see she was learning, just soaking everything up like a sponge. Everybody liked her and before too long they were inviting her to sing background."

Many people at the studio that day were impressed by Cissy's sixteen-year-old daughter, whom they heard so much about. Of course, she could sing just like her momma, but she was also so striking with a dewy, fresh-cut kind of beauty. She was already working as a model for such magazines as *Seventeen* and *Glamour*, after a fashion photographer spotted her at a United Negro College Fund Benefit with her mother.

So talented and so pretty, folks thought, she might just be somebody one day.

The song Luther, Whitney, and Cissy worked on was the charging "Our Love Is in Danger," a gospel-powered cut especially written for Chaka by Ashford and Simpson. The three, along with a few other singers, provided powerful backing, echoing Chaka's words and at one point belting out a forceful "yeah . . . woo hoo!" After the session, everyone was still talking about what a fine job Whitney did.

Even Chaka was impressed, if somewhat reserved in her praise. "She had a good voice, I saw that," Chaka remembered. "But I didn't detect any real drive. Maybe she wasn't even there yet, you know—it's possible. I think at the time she still wanted to be a model, and that's where she was really putting her cookies. So who knows?"

Luther was more enthusiastic. He wrote Whitney a note which she keeps to this day. It said: "You're going to be one of the greatest singers that ever lived."

"The Glow of Love"

"The Change situation . . . got my name out there. It brought Luther Vandross to people's attention—and it sold a lot of records, too."

—LUTHER, ON THE GROUP
THAT CHANGED HIS CAREER

By 1979, something that started small, at out-of-the-way places attended by those on the margins of the mainstream, had reached a peak, infusing everything from music to movies, clothes to TV. Its influence spread like a virus: *Disco Fever!*

The scene's life pulse came from a mix of influences: black, white, Hispanic, gay, straight, male, and female. In just a few short years, it had produced a host of hit songs, and Luther was a key voice on many of them. He could be heard on some of disco's biggest hits: Chic's "Le Freak," Sister Sledge's "He's the Greatest Dancer," and Barbra Streisand and Donna Summer's "No More Tears (Enough Is Enough)." He was becoming the genre's best-kept secret.

Ambitious producers even began asking Luther to sing lead on their vocals tracks. This served as a promotion of sorts. Not only was he being recognized for how his voice could meld with others, he was now wanted for his own unique sound. The only catch was that these weren't his own records, under his own name. He was a hired hand—very respected, but a hired hand nonetheless.

Producers used Luther as the voice behind a number of studio-created acts that existed in name only: Bionic Boogie, Charmé, Mascara, and the New York City Band. He even served as a featured voice in a mock group called the Good Vibrations, which performed disco-fied versions of Beach Boys' songs.

His performances on many of these records came off beautifully. He was light and breezy on Bionic Boogie's lush, mid-tempo "Hot Butterfly" (later covered by Chaka Khan), earnest and romantic on Mascara's "See You in L.A.," and bouncy and seductive on the New York City Band's throbbing romp "Got to Have Your Body."

Yet, for Luther, this felt unfulfilling. It wasn't because of what he was being paid. "I made so much money it was obscene," Luther recalled. He requested top dollar, and most producers gladly paid, knowing they were getting someone with expertise. "I was probably making more than other backup singers," Luther observed, "partly because I had the chutzpah to ask for it, and partly because I was bringing in a vocal arranger's perspective and ideas."

What bothered Luther was the anonymity of it all. He knew that all across the country people were dancing to records with his voice, but no one was aware of it. It was the same as with jingles. Millions of people had heard him, but no one knew his name.

Certainly the covers of the albums downplayed his contribution. The front of the Good Vibrations album featured a bathing-suited blonde. The New York City Band's image was a bitten apple core. Bionic Boogie showed a brown beauty clad largely in ribbons, and the Mascara album pictured two women getting ready for a hot night out. To find Luther's name, you had to search through the credits on the back covers of the albums, and even then it was often in nearly microscopic print—and repeatedly misspelled. Luther's last name was frequently listed as if he were a member of a Swiss singing family: Van Dross.

This sort of anonymity didn't bother Luther as much when he was just a background singer, but singing lead was different. He wanted credit where he felt it was due.

That wasn't the only thing bothering him, though. He also didn't like using his solo voice to sing other people's words and bring their ideas to life. He had his own songs, his own words to sing.

Sometimes with these disco projects, he'd be expected to sing lyrics he'd never write himself. The New York City Band album had him relishing in someone's "naked delights"—something that was far outside the tastes of the shy boy from the Bronx, who always preferred songs that were subtle and romantic rather than blatant and sexual. However, he felt it wasn't his place to complain.

"[Disco] was a producer's medium," Luther explained. "It was all the producer's vision, and the lead singer was just as incidental as the trumpet, the trombone or any other instrument on the track."

This lack of influence in all aspects of his career depressed him. This wasn't what he wanted. It wasn't why he started singing. It had nothing to do with the way Dionne Warwick made him feel that night many years ago at the Brooklyn Fox Theater.

He even grew tired of his background work, being told what to do and dealing with all the superstar drama. "I was usually able to defer my own insanity to deal with certain people and projects," Luther said, "but I was becoming a very unhappy man. It was frustrating dealing with one personality and then another. I got tired of playing Tonto to everyone's Lone Ranger. No one outside of the music industry knew who I was."

All of these issues weighed on Luther's mind when he almost passed on a project that would come to change the entire direction of his career, laying the first step for his later rise to superstardom. The song he came to record would become one of his biggest hits. But it almost didn't happen at all.

The story of this record started in the 1950s on the green and plentiful island of Guadeloupe in the French West Indies, where a brown-skinned half Creole, half Haitian boy named Jacques Fred Petrus grew up loving American R&B. By the early 1970s he found himself studying music at the Conservatory of Bologna. There he joined forces with a jazz-trained instructor, Mauro Malauasi, who was known as a keyboard whiz. Together, Jacques and Mauro forged a goal, to become the Italian version of Gamble and Huff, those industrious producers behind the Philly Sound that had so influenced David Bowie and countless others.

They quickly became involved in the Milan-based Italian disco industry, a notoriously shady scene that was as cutthroat and allegedly mob-ridden as the worst parts of the U.S. music business. They recorded a number of songs using group names like Macho, Revanche, and the Peter Jacques Band, but they didn't score any hits, especially none big enough to fulfill their goal of making an impact in the States. Still Jacques continued to dream, thinking up even bigger plans. He felt he needed a grand concept to cross over in America, something cool, sexy, and sophisticated, something like the group Chic. Then he suddenly had it. He'd call his act "Change."

The plan was for Jacques and Mauro to record all the music in Milan, but in order to give the record a U.S. flavor they would later fly to New York and get American writers for the lyrics—Jacques and Mauro barely spoke English—and American singers for the vocals.

They quickly recorded the musical tracks, and by summer 1979 were ready to head to the States. Through a mutual friend, Jacques asked Wayne Garfield, a New York–based singer/songwriter who once sang with the inspirational Voices of East Harlem, to write lyrics for two songs. Jacques wanted the words to have a fresh, edgy, and hip attitude. Jacques was less a hands-on musician than a hard-line moneyman. Yet the project was still largely his vision. He knew what it should look, sound, and feel like. He often ended arguments by firmly stating, *"I am Change."*

Wayne quickly got to work writing lyrics, trying to capture disco's broad, all-embracing spirit. One of the songs he wrote was called "It's a Girl's Affair."

"It's about a lesbian party," Wayne explained.

Another song, "The Glow of Love," captured the exhilarating rush of newfound romance, where it seems as if the sun is shining and the flowers are blooming just for you and the one who holds your heart. Wayne even coyly slipped in a double entendre as a wink to disco's founding audience: "It's a pleasure / when you treasure / all that's new and true and gay."

When Jacques heard what Wayne had done, he was thrilled. He even asked Wayne to suggest a male vocalist for the song. Wayne answered, "Luther Vandross."

Wayne was friends with Luther. He knew Luther had been turning in wonderful lead vocal performances on records by Bionic Boogie and others, and he felt Luther deserved the shot. "He was overdue for his break," Wayne reasoned.

That's why Wayne was so surprised when he showed up at Manhattan's Hit Factory Studios and saw that the producers weren't using Luther at all.

"What happened with Luther," Wayne asked Jacques.

"We talked to Luther but he wants too much money," Jacques answered.

"Well, do you want a big record?"

"Yes."

"Then my advice to you is to work out the best deal you can with Luther. Give him whatever he wants."

Jacques failed to heed Wayne's suggestion. Instead, he tried other singers on the track. He went through vocalist after vocalist, but he couldn't get the sound he wanted, that smooth, fresh uptown vibe that he was so desperate to capture. Meanwhile, he was racking up bills and the whole Change project was providing industry gossips with some good material.

Desperate, Jacques decided to completely regroup. He moved from Hit Factory Studios to Media Sound Studios, a refurbished church that incidentally was one street over from Luther's West Fifty-sixth Street apartment. Jacques knew Luther would sound great on the record. He had heard his work and was familiar with his impeccable reputation, but Luther was asking for so much money. Other singers were thrilled just to be on the record. Besides, Jacques—with his alleged underworld connections—was a hardened negotiator, known to be intimidating to those meeting him for the first time. He wasn't ready to give in to some session singer, no matter how talented—at least not so soon.

Recording for the album continued and yet another vocalist was chosen for "The Glow of Love." This time it was Marc Sadane, a protégé of the sultry, statuesque jazz/R&B stylist Phyllis Hyman. Sadane was in the recording booth with Wayne teaching him the song, when suddenly Luther walked into the control room. Wayne watched as Luther traded words with Jacques for a few minutes. Then Wayne was called into the control room. Jacques told him that Marc was out and Luther was in.

After weeks of negotiation, Luther finally got what he wanted. Not just the money, which he knew he was worth, but something even more important, something lacking from so many of the other records he sang on.

"I said something that was at the time unheard of," Luther re-membered. "I said I also want my name on the album cover. Back-ground singers had never done that before."

Moments later Luther was in the recording booth with Wayne teaching him the dreamily romantic number. Just before Luther started recording, he said to Wayne, "I just gotta tell you, man, this is the most beautiful song I've ever sung in my life."

Luther started singing, the page of lyrics in his hand, and by the time he was done, Jacques had finally gotten that mood, that spirit, that energy that proved so elusive. Michael Brauer was the record-ing engineer for the session, and he remembered the waves of joy that ran through the studio while Luther sang.

"He went in there," Brauer recalled, "and suddenly that song had spirit. He just nailed it unlike everyone else before him. They had had ten other people singing that song who were all Luther's equals in the industry, who were just as busy and got just as much work as he did, but they couldn't nail it the way Luther did. He was already onto something. He had a more unique tone than any of his peers. The other guys were great, but they were lacking a lit-tle of the originality Luther offered."

Luther infused it with an emotionality often missing from many assembly-line dance-floor fillers. "There are those who consider 'The Glow of Love' to be a disco song," Luther observed, "but I consider it to be a soul song. When I sang it, I didn't think I was making a dance record. I didn't think I was making a disco record. I thought I was making a fabulous up-tempo soul number. I was feeling it like that."

Thoroughly pleased with Luther's performance, Jacques also asked him to sing on another song, "Searching." It tells the story of a lonely man, driving the cold night streets looking for someplace to go, someone to make the evening a little warmer. Luther conveyed the tale as if it were his personal reflection, a page from his diary, while an infectious melody swirled around him.

After he finished recording the number, he felt triumphant, closer to becoming the affecting vocalist that he so wanted to be. "A lesser singer would have gotten [musically] lost amid everything that was going on in 'Searching,'" Luther said. "The vocal performance could have been trivialized, suppressed. I'm not trying to blow my own trumpet, but it's like riding a bull in a rodeo—you've just got to stay on top. I rode that bull to the fade,'til the drummer dropped the sticks."

The Change album was released in April 1980, and although executives at the label, RFC Records, loved the product, they were concerned about whether it would find an audience. There was an increasingly hostile disco backlash developing. The previous summer, a riot exploded during a baseball doubleheader at Chicago's Comisky Park, when a local radio DJ staged what was supposed to be a mass demolition of disco records between games. About seven thousand mostly white male fans stormed the field breaking records, wrecking the batting cage and pitcher's mound, and setting small fires. There were numerous arrests and injuries, and the evening's second game between Chicago's White Sox and the Detroit Tigers was called off.

Industry observers started commenting on this new "disco sucks" movement. *New York Times* music critic John Rockwell wrote: "Even with the embrace of disco by the white masses, symbolized by John Travolta and The Bee Gees, disco is still regarded by rock loyalists as a black and homosexual phenomenon. It's not always clear when whites profess a dislike of disco as to whether they dislike the music or whether they dislike those who like it."

Nevertheless, once the Change album was out, it was quickly embraced by the disco and R&B crowd. "It was just so polished," remembered RFC executive Vince Aletti. "It was so sophisticated and the sound was so well pitched to that moment. They really had a good sense of where the dance floor was going. By 1980, disco was supposedly over, but what made the Change record work is that it really had a strong R&B base. It didn't have that Eurodisco thump-thump-thump. It had a real American feel to it."

Jacques had accomplished his mission.

What's more, Luther's voice was now more ubiquitous than ever. Radio announcers started crediting "Searching" and "The Glow of Love" to Change *featuring Luther Vandross*. Sometimes, they would just say *Luther Vandross*. People now knew his name.

Critics loved the record. Britain's *The Face* magazine called it "perhaps, the first great soul record of the Eighties . . . news from somewhere that there was still some soul left in the heart of black America."

"[Luther] was faceless," the article continued, "brought in by a pair of disco producers who pulled out all of the strings and put synthesizers in their place [but] Luther sang so well that the passion just burnt through all the precision."

With the Change record rapidly rising on the charts and being played everywhere from nightclubs to backyard barbecues, Luther felt certain that it would only be a short while before a record company came calling offering a record deal. His only stipulations were that he wanted complete creative control, to be able to write his own songs and produce himself, or at least be the one deciding who he should work with. After years of selling products and singing other people's music, it was the bare minimum that he would settle for.

"I wanted to be my own producer," Luther said. "That's almost unheard of when someone's untried and unproven in the industry. I can take directions as well as anyone—you can't make it as a background singer or a jingle singer unless you can—but this time I wanted to be in charge."

Shortly after "Searching" and "The Glow of Love" came out, an interviewer from Britain's *Blues and Soul* magazine asked him about the impact of Change's success. "There's been no immediate tangible result for me in terms of career at this point," Luther answered, "but I anticipate that . . . we should be getting even more interest from companies for me to get the right kind of deal."

However, weeks then months passed by, but there were no offers for the type of deal Luther desired. "They all liked my voice," he said, "but across the board they didn't want me to produce myself. They're so used to pairing producers with black artists—that was the success story."

Compounding this disappointment, Quincy Jones had yet to fulfill his promise of helping Luther make a record. The album Quincy had been working on with young Michael Jackson, *Off the Wall,* turned into an unexpected smash, selling a few million copies, which was nearly unprecedented for an R&B act. Quincy then had to start working on the follow-up.

"Luther was on my record and you could hear his talent a mile away," Quincy explained, "but I was too busy to do more with him."

That wasn't good enough for Luther. "I grew a little tired waiting for Quincy," he remembered.

All of this added to the funk Luther was beginning to feel before the Change project came his way. It wasn't that people didn't appreciate him. Four years in a row, he won a special award given to behind-the-scenes musicians by the New York chapter of the National Academy of Recording Arts and Sciences. Plus, he was making "mountains of money from jingles." However, none of this was getting him closer to signing a record deal.

"No one wanted me," Luther said. "Either they didn't like my sound or they didn't like the idea that I wanted to produce my-self—something I was very adamant about—or they were turned off by my six-feet-two-inch, two-hundred-eighty-pound image."

Luther plunged into the deepest depression of his life. It in-creasingly seemed like he was already, at age twenty-nine, all he was ever going to be: a highly valued session singer. It began to look like all the dreams he'd been carrying would never come to life.

The sadness threatened to overwhelm him, and he dealt with it the way he always had. It was the only thing that buffered the pain. He needed food. It filled him up and gave him something to do other than sitting around obsessing over what wasn't happen-ing with his career. He knew he shouldn't do it, knew that his weight was one of the factors keeping him from signing a record deal. Yet he couldn't control it, couldn't stop himself from repeat-edly calling the neighborhood deli and having them deliver what-ever they could to his door—more, more, and more. It was an addiction, as much of an emotional salve as downing vodka or snorting cocaine. He also knew that, in its extremes, it could be just as damaging, just as deadly.

In the midst of this turmoil, Luther got a call from one of the people that he most enjoyed working with: Roberta Flack. She, however, was having hard times of her own. Just a year earlier, she was planning a reunion with her old college buddy and duet part-ner Donny Hathaway. They had been estranged for a few years. She was dealing with her issues; he was battling some of his own.

Donny often thought audiences preferred acts like Stevie Won-der and Al Green to him. He heard the cheers and screams of his audience and wondered why he deserved it. For a time, he was hos-pitalized for depression.

However, everyone around him thought he was slowly begin-ning to manage these sometimes consuming doubts. It seemed the perfect time for Roberta and Donny to revive their musical partnership, to stir up some of that chemistry that bound them so closely. Their reunion even provided the theme for one of the songs they were recording: "Back Together Again."

One winter evening, Donny was over at Roberta's Dakota apartment for dinner to talk about the new album. They chowed down on fish, rice, salad, and spoon bread, as they caught up on each other's recent past and discussed plans for the future. Roberta dropped him off at his hotel room after they finished eating. He was staying at the ornate Essex House Hotel, a towering block-long reminder of old New York that sits right by Central Park.

Before heading to his room, he asked Roberta: "Do you have any more of that cake?" referring to a dessert her housekeeper had brought back from a trip to Jamaica.

"No, you guys ate it up," Roberta said, amused, but she promised him they could get some more.

He smiled just thinking about the cake. "That was so good," he said before heading into the building.

Sometime later that night, alone in his room, he walked over to the window and removed the safety glass. He placed it down neatly on the bed. Then he walked back to the window and hurled himself down thirteen stories, a free-falling attempt to escape from . . . something.

After a starling, painful phone call, Roberta found herself in the New York City morgue identifying his bruised and broken body. When he died, Donny left a wife and two young daughters. The music world lost one of its most precious voices. Roberta lost her friend.

By the time she called Luther, Roberta was slowly trying to move on with things. She had completed the album she had been working on with Donny—you could hear his voice on two cuts— and she was planning to go on tour with another male vocalist, Peabo Bryson, with whom Luther worked back in 1975. Roberta wanted Luther to come on the road with her and be in charge of all the background vocals.

He said yes and was happy to go. Sometimes touring with Roberta was like going on a holiday because she often played places like St. Thomas. "To me, those were vacations," Luther said.

But as they headed out on the various dates, darker thoughts sometimes came to him. He was on the cusp of turning thirty, but his life seemed like it was on pause. Luther remembered thinking, "Here I am five years later and I'm getting ready to back Peabo again."

The tour rolled on, and Luther soon got into the spirit of things. He remembered how the Sweet Inspirations backing Aretha had inspired him all those years ago. Sometimes on a whim, Luther would completely rearrange all of the background parts, leaving Roberta surprised and amazed.

"I'd think we were getting ready to head one way on a song," Roberta recalled, "and then the singers—led by Luther—would do this little change, some little twist, and I'd just go, 'Whoa.' It was so exciting for me, like being in a jazz band when the music just took over and carried you away."

Roberta trusted Luther completely. "He is just an excellent musician," she said, "real smart and real sober in his judgment of music." Often, she'd ask Luther to fill in for her at sound check, while she was off doing interviews and taking care of other business.

One of these times occurred at the Holiday Star Theater in Merrillville, Indiana, about half an hour outside of Chicago. Luther sat onstage singing with the band while the lighting director shone a single spotlight on him. Luther went through several of Roberta's hits, just pouring himself into it, enjoying the pure sound of his voice. He especially enjoyed singing her smash ballad "Killing Me Softly," about the effect a performer can have on a listener. Luther loved the song because it expressed the way he wanted people to feel about him and his music. It summed up how he felt that night watching Dionne Warwick at the Brooklyn Fox Theater, how her melancholy delivery made him feel a little death that opened him up to a whole new life.

When Luther finished, the lights came back on. He looked into the nearly empty house and was shocked to see Roberta sitting there watching him. She got up and walked over to where he sat onstage.

"You know," she said, "you're getting too comfortable sitting on this stool singing 'ooh' and 'aah.' You must go pursue your own solo career. We deserve it and you deserve it."

Luther protested. He had told her how hard it had been for him, how nobody wanted to sign him. Roberta, however, wasn't interested in hearing excuses. She had seen firsthand what could happen when people didn't believe in themselves, when talent went tragically to waste.

"Luther," she said, "you've got a choice here. You can sing background all your life. Or you can do what you're supposed to do. You can get out there and let the world hear you."

Then, according to Luther, she dropped a bomb of sorts, saying, "I'm lovingly firing you."

Roberta later denied that she specifically said that, but she admitted that her intent was for him to commit himself to his career. "Luther Vandross likes to say that I fired him," she said, smiling, "but I never really fired him. What I did was encourage him to believe in his own ability."

Either way, Luther got the message. Maybe it was the timing, or perhaps it was how she said it, but whatever the case, he decided that he would take one more shot at his dream. He wouldn't wait on those tired record companies. He wouldn't worry about whether they *allowed* him to take control of his career and produce himself. He was just going to take a chunk of all the money he had piled up over the years and make his own record on his own terms, come what may.

The surprising thing about it all is that once he made this choice, it wasn't scary at all. Rather, he felt strong, proud even, that he finally recognized that he—and only he—had the power to change his life.

"I've been around people," Luther said, "seeing them get over and do things and helping them get over by singing background and arranging things for them. But success for me now is growing out of that period and coming into my own. And I feel pretty good now because it's happening. It's strange to want something for so long."

"Never Too Much"

*"It was like a desert,
and Luther had water."*

—COLLABORATOR MARCUS MILLER,
ON LUTHER'S SOLO DEBUT

It was only ten P.M., but you could barely move inside the Savoy nightclub on West Forty-fourth Street in Manhattan. The show wasn't scheduled to begin for another hour, but people had turned out to see this hot new R&B singer, Luther Vandross. His voice seemed to be all over the city throughout 1981. You could hear his music coming out of cars, in beauty shops, tony department stores, downtown dance clubs, out of open windows in the summer heat, on the lips of people singing to themselves on the subway train, and blaring out of those huge radios that some young brothers carried perched on their well-toned shoulders. It seemed like Luther had tapped into the spirit of this metropolis, like his music provided its beat. Now a whole roomful of people were gathered at the Savoy to hear him deliver it live.

It was a well-dressed crowd, styled in their evening best. Gold and diamonds flashed through the smoky air, and there was a woman resplendent in green mascara and a white mink.

The show began with four pink-clad background singers—two men, two women—walking onstage, smiling, snapping their fingers, and moving their bodies to the band's full-bodied groove. Once they settled behind their microphone stands, Luther walked on. His face shone with a broad smile, and he literally sparkled, wearing a cropped jacket covered in green sequins that was set off against a pair of black slacks.

All of his friends and associates in the crowd would have noticed that not only did he look good—the often disheveled studio caterpillar transformed into a glittering onstage butterfly—but he also appeared to have lost a considerable amount of weight. Success agreed with him, and they felt happy and proud watching his hard-won metamorphosis.

He started singing, taking the crowd through some up-tempo numbers. The audience responded warmly, clapping, singing along, moving to the sharp, snappy rhythms. However, there was a sense of anticipation as if they hadn't yet gotten what had made them come out on this cold winter night. The show went on, one song followed another. Then, finally, the moment arrived.

Luther addressed the assembled throng. "On all of my albums," he said, "I intend to sing one song in honor of each of the reigning black divas. This song is in honor of Dionne Warwick." The music began: a quick run of notes like piano raindrops, followed by a slow watchful bass. Luther started to sing. First, it wasn't lyrics, but simple stuttered moans, the kind of sounds someone might make while sitting alone at a window on an overcast day. Soon, the words came out: "A chair is still a chair . . ."

Most anyone who wasn't sure what he was singing before now knew. It was Dionne Warwick's classic ballad of loneliness "A

House Is Not a Home." However, it had never sounded like this until Luther got ahold of it. Dionne's version, while affecting, was poised and mannered, the reflections of a forlorn woman with a stiff upper lip. Luther changed this song, one of his favorites, from a plaintive reflection to a testament to hungering desire and devastating loss. He made the song sound like Dionne's version had always made him feel.

When he finished, the audience broke out into claps and shouts, overwhelmed with emotion. The woman in the white mink had green mascara running down her cheeks.

This song, which was receiving constant radio airplay, was touching people all over the country. It was one of the reasons Luther's debut solo album was such a winner. That night at the Savoy, record company executives presented Luther with a gold plaque, commemorating 500,000 albums sold. Luther embraced the plaque, then told the audience, "This is my diploma." The former Western Michigan University student had made good.

It had been nearly two years since Luther had that conversation with Roberta Flack, when she urged him to pursue a solo career. In the meantime, so much had happened, each thing serving as a little building block that led to this triumphant night at the Savoy.

In that time, Luther had fully committed himself to recording an album that he would produce and finance himself. However, he did agree to lend Bette Midler a hand on her *Divine Madness* tour, which was shot for a concert film. It was easy work, and he was helping an old friend. He didn't even have to appear onstage. Instead, he sat on a stool behind a screen, munching on hamburgers in between singing his parts.

The other thing he had to deal with was the second Change album. *The Glow of Love* was such a big hit that the record company wanted to rush out a follow-up. Luther was interested. After all, his own album was still in the works. He didn't even have a label. Change, on the other hand, seemed like a sure thing. Yet he wasn't willing to do it for the same terms as the first record. Not only did he want his name on the cover, he also wanted to get a percentage of the album sales as opposed to simply a flat fee for his vocals.

He brought these terms to Change's tough-minded visionary Jacques Fred Petrus, who immediately balked at Luther's demands. "They didn't need Luther," he thought.

Jacques and his team soon initiated another search, but this time it was clear that they wanted a Luther soundalike. After two frustrating weeks, they settled on New York–based vocalist James "Crabs" Robinson, who has a deeper tone than Luther. Throughout the second album, titled *Miracle*, Robinson attempted his best Luther interpretation, trying to make his heavier voice sound springy and light. The result, however, is much like a hefty boxer trying to do ballet. It just didn't work, and the album fared poorly.

While all this transpired, Luther toiled on his album. The songs came quickly: the fleet "Never Too Much"; "Don't You Know," with its thick, insinuating groove; "She's a Sugar Lady," based around a funky, plucking bass; and the rejoicing "Sugar and Spice (Found Me a Girl)." Then there was that song that Luther had always wanted to record, "A House Is Not a Home."

The night Luther sang it in the studio, he was alone in the recording booth, while a group of his friends and other musicians sat in the control room. There wasn't a person there who didn't know how special this song was to Luther, how long he'd been waiting to record it. They saw him in the booth, looking like he was nurturing each note coming out of his mouth. Suddenly something happened that Luther's recording engineer Michael Brauer called "one of the most special things I have ever experienced."

"Everybody is watching him," Brauer recalled, "and he's just

holding this one note, and you can hear that there's this little tim-
bre, just a tiny drop in his pitch a couple times while he's holding
his note. That was his heartbeat causing the note to vary just that
little bit. It was so intense."

When Luther walked out of the booth, everybody cheered. "We
were all freaking out," Brauer remembered. "It was so great."

Luther completed work on this batch of songs and went to play
them for the person who had given him the push to record them in
the first place, Roberta Flack. They were together at a theme park
when he handed her the tape. She started playing it and could hear
all the hard work he had put into it, all of the lessons he had
learned.

When Luther looked over at her, she was crying. "You're em-
barrassing me," he told her. If her tears bothered him so much, she
responded, he should just go sit someplace else.

Encouraged by Roberta's enthusiasm, Luther took his songs
around to record companies again. This time he wasn't asking
them to let him produce himself. He was presenting them with already complete recordings that they could either put out or not.
Initially, every company chose to do the latter. It seemed that no
one was interested in him.

This was during the era when black music was largely dominated by huge bands with a small army of members. There were
the Commodores, Parliament/Funkadelic, LTD, Lakeside, Kool
and the Gang, and the S.O.S. Band, among others. They made
walloping horn-blasting, bass-slapping funk.

The biggest male singers on the scene exuded sex. Buffalo's Rick
James talked dirty while wearing tight leather pants. That flowery,
long-haired dandy Prince seductively chirped "I Wanna Be Your
Lover." Teddy Pendergrass, formerly of the powerhouse Philly
Soul outfit Harold Melvin and the Bluenotes, held "For Ladies
Only" concerts, and Mississippi-born singer Michael Henderson

often made the R&B Top 20 by combining smooth ballads with provocative album covers, one even featuring him nearly nude, clad only in a sky-blue Speedo. In this musical landscape, there didn't seem to be any room for a heavy-set romantic like Luther.

Since his music wasn't funk and didn't have an erotic edge, he was sometimes told that it wasn't black enough. This outraged him.

"To be black and to be part of the black experience, you don't have to be Funkadelic or Grandmaster Flash," Luther said. "They are legitimate, but I am also legitimate. . . . That kind of prejudice stopped me from getting a deal for a long time, the fact that I'm not raunchy. But I held out because I knew what I did was real."

Finally things started to turn around when Luther found out that somebody who once tried to sign him in the past, an executive named Jerome Gasper, had recently taken a new position at Epic Records, a subsidiary of the all-powerful CBS Records. In 1978, Gasper had been working at RCA Records, where he tried to sign Luther, but his higher-ups refused to OK the deal. It didn't matter that Luther had an impeccable industry reputation. They couldn't see past his weight. Gasper's new boss, however, held a different view. His name was Larkin Arnold, and before coming to CBS, he had played a major role in shaping the careers of Peabo Bryson and crooner Nat King Cole's soul-singing progeny Natalie.

Arnold saw the potential of Luther's recordings and agreed to his terms. As Luther explained, "The deal was simple—'I'll deliver the [tapes] and album covers, you guys put them out. No interference.' That was it."

Pretty soon, Luther's signature was dancing across the contract page. He called it the happiest moment in his life. "Up until that time," he remembered, "it had been a long struggle with many disappointments. The more I was turned down, the stronger I felt inside that I could be a solo performer. So, it was a happy period in my life when my belief in myself met reality."

Sesame Workshop

On the first season of the TV show *Sesame Street,* a smiling, teenage Luther (far right) sings with the Apollo Theatre's youth group, Listen My Brother, and helps spread the message that "children are beautiful." Also pictured are his high school friends Robin Clark (far left) and Fonzi Thornton (kneeling).

In 1974 a chance meeting with British rocker David Bowie changed the course and color of twenty-three-year-old Luther's life. Here, he sits back while the flamboyant rock star receives attention from a gushing fan.

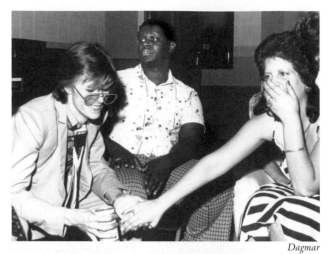

Dagmar

Michael Ochs Archive

With hope and ambition shining in their eyes, Luther's group, simply called Luther, poses for a publicity shot to accompany their first album released in 1976. Pictured from left to right are Diane Sumler, Luther, Anthony Hinton, Christine Wiltshire, and Theresa V. Reed.

You'd never know that Luther often felt uncomfortable performing by this picture of him working the stage at the Montreux International Festival in 1977. This was when Luther was fast becoming the secret voice of disco, singing background on such smashes as Sister Sledge's "We Are Family" and Chic's "Le Freak."

Life was good as Luther took photos for the cover of his 1981 solo debut, "Never Too Much." Luther had lost weight and, after years of hearing him in the background, the public was finally about to experience the uncompromised purity of his voice and vision.

William Coupon / CORBIS

"If I were not a singer, I'd be an interior designer," Luther often said. He outfitted the foyer of one of his first apartments entirely in his favorite color—pink. He'd sometimes joke that he was "cursed with good taste."

Lynn Goldsmith / CORBIS

Growing up, kids would laugh at Luther because of his weight. But, as he got older, he decided to laugh back. In response to comedian Eddie Murphy's joke that Luther was a big Kentucky Fried Chicken eater, Luther once brought a whole bunch of buckets onstage with him.

Lynn Goldsmith / CORBIS

Back among old friends, Luther sings background vocals for David Bowie's 1986 single, "Underground." Alongside Bowie are the fiery and blisteringly talented Chaka Khan (far left) and Luther's all-time favorite vocalist, Cissy Houston (far right), mother of Whitney.

AP Photo / Harrison Funk

Before a tragic car accident changed everything, Luther worked closely with fifteen-year-old budding pinup dream Jimmy Salvemini.

Michael Ochs Archive

AP Photo / Mark Terrill

Leaving the Van Nuys Municipal Court of California where he was on trial for vehicular manslaughter, Luther looks distressed after the death of Jimmy Salvemini's brother/manager, Larry, whom he called "my friend for life."

By the mid 1980s, Luther was the undisputed voice of black love, but he was also dogged by rumors about his health and sexuality. Luther poses here in a romantic shot with a female model, but in interviews he never revealed the name—or gender—of anyone he's dated.

A newly svelte Luther is dapper and dazzling in July 1987 singing at London's Wembley Arena, where he set a box office record by selling out ten straight nights at the venue.

© David Corio / Retna Ltd.

Phil Roach / IPOL / Globe Photos Inc. © 1988

B acking Luther is the Chicago-bred stunner Ava Cherry, a former Playboy bunny who once had a twister of an affair with David Bowie.

Background vocalist Lisa Fischer helped Luther fulfill his dream of being surrounded by beautifully styled singers and dancers. Like Luther, Lisa hailed from the rougher parts of New York City, but she remade herself as an enchanting diva-for-hire touring with the Rolling Stones, and even scoring her own solo hit with the 1991 single, "How Can I Ease the Pain."

In 1988 what seemed like a brilliant idea—putting Luther on a co-headlining tour with his smooth R&B female counterpart, Anita Baker—quickly devolved into a mess of he said/she said accusations. Here, Baker performs at New York's Radio City Music Hall.

"I'd like to thank my diet doctor," said a strikingly thin Luther when accepting one of his awards at the 1992 Grammys. This marked one of his few wins after nearly a decade of devastating losses.

AP Photo

Robin Platzer / Twin Images / Time Life Pictures / Getty Images

When thirteen-year-old Luther first saw Dionne Warwick (left) perform, he knew he wanted to touch others the way she touched him. He later became friends with her, as he did with many of his other beloved female singers, such as Gladys Knight (right), who would sometimes cook dinner for Luther and his family.

Luther called himself an "Arethacologist" because of his enduring, studied love for the Queen of Soul, Aretha Franklin, seen here with her biggest fan at the inaugural celebration for President Bill Clinton in 1993. Luther and Aretha briefly fell out of each other's favor in the mid 1980s starting with an infamous recording studio blowup.

Lynn Goldsmith / CORBIS

David Williams / Allford-Trotman

Things got so bad that the police had to be called during Luther's 1993 tour with the girl group En Vogue. He said the young women were "spoiled, non–truth-telling, contract breakers," and they dubbed him "Lucifer." Shown backstage at a concert in the early 1990s are Maxine Jones, Dawn Robinson, Cindy Herron, and Terry Ellis (left to right).

Sharing the kind of laughter that comes from years of love, memories, and trust, Luther and Whitney Houston, whom he first met in the late 1970s, hang out backstage at the Soul Train Music Awards in 1999.

As a teenager, Luther admired Patti LaBelle so much that he became the first president of her fan club. Standing onstage at the 2000 Democratic Convention in Los Angeles, Luther had become not only her occasional duet partner but also her friend.

AP Photo/Michael Caulfield

When Luther dyed his hair red in 2000 he was trying to shock his friends before a Hawaiian trip. He later showed up with his new do at the 31st Annual NAACP Image Awards where he linked arms with legendary Motown crooner Smokey Robinson, who once said, "There are vocalists, and then there's Luther."

Camera bulbs flashed as Luther showed up at the opening of the Broadway musical *Nine* on Thursday, April 10, 2003, six days before his debilitating stroke.

Across the nation, fans dropped to their knees or lifted their hands and voices in prayer to show support for a hospitalized Luther. On May 29, 2003, a fan participates in a vigil at Harlem's Convent Avenue Baptist Church for Luther and Barry White, who was also ailing and died a few months later.

Two of Luther's favorite songwriters, the married team of Nick Ashford (left) and Valerie Simpson (right), take part in the Harlem vigil with Luther's devoted mentor, Roberta Flack (center), who initially pushed Luther to move from the background and pursue a solo career.

AP Photo / Bebeto Matthews

Luther's mother, Mary Ida Vandross, photographed in June 2003, raised her youngest son alone after her husband died in 1959. Fate has since forced her to bury her other three children. Yet she still has the strength to promote her ailing son's album *Dance with My Father*.

Luther sits in a wheelchair at a New Jersey rehabilitation center while J Records President, Clive Davis, presents him with a platinum plaque in December 2003 indicating that his *Dance with My Father* album had sold more than one million copies.

AP / WorldWide Photos

By April 21, 1981, Luther was under contract as a solo record-ing artist. He was thirty, and he was no longer singing backup for Peabo Bryson. With contract negotiations completed, Epic Rec-ords started strategizing Luther's debut. Luther spent a lot of time at the Epic offices, meeting with executives, charming them with skillfully deployed humility. There were pictures to be taken, biog-raphies to be written, regional representatives to meet.

All this hustle had two effects. One, it endeared him to those in the company. He didn't come off as a snotty prima donna. He proved he was willing to work, and that made people feel invested in his success.

Two, by constantly being on the go, Luther found himself shed-ding pounds like never before. "The more [work], the better," he remarked. "I have an ongoing battle of the bulge. . . . So as long as I'm working, I'm distracted from eating."

Setup work on the album continued through late spring, and by early summer they had decided on Luther's first solo single: "Never Too Much." Everything about the song felt fresh. His singing seemed so breezy and effortless. It had a deep-seated groove that you couldn't stop snapping your fingers to. There was something more, as well. It was in the way Luther sang the flurry of words that made up the song's rapid-fire verses. His styling seemed to lightly reflect an energy that was taking shape in the streets with all those colorfully dressed kids spray-painting subway cars and saying rhymes over songs booming from their handheld radios. "It kinda is like a rap syncopation," Luther acknowledged, "and then it smooths so breezily out for the chorus."

Epic commissioned a video of Luther performing "Never Too Much." This was a relative novelty in the business at the time, but they figured the clip could be shown in stores and on TV shows when Luther couldn't appear himself. Most of the video focused on a trim Luther in a shiny black jacket with a burst of pink trim.

Giant headphones sat on his head as he mouthed the lyrics to his own hit record.

"I was always good at lip-syncing," Luther recalled. "I could lip-sync all the Temptations' songs, so there was no problem with that." The other parts of the video showed a bevy of people walking down the street eating lunch on the sidewalk and roller-skating in the park, all grooving to Luther's tune.

The song steadily rose up the R&B charts, and before long it had replaced the Four Tops' ditty "When She Was My Girl" at the number-one spot. Luther was ecstatic. A full decade after he first left school to pursue a music career, people were calling him an overnight success.

Everything was going so well. Luther's only problem concerned the progress of "Never Too Much" on the pop charts, where it never broke into the Top 20. This nagged him, but he didn't have time to focus on it too much. There was so much else to do.

Epic was thrilled at how well the record was doing. The company's only concern was about Luther's numerous side projects. "My record label wants me to cut way down on doing lead vocals on jingles because of the overexposure factor," he explained at the time. "You might hear 'Never Too Much,' followed by Burger King and Miller Beer spots with my lead, followed by Chic's 'Le Freak' with me very close to the mic on lead vocals followed by Donna Summer and Barbra Streisand singing 'Enough Is Enough,' again with me very close to the mic on backgrounds. So, I'm keeping new lead vocal projects down to a respectable minimum, although I'm not turning down an American Airlines jingle since that can mean the equivalent of a platinum single in this business."

The album, also titled *Never Too Much,* came out in August and received great reviews. What was especially rewarding for Luther is that they often praised the two things that he had fought so hard for: the ability to produce himself and pen his own tunes. *Sepia* magazine wrote: "Vandross' talent extends beyond his smooth vocal delivery. Those words that pass his lips and play masterfully with the ears are his own." The *Village Voice* concurred: "In a situation that would seem to invite gross self-indulgence, the Vandross album is remarkable for its restraint and subtlety—a fine understatement that for all its care and polish, is not chilly but wonderfully warm."

Luther was vindicated. "I feel really excited about what is happening to me—and ecstatic about the album itself," he said. "It's the best thing that has ever happened to me and I was able to express myself artistically for the first time. There honestly is nothing about the album that I would want to do differently if I had to do it all over again."

In addition to Luther's newfound solo success, there were other changes in his life. He had outgrown 330 West Fifty-sixth Street and moved into a grand new apartment near Lincoln Center. Looking out the window, you could see the Hudson River stretch out across the length of the city. Inside offered a dazzle of brass trinkets, floor-to-ceiling mirrors, shiny black leather furniture, and walls painted in Luther's favorite color: pink.

He would park his recently acquired gray Mercedes, detailed with his initials on the doors, in the downstairs garage. There he'd sign autographs for the workers and their families and jokingly ask them not to hurt his "baby."

Luther adored this new place, but in the months following his album's release, he had little time to enjoy it. The record company wanted him out on tour—an idea that initially terrified Luther. "It scares you to death," Luther remembered, "especially after being a session singer—you come in with your hair nappy, in sneakers, your shirt hanging out. It doesn't matter what you look like, you've just got to *sound* good. Now all of a sudden to have everybody looking at you is a *deep* transition."

His first solo gig took place in his hometown New York City, opening up for someone he once sang backup for: the fiery, inimitable Chaka Khan. In order to ease his nervousness, Luther surrounded himself with many of his old friends and colleagues. Nat Adderly, Jr., a former Listen, My Brother member, manned the keyboards, and the background singers included Fonzi Thornton, his high school buddy.

It was like a family onstage, one that he had nurtured over the years and finally was able to bring together. What a rewarding feeling it was to be able to give work to his friends. That wasn't the only reason there was a familial atmosphere in the room that night, however. Seated in the audience was his mother, Mary Ida. He was finally ready to let her see what it was that he did. It still made him nervous to have her there, though, and he avoided making eye contact most of the night. Yet just before he was about to leave the stage, he glanced over at her and saw an expression that he never forgot.

"I looked up," Luther remembered, laughing, "and my mother's face was like, 'Did I raise *that*?'"

Her shock came from how accomplished he was, how much the crowd loved him and wanted to hear his songs. Not only had her baby become a man, but the once shy boy she still called Ronnie had transformed into a polished entertainer. All that time spent listening to records, watching Ed Sullivan, and hanging around the Apollo suddenly had new meaning.

Luther felt energized seeing his mother's response, and he loved the reaction of the crowd, how they knew his songs and were mouthing the lyrics. It was different than the thrill of creating something in the studio. This was about connecting with people, making them feel what you wanted them to feel, killing them softly. He wanted more.

"I can't wait to really get out there on the road," he said shortly after the show. "I have a *need* to perform—it's an urge inside of me."

Luther went off on tour. He opened for Natalie Cole in Boston, then later did shows with Brooklyn's eight-piece Skyy and the sometimes ten-member-strong Kool and the Gang. Luther played ten nights opening for the Commodores, a nearly unstoppable pop/R&B behemoth led by singer and songwriter Lionel Richie. Life became a rush of airports and braving flights through dense fog in order to make it to the stage on time. It was very different from when he toured behind others. This time all the responsibility and burden fell on him.

He enjoyed the cheering crowds. When he played the Greek Theater in Los Angeles, women rushed the stage bearing flowers. "Girls *do* scream when I sing," he observed following the gig. "I thought you had to have a thirty-inch waist to get screams."

There were also times onstage when he felt like he was living a teenager's dream. Once, promoters asked him to open a show for Aretha Franklin in Washington, D.C. It was a moment he had thought about for so long, fantasized about as he listened to her many records, and now it was going to happen.

He arrived in D.C. and went to Constitution Hall, the city's primary venue for R&B acts. He made his way backstage and anxiously awaited his idol.

"At first I was very scared," Luther recollected. "You know, the legend precedes the body with her. I was a nervous wreck when I went to her room. She was standing there, and on that particular day, she had on a burgundy-and-gold gown. It was one of those gowns like from *The King and I*. So she looked very majestic."

Aretha spotted her opening act, but instead of saying "Hi" or "How are you," she simply said "Hmmm . . . 'Never Too Much,'" and walked away. Luther wasn't sure what to make of it. "I knew nothing about her manner," he remembered. "I didn't know she was slightly shy, a little quiet in countenance and texture."

Still, whatever she was feeling, Lady Soul was obviously impressed enough with the buzz surrounding the enthusiastic, worshipful upstart that she invited him to later come onstage and duet with her. When the crowd that night heard the princely R&B newcomer join together with the now-and-forever queen, they went wild. "We killed them," Luther said. "They're still removing the bodies from the audience."

Sometimes he even stole the show from the headliners. In November 1981, he opened for the mellow R&B act Maze at New York City's Palladium, yet Luther was the act who many ticket holders came to see. A reviewer for the *New York Times* wrote: "It was apparent from the audience response . . . that the second-billed Luther Vandross, a New York singer with a smash-hit album riding the charts, was the chief box-office attraction. A portly wide-eyed entertainer with a flowery, good-humored stage manner, Mr. Vandross has the potential to become one of the most important pop-soul crooners of his generation."

With all these well-received concert dates and healthy record sales, Luther drew the fickle attention of the press. Interviews were as important as live shows when it came to boosting record sales, but the schedule was completely different. Concerts took place at night, while interviews often happened during the day. Luther was working almost around the clock, which led to interesting situations. One reporter expressed shock when he showed up for a meeting with Luther and heard a raspy neo-baritone instead of a silken tenor.

"This is my morning voice," Luther explained. "Now I sound like Melvin of The Temps. That's just a characteristic thing about my voice. It gains a few notes as the day goes on."

The interviews Luther gave during this time reveal a man bursting with ambitions. The guy who was once intimidated to sing in the studio now spoke of grand plans for the future. "I want to be an entertainer," Luther said. "I don't want to be just a singer or a stand-up comedian or an actor. I want to combine all three resources. . . . Within the next two to three years, I want to spend six months on Broadway in a musical."

Luther came across differently than most new pop, rock, or R&B artists. He flaunted his clean-cut lifestyle. "I don't do any drugs," he said. "I don't drink and I don't smoke." Though his weight was down, he admitted that his primary indulgence was food. "I go for the starchy stuff," he said. "I go right for the bag of potato chips, the extra leg of chicken or the Häagen-Dazs. I never crave broccoli."

This wasn't the only way Luther differed from most new artists. Since he had been successful doing jingles, he also didn't share the financial burdens that saddled scores of debut acts. "The business I take very seriously," Luther explained. "I have my own corporation, Luther Vandross LTD of which I am the president. My tax situation is impeccable. I'm not going to get in trouble. I'm taking care of business."

The only problem reporters had with Luther is that he seemed so wrapped up in his own musical world that he had little awareness of what was happening around him. While en route to lunch at the trendy Pier 52 restaurant, Luther noticed piles of trash lining the sidewalk. "Is there a strike on or something," he asked a writer from *New York* magazine, who then informed him that city sanitation workers had walked off the job ten days previously. Later, the same writer asked Luther if he would perform in South Africa, where apartheid divided the country between blacks and whites. Luther responded that he would have to read up on the situation before he could answer.

The man who once thought Diana Ross leaving the Supremes was a national crisis still lived in a world where only music mattered. It had always been that way, whether growing up in the

Lower East Side projects or being a teenager in the Bronx. His single-minded focus on music is what drove him, sheltered him, kept him company, and warmed his soul. It was the reason he was now so successful. Yet with increased fame came more scrutiny. Another reporter directly challenged Luther for not addressing politics in his music.

"I can't speak for anybody but me," Luther answered, "and there's a lot about life that I haven't really experienced. What I write may seem mundane to some people, but I don't care because it's obviously hitting somebody. It's the overall impact of what I do that gets over well. I just haven't made a 'What's Going On' record yet."

The writer pressed and asked Luther if he ever planned to make a political record like Marvin Gaye's influential classic.

"If I feel like it, I will," he said. "If I don't feel like it, I won't apologize for not feeling like it."

Luther didn't understand why people couldn't just focus on the music. Why did they care about politics and what was going on in his personal life?

Someone asked him if he was in a romantic relationship, and Luther admitted that, despite his success, it was the one thing he yearned for.

"You can't talk to your Dreyfus Liquid Assets," he remarked, "and the bank book doesn't keep you warm at night."

13

"Jump to It"

"Dreams were coming true."

—LUTHER, ON PRODUCING ALBUMS
FOR ARETHA FRANKLIN AND
DIONNE WARWICK

Luther woke up anxious on the morning of January 12, 1982. It was the day when the National Academy of Recording Arts and Sciences would announce the nominees for its annual Grammy Awards, the music industry's most prestigious honor since they were bestowed by musicians themselves. The statue was a little golden gramophone that anointed stars would often dramatically display on polished mantels in their living rooms. Dionne had four of them; Aretha owned eleven; Luther wanted at least one.

In the days before the nominations were read, critics and industry watchers had predicted it would be a sad and sentimental year for the Grammys. Only thirteen months had passed since much-beloved Beatle John Lennon was murdered outside of his Manhattan home. Since his death, a posthumous album, *Double Fantasy,* had became a top seller and critical favorite. This record had the potential to sweep the Grammys.

Another big album that year was Quincy Jones' *The Dude*, his follow-up to the record that featured Luther. Including hits like "Just Once" and "One Hundred Ways"—both sung by a promising raspy-voiced Ray Charles protégé, James Ingram—*The Dude* seemed certain to rack up a bevy of nods.

The brief nominations announcement occurred in the morning, and when it was over, there were a number of multiple nominees. Quincy picked up eight for *The Dude*. Lionel Richie—lead singer of The Commodores, a group Luther once opened for—received six nominations for "Endless Love," a duet with Diana Ross. (This success only fueled the intense rumors that Richie was about to leave the group.) The John Lennon album scored the next highest number of nominations, earning three.

Each year, one of the most closely watched categories at the Grammys is Best New Artist, an award that's intended to signal that an act has significant promise. Often this fails to be the case and the award goes to folks who are never heard from again. Nevertheless, the award retained a certain cachet, an idea that the artist who wins might turn out to be one of the greats.

In 1982 the best new artist nominees came from several different musical worlds. There were the brightly decorated British new wavers Adam and the Ants, Los Angeles–based women rockers the Go-Go's, demure Scottish pop princess Sheena Easton, Quincy's discovery James Ingram, and that year's biggest news in R&B, Luther Vandross.

When he heard the news, Luther wanted to shout with joy. A Grammy win would get a lot of people talking, even those who didn't keep up with R&B. His name, once buried in a long list of album credits, would be on everyone's lips.

In the weeks following this announcement Luther had little time to obsess over his chances, though. He had received an opportunity that seemed to come straight from his teenage fantasies. He was asked to produce an album for Aretha Franklin.

It came about because of something Luther had said to a reporter from the rock-and-roll bible, *Rolling Stone*. The writer asked about future plans, and Luther answered, "Now, I'd wrestle [twelve-time World Wrestling Federation champion] Bruno Sammartino to get to produce Aretha Franklin."

Clive Davis, the president of Aretha's label, Arista Records, saw the interview and thought a Luther-Aretha matchup sounded like a good idea. The challenge with a living legend like Aretha was always to keep her sound fresh, and this newcomer everyone was talking about seemed like he'd be just the person to do that. "It's not easy coming up with not only hit songs but also songs that would stretch Aretha musically, and provide her with a black base that she, of course, so naturally has," Davis recalled. "Having read the interview that Luther gave to *Rolling Stone*, and with his success at the time as a producer, and as an artist, I thought that it would be a good association."

Davis introduced the idea to Aretha, who quickly warmed to it. Ever since they performed together in D.C., Aretha had become fond of Luther's album. "I like the record," she said. "It's a funny thing, but he did something on that particular recording that I was working on at home: 'A House Is Not a Home.' I said, 'Aha, he beat you to the punch!' But I still hadn't quite settled on Luther producing me. I had been thinking about him as well as some other people. And then my cousin Brenda, who sings with me, mentioned his name again. 'Why don't you let Luther Vandross produce your next album—he is really hot!' she said. Coupled with the fact that there was a relatedness and a similarity in stylings, I said, 'Why not? He obviously knows what he's doing.'"

Aretha called Luther to discuss the idea. He immediately found himself gushing.

"I just love you so much," Luther told her, "and I have some ideas that I think would work on you, that I think you would wear well."

"Well, I love 'Never Too Much,'" she responded, "and when I heard 'House Is Not a Home,' I thought you had lost your mind."

Luther told Aretha that he would start writing some songs for her, and she said, "Do your thing and send it to me."

The only trouble was that Luther already had a fully-booked schedule. He was still promoting *Never Too Much* with TV appearances and concert dates, and he was already slated to produce an album for label mate and onetime disco queen Cheryl Lynn, whose joyful 1978 hit "Got to Be Real" still filled dance floors. The pressure became intense.

During the week of February 20, Luther spent most of his time preparing for an appearance on the hit comedy show *Saturday Night Live.* Oscar-nominated actor Bruce Dern hosted, and Luther was the musical guest. Between rehearsals, however, Luther would think about songs for Aretha. Once during a break, he and bassist Marcus Miller, his former Roberta Flack band mate, sat at a piano that had temporarily been placed in a hallway of the TV studio. They started playing, creating a punchy, upbeat, gospel-like melody. Inspired, Marcus worked on their idea at home that night, then Luther, impressed by what Marcus had done, started fleshing out the chorus and the hook. Before long, they had lyrics and a name for the song: "Jump to It."

Aretha loved what she heard when Luther sent it to her. "[It] had all the sugar and spice I required," she recalled. "The groove was extra mellow and the message right on time." She asked him to do her whole album.

Before Luther could turn his full attention to Aretha, however, he had to attend the Grammys and see how far his lucky streak was really going to stretch. The awards ceremony took place four days after the *Saturday Night Live* appearance, on a Wednesday evening, February 25, 1982. As expected, the mood proved melancholy. John Lennon's widow, Yoko Ono, and the couple's six-year-old son, Sean, caused many in the audience to tear when they accepted an Album of the Year award for *Double Fantasy*. Another poignant moment came when children of the late jazz saxophonist, John Coltrane, received an award on behalf of their father for *Bye Bye Blackbird*, a posthumously released disc of live recordings.

Quincy nabbed four statuettes for *The Dude,* and showbiz legend Lena Horne received two for the cast album of her acclaimed one woman show, *Lena Horne: The Lady and Her Music Live on Broadway*.

When it came time to hand out the Best New Artist award, all of the names were called: Adam and the Ants, Sheena Easton, the Go-Go's, James Ingram, and Luther Vandross.

Sitting in the audience, Luther felt himself quivering with nerves. His hands trembled, and his palms started to sweat. Finally—after what seemed like forever—the announcer opened up a white envelope and read from the small card inside: "And the Grammy for Best New Artist goes to . . . Sheena Easton."

Suddenly, all around Luther, there was noise, people clapping loudly as Easton found her way through the crowd to pick up her award. Luther was devastated. He'd wanted it so badly and thought he had a good shot given how well *Never Too Much* was doing and all the great reviews he'd received. Then again, Sheena had something going for her that Luther didn't. Her debut single, the singsongy "Morning Train," reached number one on the pop charts and stayed there for two weeks. Overnight, it seemed like everyone knew who she was. "Never Too Much," on the other hand, failed to reach the pop Top 20. After all the years he'd been toiling in the business, Luther lacked the name recognition of newcomer Easton.

The disappointing loss made Luther feel worse than he'd felt since recording his album. The pain left him reeling and looking for a way out.

After the awards, Luther, who had been so diligent about keeping his weight down, went grocery shopping, and as he recalled, "emptied the store out."

Using food to erase his disappointment over the Grammy loss, Luther somehow remained focused on work. He had to. The jobs were piling up, making his schedule more frenzied than ever. For starters, he needed to complete the Aretha Franklin and Cheryl Lynn albums, and on top of that he had signed on for a new round of tour dates as a headliner.

"I would perform on Thursday, Friday, Saturday, and Sunday in four different cities," Luther recalled. "On Monday I would fly back to L.A. to produce Aretha or Cheryl for four days, and fly back just in time for my Thursday performance."

Food helped him manage his stressful schedule. "I used to go on stage at nine-thirty having just eaten three hamburgers and french fries at nine-fourteen," Luther remembered. "When I was 320, I would do that in a second."

The stockpile of commitments would've proved impossible if Luther didn't love the work so much. He felt satisfied that the industry was finally acknowledging his production and songwriting talents. Plus, he was working with his idols and other artists whose voices he truly loved.

As the sessions for Aretha's album approached, Luther became slightly unnerved every time he thought about the fact that he was in charge of a record by someone he had adored since he was sixteen. "You can imagine the fright in my heart when I was asked to produce her," he remembered.

Her scorching meditations on love had eased his teenage heartaches and taught him a textbook's worth of lessons on the ways of romance. He thought by producing a hit record for her, he'd be returning a favor of sorts, giving back to someone whose work had given him so much.

At the same time, he knew that keeping his composure was key. The Queen of Soul wouldn't tolerate some fumbling, inexperienced producer. Industry lore was full of tales of upstarts who crumbled in her presence. If he showed how nervous he was, the gig would be over before he ever got the chance to prove what he could do.

Days before recording began, Luther started psyching himself up. "I had to confront myself," he explained, "and say 'OK, it's fine to be a fan, but you're going to blow this gig if you go in there as a fan.' You have to put that on the back burner and go in there authoritatively and gently tell her what you'd like to accomplish with this and get her through it, because she's looking to you for direction and for some guidance."

Still, when the first day of recording finally came, Luther found his insides shimmying with nerves. "I remember sitting there waiting for her to walk through that door," Luther recalled. "When she came in, my heart stopped. She just looked at me and said, '*Vandross*'—she never calls me anything but *Vandross*—'I like that "Jump to It." Do your thing . . .' "

From that moment, the two got along well. Luther overcame his anxiety, and Aretha proved to be receptive to his ideas. She needed him as much—if not more—than he needed her. It had been years since her last big hit, and although she was still the undisputed

Queen of Soul, there were a whole bunch of wailing ladies-in-waiting gathered at the hem of her gown.

Some of her biggest admirers thought that she had lost her way amid misguided dabblings in disco and overblown Barbra Streisand–like balladry. Rock group Steely Dan even summed up these feelings in lyrics: "Hey Nineteen, that's 'Retha Franklin / She don't remember the Queen of Soul." Aretha, who was about to turn forty, seemed in danger of becoming a relic of an earlier era.

That wasn't all the singer was dealing with, or the only reason she desperately needed a big record. Aretha's finances had been rapidly draining since two years earlier, when her father, the Reverend C. L. Franklin, was shot twice during a robbery at his home. The famed church leader languished in a coma, and Aretha spent nearly $1,500 a week to ensure he received top-notch care. A hit record could do a lot to refill her coffers.

Once Luther and Aretha started working, there was a good, fun-loving vibe in the studio. They freely shared gossip, updates on their favorite soap operas, jokes, and lots of food. "He had me laughing like crazy," Aretha remembered. "He's a great guy, and in some of these sessions, boy, we had us some fried chicken . . . wow! We had a lot of fun together, I can tell you." Before they finished, the studio was a mess of Kentucky Fried Chicken buckets, used tea bags, and bottles of Wild Bee Honey.

Luther was consistently impressed with Aretha's professionalism. "The thing about her that's so incredible is that she comes to the studio so prepared," Luther remembered. "If you are ever witness to a recording session, you'll notice that an artist will step up to the microphone and a couple hours later they start to sound like who you know them to be. Aretha Franklin becomes Aretha Franklin immediately. She gets to the essence of her talent very quickly. It's startling. . . . Anybody that records her should know to have the microphone on even for the second check, even for the first take. Because 'Jump to It' was basically the first take.'"

Aretha felt great about what they accomplished. She'd sit in the control room, close her eyes, and point one finger to the ceiling, signaling, "I like this."

Straight from working with Aretha, Luther shifted his attention to singer Cheryl Lynn, who was excited about working with this hot new talent. "I wanted to meet the man who put the song 'Never Too Much' together," Cheryl remembered, "and he wanted to get together with the woman he called 'the diva of CBS Records.'" The two hit it off at a listening party for Chic. They ducked out of the affair and spent the rest of the evening trolling about Manhattan in a Rolls-Royce, singing to music and telling jokes. "It was as if we'd known each other for a long time," Cheryl remarked.

She and Luther shared much in common. Both were the children of deeply religious mothers and both waged long struggles with their weight. Cheryl's weight, at the time, was scaling to a personal high. "I was truly a monster," Cheryl said, reflecting on that period, "but I thought I was real cute."

Doing Cheryl's album was grueling for Luther. He was still on tour, so sometimes he would be in the studio working with her until two in the morning, then he'd immediately have to fly out to his next concert stop. It was thoroughly exhausting, but he enjoyed it. Working with Cheryl was different from working with Aretha. Even though Cheryl had been making records longer than Luther, she was six years his junior. He could adopt a supportive, nurturing role with her. When they were scheduled to record on Valentine's Day, he made sure that one thousand Hershey's Kisses were waiting for her at the studio. "He was very very sweet," Cheryl recalled.

A high point of their work together was pairing on a cover of Marvin Gaye and Tammi Terrell's duet "If This World Were Mine." The song had been a number-one R&B hit when Luther was seventeen. They initially planned to record Gaye and Terrell's

"Your Precious Love," but jazzy crooners Randy Crawford and Al Jarreau had recently done that. The idea of doing "If This World Were Mine" came, as Cheryl described it, in "a moment of lightning-bolt inspiration."

As with "A House Is Not a Home," Luther turned a rather simple song into an emotional journey. He ensured that he got the performances he wanted by creating a mood in the studio. "The lights were low," Cheryl remembered. "We were looking into each other's eyes, and I was thinking, 'Oooh, he's gonna sing for me.'" The passionate yet controlled way they trade verses over the lush string-laden track makes what was once a twinkling expression of youthful whimsy become a full-blown adult fantasy.

Not long after they recorded it and the song started getting airplay late at night on R&B radio, Cheryl joined Luther to sing the song on tour. They staged an elaborate number, where Cheryl would appear at the top of a tall winding staircase. Then Luther would meet her halfway up the stairs and slowly escort her down to the stage, as they sang dreamily of moonlight, forever-blue skies, and pretty lovin'.

This was the type of showmanship Luther was becoming known for as he toured the country. Although he was still essentially a new artist, he had learned from some of the most skilled performers around. "All the singers I love, like Dionne and Aretha and Bette Midler, have great wit, taste, and drama," Luther explained. "I've tried to learn from watching and working with them. Being able to use all those things now is really the biggest thrill for me."

He had overcome his former reticence about being onstage, being seen, being scrutinized, and now he loved standing in the spotlight, moving people with his music, and hearing their roaring appreciation. He was selling out concert halls and even winning critical raves. A reviewer described a Radio City Music Hall show as "an hour-and-forty-minute vocal and musical smorgas-bord garnished with campy theatrics and one-liners. Vandross' shyness has been replaced by a much stronger rapport with the audience. He's also footloose and charismatic, as are his dazzling backup vocalists."

These were good times within Luther's camp. It was hard work, but everybody felt like they were part of something special. Michael Brauer was the recording engineer for all of Luther's studio work, and he was also in charge of sound for the live shows. He remembered these early days touring with Luther and the band as "genuinely the most amazing time I ever had in my life."

"Things were happening so quickly," Brauer recalled, "and when Luther would perform, people were just flipping out over what he was doing. It was great. The band could feel that we were all on a very good road."

There was a family vibe in the band. Nat Adderly, Jr., led the outfit, which included people Luther had worked with in some capacity for years. One of those musicians was drummer Yogi Horton, a Teaneck, New Jersey, resident whose career followed a path similar to Luther's. He had been the key timekeeper at high profile sessions all over New York City, whether for lucrative jingles or top stars like Aretha Franklin, Diana Ross, and Ashford and Simpson. He and Luther found themselves in the same place, booked by the same people, all the time. So when Luther started putting together his own band, he knew exactly which drummer he wanted.

Yogi's skills were so precise that people often mistook his playing for the steady ticking of a drum machine. Whenever Yogi heard this, he'd laugh and say, "That ain't no damn drum machine. That's me."

Yogi kept the band chuckling and having fun throughout the

long months of touring, the flurry of cities, planes, and buses, and the lonesome, sleepless nights. "Yogi Horton was the funniest person I'd ever met," remembered Brauer. "He would keep all of us laughing from the time we got into the van until we got to the airport to being on the plane. Then, on the plane, we'd be laughing hysterically the whole time. I'm not kidding. Then we'd be in the van to the hotel and we'd be roaring."

Everything would've been perfect if it weren't for the punishing schedule and the increasing demands on Luther. The summer of 1982 saw the release of the two albums he had been working on— Aretha Franklin's *Jump to It* and Cheryl Lynn's *Instant Love.* Both became big hits, and Aretha's album even went gold, indicating sales of 500,000 or more. It was her first gold record in six years.

At the same time, executives at Luther's label, Epic, were pushing him to deliver the follow-up to *Never Too Much.* Fans hungered for another album, and the record company wanted to rush to feed the demand.

Luther returned to the studio, but the atmosphere differed dramatically from the creative flowering that produced *Never Too Much.* "By the time we did the second record we were coming close to a deadline," Brauer remembered. "He didn't even have lyrics for most of the songs." This was very unlike Luther, who thrived on being hyperprepared.

Brauer also noticed a change in Luther's attitude, a restlessness that often took on a cutting edge. "This was a really happy guy," said Brauer, "but the pressure really got to him. It was difficult to balance all of that out. These were extraordinarily tough times. He was trying to do his own records, and he was trying to write and produce three other records."

One of those projects was particularly special since it involved an adored R&B singer whose life and career had suddenly gone tragic. It happened in the early morning hours of March 18, 1982, when growling sex symbol Teddy Pendergrass was driving his green Rolls-Royce Silver Spirit in Philadelphia. This was the city he called home, where at age two he stood up at the Holiness Baptist Church and sang his first solo, "Jesus Loves Me This I Know," and where he later found fame as the lead vocalist of the suave Harold Melvin and the Bluenotes. That night, the power steering gave out in his car, causing it to jump a guardrail, slide across a two-lane street, careen off of one tree, slam into another, and get pinned against a third. It took nearly two hours to cut Teddy and his passenger, transsexual performer Tenika Watson, out of the vehicle. Soon after Teddy arrived at the Thomas Jefferson Hospital, doctors discovered extreme damage to the bones and nerves in the lower half of his neck.

Then all the questions started, posed by everyone from friends to associates to fans: How could this have happened to Teddy? Will he ever walk again? What was he doing in the car with a female impersonator whose rap sheet included thirty-seven arrests for prostitution?

No answers were immediately forthcoming. Still, love poured in for the singer during his long, surgery-filled days at the hospital. Celebrities like basketball's Dr. J and Teddy's sometime duet partner Stephanie Mills put in visits. Fans sent balloons, get-well cards, and sometimes money, fearing Teddy would end up sick and broke like R&B great Jackie Wilson and so many sad others. Then there was his family, who kept a long vigil by his side. As the days added up to weeks and months, his mother lifted Teddy's spirits by hand-feeding him homemade fried chicken and buttermilk biscuits.

His recovery progressed rapidly, and by the end of May he was on radio stations coast-to-coast sending a message to followers: "I'll be back in a year." However, when he returned home, he discovered that getting back in the music game wouldn't be as easy as he thought. It turned out that his record company had no interest in making any more music with him, thinking that there was no market for a sex symbol who was now paralyzed from the chest down.

Teddy remained hopeful, however, and soon his handlers were phoning the man everyone was talking about that year, Luther Vandross. Although he was already overtaxed, Luther quickly signed on to help Teddy make a demo recording that could get him a deal at some other company. Everybody knew that Luther preferred working with female singers, but this was something different. This meant brotherhood, one black man helping to raise the hand of another.

Luther wrote a song especially for him, a swoony ballad called "You're My Choice Tonight (Choose Me)." To record it, Luther traveled to Teddy's thirty-four-room English Tudor mansion in Philly's Gladwyne suburbs. They had to do the song there because Teddy couldn't get to the studio. Instead, they set up a remote recording truck outside the sprawling home.

Although Teddy was excited to get back to singing, everyone could tell he was nervous, and no one—including him—knew if he would sound as commanding as he once did. The situation terrified Teddy and all of those close to him. Everyone knew the stakes. If this didn't work out, Teddy might never be a recording artist again. "Here's a guy who was just the king for so many years," Brauer recalled. "You could see that he was very humbled by it all, and was hopeful that he could actually sing again." In the end, everything worked out. "Teddy did fine," Brauer recalled. "Luther was really happy for him."

Bob Krasnow of Elektra Records heard "You're My Choice Tonight (Choose Me)," and the news got even better. Teddy had a record deal again.

Luther intended to produce Teddy's entire comeback album,

but he quickly had to bow out. More jobs were coming and pressures increased. Plus, he needed to focus on his second album, *Forever, For Always, For Love.* This, in many ways, was his make-or-break record. So many acts had started out as promisingly as Luther but then failed to reconnect with an audience on their second release.

Luther finished the album quickly, largely sticking to the formula that made *Never Too Much* such a hit. The album opened with the bouncy number that mixed a Luther original "Bad Boy" with Sam Cooke's 1962 hit "Having a Party." This cut established what would become a Luther trademark. He dusted off a forgotten sound from the rich black musical past and shined it up like a treasured heirloom. In his hands, the rhythm and harmonies of doo-wop and Motown became new—classic but thoroughly contemporary. The album's other highlights included the irresistibly punchy "You're the Sweetest One," which, like most of Luther's records, now included his beloved Cissy Houston on background vocals, and the mournful "Since I Lost My Baby," a Smokey Robinson–penned number that was once done by Luther's favorite male group, the Temptations.

When critics heard the album, some felt they could sense the strain of him doing so many different projects at once. In a *Village Voice* review, black music chronicler Nelson George noted that, since his successes with Aretha Franklin and Cheryl Lynn, Luther had been deluged with "offers to rescue the lame, the blind, and the baffled." George thought this impaired Luther's ability to focus on his work. "I'm disturbed by signs of creative stagnation on Vandross's *Forever, For Always, For Love,*" George wrote. "Listening to it, I wonder whether Vandross's ascendance from background singer to jingle singer to featured vocalist in Change to solo act to producer-writer in the space of three years doesn't contain the seeds, not of disaster, but of a missed opportunity for Vandross to establish himself as the foremost singer of his generation."

One comment of George's must have seemed especially cutting given Luther's struggle to control his own creative direction. "He's hardly his own best screenwriter," George wrote, calling much of the album "barely tolerable filler." "[And] a great singer needs strong material."

Luther had little time to nurse any wounds inflicted by this review because he was soon off working on more albums. He received yet another opportunity he couldn't turn down, the chance to produce the woman who inspired him to sing in the first place: Dionne Warwick.

Like Aretha, Dionne was signed to Arista Records, run by impresario Clive Davis. Since Davis was so impressed with the quality and sales of Aretha's album, he immediately tapped Luther for Dionne. They got to work and discovered that, in addition to music, they shared another passion: spending hours playing Ms. Pac-Man.

It was amazing to think about. Luther once was so hungry to have a connection with Dionne that he lied about being her brother. Now he was directing her next career step and challenging her at video games.

As with most of the people Luther produced, Dionne deeply needed a musical makeover. Her career had floundered so much since her 1960s heyday that she once thought, "I'm not a recording artist anymore." Her personal life hadn't fared much better. Throughout the early 1970s, she had made desperate attempts to save her marriage to actor/musician Bill Elliott, who openly disdained standing in his wife's superstar shadow. She nearly lost herself in the process. Following the advice of astrologer Linda Goodman, she added an "e" to the end of her last name for "vibratory reasons" and to signify Elliott's place in her life. She became Dionne Warwicke.

Contrary to her expectations, though, things got much worse. "As soon as I put the 'e' on," Dionne once said, "all hell broke loose." Her marriage ended. Then, in 1977, her father died, and her mother suffered a debilitating stroke the very next day.

After dropping the eerily unlucky "e," her fortunes started changing for the better. She recorded hit albums with pop piano man Barry Manilow and Bee Gee Barry Gibb. Yet they failed to reconnect her with a black audience. This was where Luther came in. He was supposed to make Dionne cool again, the way she was in her early days, able to play a posh supper club one night and the Apollo the next.

Luther followed much the same path that proved so successful with Aretha and Cheryl. The album featured a charging, retro-Motown number, "Got a Date," and a thoughtfully selected cover tune, "Will You Still Love Me Tomorrow" originally recorded by the Shirelles, Dionne's longtime friends and among Luther's first musical loves. Luther even fulfilled a lifelong dream of dueting with Dionne on the elegant "How Many Times Can We Say Goodbye."

The album's most special moment was a ballad Luther wrote just for Dionne, "So Amazing." It's a sweeping realization of love's power to change a life, and it's one of the first great ballads that Luther ever wrote himself.

To record the songs, Luther would give Dionne a tape of him performing the tunes and then she would sing along with his voice. He wanted her to do the songs exactly as he sang them, and sometimes this caused mild friction. "In producing," Luther explained, "there's a fine line between direction and badgering. I decided that if I badgered, I wouldn't care because I knew [she'd] wind up loving the finished product. Dionne did."

Luther felt invigorated when artists were pleased with the results of his work. That's why he clocked so much time in the studio. He had struggled for so long to establish himself as an artist, songwriter, and producer. He wasn't about to let it be wrested from his grip just because friends, associates, and sometimes even his own fatigued body suggested he should slow down.

"I guess it's something in my personality," Luther once said. "I have a built-in guilt reflex when I'm not working all the time."

His relentless schedule strained some of his relationships. Those who worked closely with him on these back-to-back projects sometimes found him very bristling. "Luther wasn't as happy as he used to be," remembered Brauer. "He had huge success, the money was crazy, but he just didn't seem to be happy.

"He'd walk into the studio at ten in the morning and I knew whether I was going to be in for a really long day, just by his demeanor. He'd come in, and he'd have a look in his eye, and I just knew the day was going to suck. He would just get this attitude. It was hard to describe. I think it was the first time I really understood the word 'condescending.'"

Luther never talked about what was bothering him, so his moods were impossible to predict or control. "He was bringing something in the studio with him," Brauer said. "It's not like it occurred in the middle of the session. His private life, I think, was very complicated. When things were going well, he was happy. When things didn't go well, he was really sad."

Complicating matters was his weight, which steadily rose in the months following the crushing Grammy loss. "He was always fighting to keep his weight down so you don't know what kind of diet he was on," Brauer continued. "He was always trying different diets, and I know if I don't eat well, I'm gonna get grumpy."

It didn't improve the situation when some of the albums Luther worked on failed to become hits. It was as if Luther was making all these sacrifices for nothing. When the Dionne album was released, it was savaged by critics. One reviewer called the album's fast cuts "disco-based shenanigans" and even disparaged Luther's cherished matchup with Dionne, saying that the "weak, syrupy ballad . . . squanders both their strengths." Another writer argued that many of the songs were "trite up-tempo numbers that are totally unsuited to [Dionne's] style," but this critic did like one tune. "'So Amazing' has a sinuous vocal line that's ideally suited to Warwick's approach."

The *Washington Post* called "So Amazing" "an exclamation of astonishment at love, which benefits from Warwick's dignified restraint as she slowly warms up to the glorious melody."

Nevertheless the album fared poorly, and none of the singles were hits. This profoundly disappointed Luther. "The biggest regret of my career," he said in 1983, "is that 'Got a Date' wasn't taken to the top of the pop charts. It's my favorite piece—ever. I get mad when I think of what happened or didn't happen to that song."

Luther didn't suffer any backlash from the failure of Dionne's album. It was soon time to again work with the woman who launched his hit-producing streak, Aretha Franklin. She was ready to make the follow-up to *Jump to It* and wanted Luther behind the boards for another round. "Luther is a very bright, meticulous, astute producer," Aretha said. "If he gets tired of singing, he could be a comedian for sure. He just cracks me up."

Both Luther and Aretha looked forward to recapturing the fun they had while making *Jump to It.* "I remember being anxious and honored to be asked to do [another album with Aretha]," Luther said. "You know how you feel after you do a successful project and you go back in for a second one, the follow-up. You feel very stoked. You feel very encouraged and very positive. That's the way I felt then."

Things didn't start out so well, though. At first, the two had mild disagreements over who would be singing background on the tracks. Luther had his core group of people and had recorded most of the background vocals before Aretha even stepped into the studio. Aretha, however, wanted to use some of her regular singers, the women who had followed her on tour for years. She felt loyal to them and always liked to make sure that they had some work whenever she made an album.

Tensions didn't end there. As he did with Dionne, Luther sang the songs for Aretha and expected her to follow his lead. Aretha had other ideas, though, and definitely didn't appreciate being told what to do. "All of a sudden Luther wanted to tell me how to sing," Aretha recalled, "when it was I from whom he had learned much about how to sing."

Luther wouldn't budge. He had written the songs and felt he knew how they should be sung. He understood why she was upset, but she had hired him to take control of the album. Plus, the two had found success together in the past. He thought it was his job to push and push until she gave the best performance. It didn't always make artists happy at first, he knew, but so far everybody had been pleased with the results.

So when Aretha continued to protest singing a line a certain way, he reminded her, "I'm the producer."

She stopped for a moment, surprised that he had escalated the situation, and responded, "Well, I'm the Queen of Soul." She thought that would put an end to it.

Luther quickly fired back, "Well, I'm the person who produced your first gold record in years."

With that, Aretha walked out of the recording booth, grabbed her fur, and was out the door.

The album was left unfinished, and one of the most valued relationships of Luther's personal and professional life was broken.

"The Night I Fell in Love"

"So Luther sang and his songs were all long, long stories. But very good, the audience loved him."

—Artist Andy Warhol
after seeing Luther perform
at Radio City Music Hall

By 1983, Luther had recorded two solo albums, *Never Too Much* and *Forever, For Always, For Love.* Both were big R&B hits, thoroughly loved by fans. The songs spoke movingly of love: wanting it, finding it, losing it, and longing for it all over again. Luther sang these tunes as if they sprang from a well filled with everything he ever felt, desired, or mourned the loss of.

Yet for all of the emotionalism of his delivery, there was a certain veiled quality to the lyrics. You could hear what Luther was feeling, how deeply he meant every word, but you couldn't necessarily tell how it related to his own life. This changed with his third album, *Busy Body.*

On this autobiographical record, he opened up, crafting a compelling portrait of an entertainer looking for romance, receiving it, and then doing almost anything to keep it from going away. The set kicked off with the thumping "I Wanted Your Love," on which he sang about how loneliness put a damper on all the good things in his life: the sold-out shows, the screaming crowds, the standing ovations. By the next song, the album's silken title track, he had found love, but it was a wandering one. The person he was involved with also rolled with many others and was seldom by the singer's side when he woke in the morning. Luther wanted to end the affair, but couldn't tell this philandering lover good-bye. He was already in too deep.

The following cut, a deceptively upbeat number titled "I'll Let You Slide," told the consequences of this decision. He decided to forgive his lover in exchange for one more moment of passion.

It was a decision he'd come to regret. " 'I'll Let You Slide' was about a romance that was already in place," Luther later explained. "I let them slide, but mistakenly so."

These highly personal songs were just a few of the album's high points. Another was one of his now trademark cover tunes. This time he merged a snatch of Aretha Franklin's pining "Until You Come Back to Me (That's What I'm Gonna Do)" with "Superstar," a yearning song that had been done by many in the past. Bette Midler recorded it on her first album in 1972, and six years later Luther even sang background vocals on a version by guitarist David Spinozza.

The song's origins dated back to 1969. Then, however, it was called "Groupie," and sung by bluesy white vocalist Bonnie Bramlett. A former member of the Ikettes—Ike and Tina Turner's shimmying background corps—Bramlett penned the tune with grizzled rock songwriter Leon Russell. It was inspired by Bramlett's crush on her onetime band mate, blues-rock guitarist Eric Clapton.

Bramlett's version piddled on the charts, but the song's profile was raised when country-rock belle Rita Collidge recorded a version in 1970 and renamed it "Superstar." One year later, Richard

Carpenter, half of the soft-rock brother/sister duo the Carpenters, was watching *The Tonight Show* when Bette Midler came on and wrenched every bit of forlorn emotion out of the sad, lonely tune. Richard thought the song would be perfect for his sister, Karen, who brought a touch of melancholy to even the happiest senti-ments. He was right, and their take on the cut was soon all over the airwaves, becoming one of the biggest hits of the year.

This is how Luther fell in love with "Superstar." He could em-pathize with the story of the naive young woman who falls for a guitarist, sleeps with him, believes it when he says "I love you," then never hears from him again. The woman in the song can't seem to grasp that sometimes people say pretty words they do not mean. She's left asking, "Don't you remember you told me you loved me, baby?"

"The beauty is in the sadness," Luther felt. "I totally under-stand how that girl must have felt, waiting, waiting for this singer in a rock band to come back to her, but he breaks his promise and never does."

In Luther's hands, the song became about more than just a groupie yearning for her idol. He turned it into a near-universal plea, applicable to anyone who has ever been willfully abandoned or carelessly left behind.

Luther's take on "Superstar" soon reached the upper part of the R&B charts, making the album *Busy Body* another certified hit. In 1983 only four black solo acts released albums that sold more than one million copies: Michael Jackson, who was soaring with his sec-ond Quincy Jones–produced album, *Thriller*; Michael's raunchier, sometime nemesis, Prince; Lionel Richie, who had, as gossips pre-dicted for years, finally left his group the Commodores; and Luther, whose most personal expression to date allowed him to connect with more people than ever.

Things would've been nearly perfect if it weren't for Luther's

ongoing problems with Aretha Franklin. The situation had escalated to a degree that he never intended or expected. Fittingly, a
feud with the Queen of Soul was proving to be a royal pain.

After Aretha stormed out of the New York studio, words flying,
fur in hand, she went back to her hotel and started packing for a return home to Detroit. The whole album was threatened. Fearing
that all could be lost if he didn't act soon, Clive Davis, president of
Aretha's label, Arista Records, called Aretha in her hotel room. He
listened patiently to all of the complaints, how Luther had just
crossed the line. He agreed that things had gone too far, but he
tried to convince her that it would be in everyone's best interests
for them to reconcile.

Aretha thought it over for a moment. Clive, after all, could be
very persuasive. Finally, she came to a decision.

"If Luther apologizes," she told Clive, "I will, too."

Davis thought this was fair and presented the offer to Luther.
For his part, Luther was anxious to complete the record he started
so he agreed to the terms. The two warring singers were soon back
in the studio making music together.

That wasn't the end of this situation, however. Years later,
Aretha wrote in her autobiography that she always felt Luther's
apology was "halfhearted."

Nevertheless, they finished up the album, which was now called
Get It Right. Aretha did some press to promote the record and
seemed enthusiastic. She told *Jet* that *Get It Right* was sure to be
another smash because Luther was such a talented producer. In the
album credits, she offered Luther a compliment: "What can I say?
You really outdid yourself."

The title track from the album went to number one on the
R&B charts, matching the success of "Jump to It." Both songs
have a very similar feel, although "Get It Right" has a deeper,
funkier bottom.

Critics seemed to enjoy Aretha's second team up with Luther. One wrote: "Vandross and Franklin have extended their collaboration into an even more consistent, more rewarding album." Another stated: "Franklin's voice hasn't sounded this confident in years, and Vandross has given her some first class material to work with."

Fans proved rather indifferent, though. The album's sales fell way short of the more than 500,000 copies that *Jump to It* moved.

This disappointment coincided with an increasingly difficult period in Aretha's life. Her marriage to actor Glynn Turman was crumbling faster than a day-old biscuit. It had once seemed so promising: the Detroit diva meets the lean black cowboy, who rode Arabian stallions when he wasn't on a movie set. They had paraded their sweet love all over. *People* magazine ran wedding pictures of the couple with the headline: "Lady Soul Aretha Franklin only sings the Blues onstage, now that she's wed Glynn Turman."

Just a year before their estrangement, *Essence* wrote an extended profile on "what makes their two-career marriage work." Even in this article ostensibly about togetherness, there were signs of strain. Turman talked about how hard it was to sometimes be considered Mr. Aretha Franklin.

"It's just not the outside pressures," he said from the couple's sprawling California home. "It's a thing of being a prideful man raised in this society with the idea of being a breadwinner with the head-of-the-household thing. I'm not used to being referred to as anyone's husband. I'm used to a woman being referred to as *my* woman. . . . After I had worked 17 years in the business at the time we got married, suddenly being recognized as Aretha's husband was a heavy burden to carry."

Aretha took a drag from her cigarette, then said, "I don't think it's so hard."

"But you're not in my shoes, baby," Turman said softly but firmly.

By the time *Get It Right* was released, Aretha had left Turman back on the West Coast and returned to Detroit in order to look after her father. Reverend Franklin's condition was worsening and the bills were piling up. When a reporter asked if she and her husband were still together, Aretha answered, "No, we're not. . . . I'm happy and Glynn is happy and that's where it is."

Her comments notwithstanding, Aretha didn't seem happy at all. In fall 1983, just a few months after *Get It Right* reached stores, Aretha brought a hefty breach-of-contract suit against Arista. Among the main charges were that the record label contracted Luther to produce *Jump to It* and *Get It Right* against her will. She maintained that he was paid with "substantial cash advances," and that if she had known how much Luther was costing, she would have tried to renegotiate the terms or chosen another producer.

With this, Aretha had just opened an unexpected new chapter in the saga of her relationship with Luther.

Meanwhile, Luther was already making plans for a new solo album, but he felt like he needed a change, something to shake up the recording routine and make it seem fresh again. "[I] got tired of going into the same studios," Luther said, "driving up the same streets and going up the same elevators I had gone up during all of my years of sessions. After a few albums, I said, 'There's got to be another way to record.'"

Indeed, there was. Rock groups had discovered it several years before. Instead of making albums in the cramped studios of New York or the sterile high-tech recording complexes of Los Angeles, they traveled to the warm Caribbean island of Montserrat, about thirty miles from Antigua. This allowed them to craft their new songs while taking in some of God's awesome landscaping.

The studio, called AIR, sat atop a four-hundred-foot green mound from which you could see the clear-blue Old Road Bay and the towering Soufriere Hills, a group of mountains whose thriving, vegetative beauty masked the temperamental volcanoes slumbering inside of them. Acts working at AIR—which charged nearly $13,000 a week—stayed in hillside villas with maid service, live-in chefs, and private pools. They slept amid cooling jasmine-scented breezes and a soothing choir of tree frogs and crickets.

When the artists weren't working, drinking champagne as they wrote and reworked lyrics, they could tour the island's bamboo forests, go to market for some fresh fish and home-baked coconut macaroons, or take mineral baths by the coved beaches where the sand came in both black and white.

This was where the industry's most prized and pampered acts traveled to record: the Rolling Stones, former Beatles Paul McCartney and Ringo Starr, Sting, Elton John, and Stevie Wonder. Thus, it was precisely where Luther wanted to be.

"A lot of people go down there because of the comfort," Luther explained. "There's a cook, there are lots of lounges. It's magnificent. Outside the control room is a big swimming pool on the side of a gigantic mountain that leads to the ocean. The mood it puts you in gives you a better perspective on the music."

Luther brought his whole regular crew with him, including band leader Nat Adderley, Jr., bassist and song collaborator Marcus Miller, and drummer and resident funnyman Yogi Horton. He felt the change in surroundings gave the proceedings a fresh perspective.

"We were out of town," Luther said, "so the band wasn't looking at their watches, having a four-thirty Pepsi-Cola jingle they had to go do. Once you get someone away from that New York session mentality, their guard comes down. They take off that bulletproof vest they've been wearing and give you the best that they've got."

The album Luther recorded there was called *The Night I Fell in Love.* It was a sensual masterstroke, full of richly textured tunes about the quest for romance and its many rewards. As usual,

Luther included some of his signature takes on other people's songs. He smoothed out Stevie Wonder's ode to a dream lover, "Creepin'." He brought plainspoken desire to "If Only for One Night," a tune by sharp singer/songwriter Brenda Russell that Roberta Flack used to perform when Luther toured with her.

Luther's own songs on the album continued, by his own admission, to reveal new dimensions of his emotional life. The soaring "Wait for Love" played like a faith-restoring prayer for the brokenhearted. The number that followed it, "My Sensitivity (Gets in the Way)," was all about a man who falls in love too easily, a man whose affections are won over with the "slightest touch," a man who can't control his heart. Luther called this one "absolutely personal."

The Night I Fell in Love was released in February 1985, and Luther began vigorously promoting the album. One of the television appearances he was scheduled to do marked a homecoming for him. Luther was asked to join such stars as Stevie Wonder, Little Richard, and one of his personal favorites, Diana Ross, in a special tribute to his old stomping grounds, Harlem's Apollo Theatre.

Luther still carried both memories and wounds from his days at the Apollo. He remembered times of magic and dreams coming true, like hanging out with his buddies Robin, Fonzi, and Carlos, and meeting Cissy Houston and Patti LaBelle. Yet there were also a host of unpleasant moments: the multiple amateur-night losses, and all of those times he didn't get the affirmation he needed from his mentor, Listen, My Brother director Peter Long.

This historic black venue had been through a lot of hard times since a teenage Luther stood on its stage, culminating with the doors being bolted shut in 1976. However, a new owner had recently taken over at the Apollo, committed to dusting it off and upgrading its image. The theater underwent a nearly $11 million makeover, including the addition of state-of-the-art audio and video equipment, and $250,000 Czechoslovakian chandeliers. The balcony, where all sorts of raucous goings-on once occurred, was now called the "upper mezzanine."

The kickoff concert, at which Luther and the other stars performed, was taped before a black tie–clad audience for a three-hour NBC TV special, *Motown Returns to the Apollo.* The evening's host was comedian Bill Cosby, who was then riding high with his number-one sitcom of middle-class African-American life, *The Cosby Show.* He introduced act after act, an intriguing mix of the new and the old. Jazz grand dame Sarah Vaughan scatted her way through the moody "Body and Soul." Fluffy British pop star George Michael sang his breezy ballad "Careless Whisper" with one of Motown's favorite and most talented grown-up sons Smokey Robinson, and scandalously dethroned former Miss America Vanessa Williams donned a sheer bodysuit and feathered headdress to perform "La Vie En Rose," in honor of the late Josephine Baker.

Luther, dressed in a black-sequined jacket and vest, appeared late in the evening. He dueted with Britain's cross-dressing blue-eyed soul sensation Boy George on "What Becomes of the Broken Hearted," that swaying 1966 hit by Jimmy Ruffin, older brother of the Temptations' lead singer David Ruffin. Almost from the start, it was clear that Boy George, who wore an emerald John Paul Gautier man-dress, was embarrassingly outmatched. Luther's notes were wet and full, where George's came off dry and flat. Then Luther went in for the kill when he employed that unique stuttering vocal technique that he developed while doing jingles.

"Where did the love go," he sang, "I wanna kn-n-n-n-n-ow!"

When the two performers walked offstage, Luther proudly smiled; Boy George looked miffed and defeated.

Later, having changed into a glittering periwinkle blazer, Luther sang the blithe "How Sweet It Is to Be Loved by You" in honor of the recently departed Marvin Gaye. Just one year earlier, this handsome though thoroughly troubled former Motown prince was shot to death by his father during an argument. Luther's tribute was nicely fitting because his group, Luther, had once opened for Marvin at New York City's Radio City Music Hall. Now Luther was helping any number of still-hurting friends and fans say good-bye at the Apollo.

He finished singing to resounding applause. More than a decade after he repeatedly lost during amateur night, Luther finally won over an Apollo crowd.

After the show, Diana Ross, who led the all-star cast in the closing number, a soulful rendition of Foreigner's "I Want to Know What Love Is," specifically requested that Luther attend a small party in her large backstage dressing area. He was overjoyed to get such an intimate audience with this woman who had been the subject of so many teenage daydreams and fantasies.

He told Diana that he wanted to produce an album for her as he had for his other idols, Aretha and Dionne. She listened to his gushing pitch but stayed noncommittal, which disappointed him.

Still, he was happy to spend time with her and was nearly blown away when he saw that she had a copy of *The Night I Fell in Love.*

"That made my day," Luther recalled, "made my month."

Shortly after the triumphant Apollo appearance, Luther made a video for "It's Over Now," one of the singles from *The Night I Fell in Love,* and he decided to invite his mother and beloved sisters, Ann and Patricia, to appear in it. Since his career started soaring, he didn't get to spend as much time with them as before.

He felt it was especially important for them to be a part of his exciting new life, since they all played such a major role in helping him develop his talents. His sisters used to buy him records, and his mother supported his decision to drop out of college to follow his musical calling.

Those who worked closely with Luther knew that he often seemed most upbeat whenever his family was near, calling him "Ronnie" and talking about old times. "Luther was always so happy when his sisters were around," remembered Cissy Houston, who by now was a regular background vocalist for Luther. "They were all so close. That's what I loved about them."

Sometimes Luther and Mary Ida had what he called "extravagant arguments," but they always made up. Frequently when he attended special events, she would be on his arm.

In the humorous, over-the-top "It's Over Now" video, his mom and sisters play Luther's nosy next-door neighbors. Luther is a vengeful lover who catches his glamorous live-in girlfriend cheating with another man. He then proceeds to cut up her credit cards, snatch back her diamond jewelry, and send her packing. Luther's mother and sisters, dressed in bathrobes and curlers, watch as this campy domestic drama transpires. At the end of the video, they come into Luther's faux apartment and dance around to the song's chunky groove.

"We had just the best time imaginable on the set," Luther remembered. "That was a fun video. It was a good time."

With the new video released, *The Night I Fell in Love* continued doing well. Over the course of four albums, Luther had developed a dependable fan base that made each of his records sell more than one million copies—then an exceptional accomplishment for an R&B artist. Only Michael Jackson, Prince, and Lionel Richie were moving the same kind of numbers.

Yet even though Luther's albums sold the same as these other acts, he was not treated the same. They were big multimedia stars while Luther flew way under the mainstream radar. This was evident in any number of ways. He hadn't been nominated for another Grammy since his first loss. By contrast, Michael, Prince, and Lionel were all well on their way to building a collection of them.

The simple fact was that most people outside of the black community still did not know who Luther was. Though he had several R&B hits, he rarely showed up on the pop charts. This is perhaps one of the reasons he enjoyed such massive success among black people. While R&B audiences had to share other big stars with the pop crowd, they could look at Luther and unequivocally proclaim: "*He is ours.*"

Luther came out at a time when R&B fans had recently lost so many talented male artists. Donny Hathaway and Marvin Gaye were dead, and Teddy Pendergrass was paralyzed from the chest down, no longer the virile sex symbol he once had been. It made folks appreciate Luther just that much more.

Luther made music that spoke directly—viscerally—to people who were very similar to himself. Many of these children of the civil rights movement had grown up poor and scrapping, but through perseverance and hard-won opportunities had reached unprecedented goals and reaped a wellspring of comforts and rewards. Luther's smooth, exquisitely produced tunes spoke deeply to both their past and present. His music had the chaste, good-time feel of the Motown-era songs his fans were reared on, along with the slick, luxuriant sound of something they once couldn't afford.

Luther's romantic songs played endlessly on black radio, especially during nighttime blocks of slow jams that stations were dubbing "the quiet storm." A Luther ballad began to serve as romantic shorthand for couples on the go.

At the same time, Luther's lonelier, more melancholy records spoke to what seemed to be a rising number of people—women, mostly—who had found themselves successful at everything but love. He addressed the pain of yearning for that one thing that increased money and education couldn't guarantee.

The passion Luther inspired could be seen in the way fans turned out in huge venue-filling numbers whenever he toured. In

Chicago, organizers needed 350 security guards to help negotiate the throngs who showed up for Luther's sold-out shows. This was more personnel than they used for those rock giants the Rolling Stones.

He caused a four-and-a-half-hour traffic jam on Interstate 95 when he played the Kings Dominion theme park near Washington, D.C. "We knew [Vandross] was popular," said a spokeswoman for the amusement facility, "but we didn't anticipate [this]."

The well-dressed crowds that were seen walking to these evening shows looked less like they were going to a concert and more as if they were headed to a swanky nightspot for some stepping and slow-dragging. Men sported finely tailored suits in colors ranging from sleek black to peacock-worthy pastels, and women, with freshly styled coifs, donned low-cut blouses, beaded dresses with thigh-high slits, and jewelry that sparkled and flashed in the twilight.

What they saw when they arrived at one of Luther's shows was an R&B extravaganza unlike any staged before. It wasn't just that it had production values rivaling the massive shows of seventies bands like Earth, Wind, and Fire and Parliament-Funkadelic. Luther, having learned many lessons from Bette Midler, offered Broadway-like staging and scenarios, with background dancers and colorful sets.

He sang "A House Is Not a Home" in a mock living room, including an armchair, a fireplace, and a window with stars and the moon shining through it. A writhing modern dancer moved sinuously atop a black grand piano on "Superstar," and for "The Night I Fell in Love," Luther created a cityscape with trees, park benches, police officers, a mother with a baby carriage, and even a flasher.

There were lavish stage clothes and accessories that had everybody talking: the gleaming gold bracelets and neck chains, the polka-dotted bow ties, the pointy Italian shoes, and the shiny black tuxedo jackets that glistened like rain.

These outfits and the stage sets were costly. Some of those around Luther worried about how much he was spending on the show.

His songwriting collaborator Marcus Miller confronted him about it. "Luther, you gotta be losing money on this, man," he said. "That's expensive."

"Yeah," Luther answered, "but I'm investing in myself. I know that after we put on this good show, people will know that Luther don't mess with your ticket money."

The folks in the audience relished Luther's carefully crafted opulence, and he always tried to get them involved in the show. When he sang a slow song, he wanted people to listen intently, but on the fast numbers he tried to get them up on their feet.

"I've got to get everyone in the room into it," he explained. "Remember, my performances are participation-oriented, not recitals. I'll get you feeling good, and you're gonna jump out of your seat. No one sat in their seat to watch Aretha or James Brown at the Apollo. That's what rhythm and blues is all about—movement."

Luther always had his regular crew of musicians with him, people like musical director Nat Adderly, Jr., and drummer Yogi Horton, who still kept everyone in stitches. They knew the ins-and-outs, the nooks and crannies of his music.

There was also someone new in Luther's entourage, a person from his past. It was David Bowie's ever-resilient, still-striking former girlfriend Ava Cherry. In the years since she last worked with Luther, Ava's relationship with Bowie had slowly and meanly broken apart. Some of it she blamed on his cocaine use, which could turn him into anything from a misfit to a paranoid and masochistic tyrant. Without this relationship, Ava was back to being who she was before meeting the rock star: just another pretty young woman with a dream.

Within a few years, she rebounded, and even recorded a few albums with soul great Curtis Mayfield. None of them, however, became hits. So when Luther asked her to don shimmering gowns and dyed fox tails to become his background singer, she was all for it. Whenever there was a spotlight and a stage, there was still a chance to become a star.

Luther appreciated those who worked for him. He sometimes spent great lengths of time doing the band introductions, stretching them out and giving each member a chance to shine.

Luther's tours operated like a giant churning machine. He knew what he needed in order to put on a good show and he demanded that they be in place. This was based on wisdom he picked up more than a decade earlier while working with David Bowie and Bette Midler. "I got to see what it was like for a name singer," Luther explained. "I saw the frustrations. I learned when to take it and when to put my foot down."

Sometimes he became enraged when things weren't to his liking. This could include anything from a musician playing a bum note to the catering not being right backstage. He brought the same perfectionism to his live show that he exhibited in the studio, telling legends how to sing and obsessing over every word and intonation. This frequently grated the nerves of those around him, and sometimes people found that they simply couldn't take it anymore.

By 1985, sound man Michael Brauer, the person who had been right there beside him ever since the Change album, felt he couldn't go on. He hated Luther's moodiness and the way he seemed to lash out at those around him whenever things weren't going the way he wanted them to. The more successful Luther got, and the more his career pressures increased, the darker his moods became.

"There were good days and bad days," Michael explained, "and I just found that the bad days started outnumbering the good."

Sometimes Luther's demands even affected audiences. He insisted, to the discomfort of many fans, that there be no air-conditioning during his performances. He thought the artificially cooled air made his throat swell. Before Luther played a concert, even during summer months, the staff of the venue would be issued a stern warning: "If the air is on, the show is off."

On July 4, 1985, the tour pulled into the Universal Amphitheatre in Los Angeles for a five-night stay. This was the same theater where Luther played with David Bowie so many years ago and spotted a glittering Diana Ross grooving in the crowd. Now he was back, and anyone seated in the audience was there to see him.

Backstage after one of the shows, Luther entertained some specially invited guests: fourteen-year-old aspiring singer Jimmy Salvemini and his older brother and manager Larry. Luther contacted them about working together after he saw Jimmy perform on the TV talent show *Star Search*. He thought the teen had promise with his brooding Italian good looks and a voice reminiscent of the teenage doo-wop idols of Luther's youth.

Jimmy was ecstatic over getting this kind of attention from someone like Luther. The youthful Long Island native had been trying to launch a singing career since before he was a teenager, when he sat in the audience of one of country singer Barbara Mandrell's concerts with a sign stating: "I am twelve years old. . . . Please fulfill my dreams to sing a duet with you."

Moved by such a cute display, Barbara invited the boy onstage where they sang, "Amazing Grace." Barbara stopped singing midway through the song to let Jimmy finish by himself. He got a standing ovation.

A few years later, Jimmy auditioned for *Star Search* and won the chance to compete on the show. This turn of events caused his brother Larry to make a difficult decision.

Larry, unlike his younger sibling, didn't thrive on the attention of the crowd. He liked keeping to himself in as remote a location as possible. After a couple of years in college, he hitchhiked more than three thousand miles from New York to the frozen tundra of the forty-ninth state. His family had a nickname for him: "Lawrence of Alaska."

This nature lover found happiness there, selling a little real estate and working at a lodge and hunting preserve. Yet when Jimmy's singing career began to heat up, Larry got tired of hearing about his accomplishments over a static-filled two-way radio. He wanted to be there for his little brother. So he packed up his northern life and moved with Jimmy to sun-dappled Los Angeles, while their parents remained in Long Island.

Larry couldn't have been happier that Luther was interested in recording his little brother. It looked like there were big things ahead.

Another night, after one of the Los Angeles concerts, Luther received a very unexpected phone call. It was from Peter Long, his decidedly stern former mentor and the man who founded and directed Listen, My Brother at the Apollo. Peter had attended one of Luther's shows and called to talk about it. After the two exchanged pleasantries, Peter said the words that Luther had been waiting nearly two decades to hear him say: "You know, maybe you can sing after all." It was a simple statement that went a long way toward easing a hardened teenage hurt.

As the tour rolled on, Luther heard from another voice from his past. This young lady, who was taking over as his opening act, was one of the biggest music success stories of the year. Already in

1985, she had four number one pop and R&B singles, and her first album was one of the biggest-selling debuts in history. She was Cissy Houston's daughter, Whitney.

She joined Luther for a few dates toward the end of August and in some cases received better reviews than he did. The *Dallas Morning News* chimed: "Whitney Houston proved why she won't be an opening act for long. Whatever it is that makes a star, Houston's got plenty of it."

Whitney charmed audiences so quickly and easily she became an instant superstar. Her beauty was bright and familiar, and where her mother's voice was full of wondrous mysteries, Whitney sounded like the wholesome choir girl next door. People loved to hear Whitney sing. What's more, they adored what she represented. She was the new black American dream, standing tall, singing proud, conquering all.

All of these moments combined to make this one of Luther's most memorable tours ever. It also managed to coincide with another dramatic happening in his life. The feud with Aretha was finally over. She dropped the lawsuit claiming that Luther had been grossly overpaid, admitting that it had largely been a ploy to get more money from her record company. It wasn't long before she'd call up Luther after watching *Guiding Light* and say, "Vandross, did you see that?"

One of the biggest thrills of his solo success was that he was now on a first-name basis with all of his idols. His newest buddy was Patti LaBelle, who he used to love seeing perform with her group the Bluebelles back at the Apollo. Since those days, Patti had reinvented herself at least twice: first as lead singer of the feminist funk-rock trio LaBelle, then later as a down-to-earth soul momma with hair that stuck out from her head like wings.

Patti and Luther had become so close that his mother, Mary

Ida, once joked that they were like brother and sister, a characterization that would certainly describe their playful competitiveness. While shopping together at the posh Beverly Hills boutique Maxfield's, they both spotted an alligator bag that each just had to have.

"I'm getting that bag," Luther said.

"No, you're not," Patti shot back, "I'm getting it."

"The bag was like twelve thousand dollars," Patti later explained, "and I knew I would have to do so many shows to pay for that sucker, but I had a credit card, so I put it on the card while he was looking at other stuff in the store."

Every time Luther saw her with the bag after that, he'd say, "You heifer, you got my bag."

Patti would respond teasingly, "You were just too slow."

In late 1985, Patti invited Luther to sing on her NBC Thanksgiving special. The appearance proved to be memorable, not just because it brought together two friends, but it also revealed something about Luther that many found shocking. He was rapidly dropping pounds, losing nearly one hundred of them since May. People following his career wondered, "How did Luther lose all of that weight?"

There was a special reason for it, though Luther kept it mostly to himself. He was in love for the first time in much too long. Though he never shared the person's name or gender, Luther admitted that this love had turned him into a "basket case." Suddenly food lost its hold on him. There were other things on his mind—beautiful, rose-tinted, hope-filled things.

He wanted to look good for the one making him feel this rush of emotions, so he started a strict low-fat, high-protein diet and bought a closet's worth of Gianni Versace clothes. In this new body and these new duds, Luther moved with ease and assurance.

Luther could, for perhaps the first time in his life, receive a compliment about how he looked without thinking the person saying it was lying.

This was a happy time for Luther, one of the most joyous he had ever experienced. It would not last long.

"Give Me the Reason"

"The valleys are a mother.*"*

—LUTHER, ON THE UPS AND DOWNS
OF HIS LIFE AND CAREER

Journalist Stanley Bennett Clay had the scoop of a lifetime. He had just received a call from one of his most reliable sources, the person who told him Lionel Richie was leaving the Commodores when everyone else still denied it. This time the source had even bigger, if heartbreaking, news. The person told Clay something he claimed to have seen with his own eyes: Luther Vandross was in the hospital and he had AIDS. That explained Luther's astonishing weight loss that still had everybody talking.

The year was 1985. Clay was an openly gay black man living in Los Angeles, and he was getting used to hearing these types of reports. "There were friends dropping left and right on each side of me," he explained.

Clay was then the Los Angeles–based gossip columnist for

Britain's *Blues and Soul* magazine. It wasn't a job he loved, but the paycheck came in handy. "I always thought of myself as better than a gossip columnist," he said.

Formerly, Clay had been entertainment editor for *Sepia* magazine, which, before it folded, was *Ebony*'s younger, flashier cousin. Then he took over as editor in chief of *Soul Teen* magazine, where he boosted circulation by implementing provocative new features. "I invented the 'Hunk of the Month,'" he said.

When he sat down to write about Luther for *Blues and Soul*, he wrestled with himself over the tone. He didn't want it to be all death and dying. He felt it should evoke the promise of healing, not just for Luther but also for all of Clay's newly stricken friends.

In his December 1985 column, he wrote: "It has been sadly but reliably reported from previously reliable sources that singer-songwriter-producer par excellence, Luther Vandross, has contracted the deadly disease AIDS. . . . Let us just hope that modern science can come up with a much-needed cure soon so that Luther and the thousands of others afflicted with this (*as now*) no-win condition will have a fighting chance. Hang in there, Luther!"

For most people in 1985, AIDS was as much of a death sentence as the gas chamber or the electric chair. There had been 22,996 people diagnosed with AIDS since 1980; nearly half of them had already lost their lives. AIDS attacked the immune system, leaving those it touched susceptible to all sorts of hostile infections. It also carried a social stigma so intense that the president of the United States had not even spoken its name. It affected some who had received infected blood transfusions, a lot of drug users—those who injected rather than snorted or drank their intoxicants—but even more so it struck gay men.

As the number of deaths increased, singer Bette Midler couldn't help thinking about her old fans from the Baths, all those shining young men done in by a simple need for another's touch.

"I began my career in 1965," Bette once explained, "and I am not lying, I do not exaggerate one minute, when I tell you that nearly everyone who I started out with is dead. . . . I never thought that at such a relatively young age I would be on such intimate terms with death. My whole adult life I have had gay friends. I've had gay collaborators, I've had gay mentors. And if I live to be a thousand, I could never repay the debt I owe to them. They gave me my vision and they gave me my career."

Not everyone felt so compassionate about AIDS and its association with gay people. The Gallup organization released a poll the same month Clay's column appeared, reporting that 37 percent of Americans stated that AIDS had changed their feelings about homosexuals for the worse. An official at the Centers for Disease Control characterized the public reaction to AIDS as an "epidemic of fear." Even celebrities who formerly flaunted sexually ambiguous personas were backtracking. David Bowie told reporters that he regretted ever saying he was bisexual. "I was so young then," he informed *Rolling Stone*. "I was experimenting."

The consequences for celebrities linked with AIDS were grave. In July 1985, after collapsing at Paris' Ritz Hotel, actor and matinee idol Rock Hudson was the target of rampant AIDS rumors, which were at first vehemently denied. Days later, however, a spokesman confirmed the rumors to be true. A collective scare rang throughout Hollywood, as people he had worked with and actresses he had kissed wondered if he had given them AIDS.

The news that Hudson had AIDS was hard for many to take. After all, he had once had skin the color of milk, shoulders so broad and strong, and legs so long it seemed like he should have been able to tower over anything coming for him. In September he issued a statement: "I am not happy that I am sick. I am not happy that I have AIDS. But if that is helping others, I can at least know that my own misfortune has had some positive worth." Less than a month later, he was dead.

For many African-Americans, AIDS was still largely considered something white folks got. This was before AIDS took the lives of newscaster Max Robinson and disco singer Sylvester in 1989. Then it felled tennis great Arthur Ashe in 1993.

It was also a full decade prior to NBA basketball star Magic Johnson announcing that he had contracted HIV, the virus that causes AIDS. In 1985, AIDS stoked the worst flames of antigay prejudice in the black community, as it had in the culture at large.

When the news about Luther hit, people were stunned. For some, it confirmed things they long thought were true; for others, it came as a complete shock. A few folks condemned him and swore off his music, but there were even more who would approach Luther in the street, sad-eyed, saying, "I understand how you feel."

There was one huge problem with all of these reactions, though. According to Luther, the news wasn't true. His lawyers immediately filed suit against *Blues and Soul* demanding a retraction. Luther made the publicity rounds, appearing on *Entertainment Tonight* with longtime gossip queen Rona Barrett. "I do not have it," he told her. Luther also denied rumors that he was gay.

Luther's responses worked to a point, but distressingly the issue lingered. On the one hand, Luther made a credible witness for his own defense. On the other hand, every star who ever had AIDS, including Hudson, initially denied it.

For Clay, this incident was nearly a career ender. He immediately lost his column and no one in L.A. would take his calls. Still, he maintained that he didn't report the apparently false news about Luther out of malice or a thirst for fame: "I was trying to point attention to the tragedy of AIDS. I saw it like 'we're about to lose another soldier.'" For Luther, it was the start of a recurring chain of rumors that would follow him for the rest of his career.

It didn't help that Luther was so cagey about his personal life. He never mentioned the name or gender of anyone he was involved with. He also was never pictured with any intimate, woman or man, holding on to his arm or running just behind him on a red carpet. Where Luther's love life was concerned, there were only questions, and many people supplied their own answers.

Luther was experiencing an aspect of fame that he never expected, never thought about when he was watching Dionne Warwick at the Fox all those years ago. This had nothing to do with wearing beautiful clothes, singing lovely songs, and making everyone in the audience feel he was performing just for them. This was different, ugly and nasty.

It was especially hard on Luther because he had always been such a private person. As a child, he used to hide his singing from his own family. Now, he was expected to share things that were far more vulnerable and dear with the whole world. But no matter what he said, people believed what they wanted to anyway. The loose talk never seemed to end.

This should've been a joyous moment for Luther. He was in love and losing weight, more than he'd ever been able to before. But instead of simply enjoying this time, he had to face down all these rumors. He had to watch people turn his personal triumphs into something tragic.

He wasn't dying at all. He felt he was just starting to live.

One thing making Luther smile as 1986 rang in was working with fifteen-year-old singer Jimmy Salvemini and his brother/manager Larry. With Luther's support, Larry negotiated a $250,000, seven-album deal with Elektra Records for Jimmy. They were so excited. All of the sacrifices they were making—Jimmy living away from his parents in Long Island, Larry moving from his cherished Alaska—were yielding results.

Luther started production on Jimmy's debut album. Although Luther still had an apartment in New York, he decided to work out of Amigo Recording Studios in Los Angeles, where Jimmy and Larry were living. They mostly worked in the evenings and on weekends in order not to disrupt Jimmy's classes at Beverly Hills High. Luther worked closely with the teen, teaching him each song word for word, note by note. Larry was always with Jimmy in the studio, never straying far from his family's boyish treasure.

Luther enjoyed the company of the Salvemini brothers. He took them around with him to restaurants, shops, and other places that a superstar like himself had to go. When Stevie Wonder asked Luther to do some soulful scatting on his single "Part-Time Lover," he took Jimmy and Larry to the studio with him. It was a woozy time for them all.

After these adventures, Larry would rush back to his West Hollywood apartment, telling his roommates, "You guys—you'll never believe . . ." The apartment bustled with the energy of Jimmy's rising career. Every time someone went into the kitchen, they saw the refrigerator papered with little notes listing all the big things Larry wanted for his brother.

As Luther grew increasingly fond of the Salveminis, he was also becoming enamored of Los Angeles. He loved its bright open aura. He experienced that emancipating feeling that many New Yorkers get when they first spend a lot of time on the West Coast. Things didn't seem as tense and penned in as they did in New York. Sure, there was traffic, but if you caught the right road at the right time, you could drive for mile upon beautiful blue-skied mile with your troubles blowing by you like the wind.

By January 1986, he had made the decision to move to Los Angeles, buying a sprawling mansion, ironically from Rona Barrett, the gossip guru who had interviewed him about the AIDS rumors. "The house is in Beverly Hills and it's newly furnished," Luther gushed, "and it will just look great." It had two stories, a gated exterior, lots of frills (a swimming pool, an elevator, a projection room, a spa, and a sauna), and a $6 million price tag. Luther made a $500,000 down payment and agreed to a mortgage of $50,000 a month. He was a long way from the Alfred E. Smith projects.

Initially, Luther worried that the West Coast move would mean he wouldn't see his mother and sisters as much, but he hoped the situation would work itself out. "We always have a great time together because I'm real close to my family," he said. "So once I'm settled here I'm sure they'll be coming out even more often." Luther planned to make the final move in February, just after he put the finishing touches on Jimmy's album.

Luther could sense how much the album meant to the brothers, and he did everything he could to ensure that the project would be special. He called in favors from many notable old friends to appear on the record: Cheryl Lynn, Alfa Anderson of Chic, and singer/actress Irene Cara, who recently had a titanic hit with "What a Feeling," the theme from the movie *Flashdance.* He asked comedian Pee Wee Herman to do a funny rap on the album's light-hearted title cut, "Roll It."

Luther penned several special songs for the album. One of the most meaningful to him was "Whether or Not the World Gets Better," a ballad about finding shelter in love. "It keeps us safely from anything outside that could hurt us," the lyrics went. To add more name recognition to the project, Luther asked singer Phoebe Snow to duet with fifteen-year-old Jimmy on the track. Phoebe, whose unique sound coolly evoked folk, pop, soul, and jazz, had been out of the spotlight for a while, but she still had one of the most immediately recognizable voices around.

At first, thirty-three-year-old Phoebe felt "a little freaked out" and unsure about singing a love song with someone less than half her age. Yet she was won over when manager Larry made an impassioned appeal to her over the phone.

"He was sweet, very protective of his brother," Phoebe recalled. "They were a very close Italian family. They all really wanted this kid to make it."

Phoebe could also sense Luther's rigorous commitment to the project. "It was just so important to him at the time," Phoebe remembered. "He was deeply, deeply involved with it."

When she came into the studio to record, Phoebe was jolted by Luther's intense perfectionism. Once she was emoting a particular line, when Luther stopped the tape. "No, the word is '*on*,' " he said from the control booth. It was the first time in her career that a producer corrected her on a preposition.

"Every word had to be absolutely enunciated," Phoebe remembered with a warm laugh. "It had to be very, very audible. No slurring allowed. He really wanted it to be right."

This exacting work, and the long hours in the studio, were worth it to Phoebe because she loved "Whether or Not the World Gets Better" so much. After Luther first sang it to her at the piano, she was overwhelmed. "I was like, 'This is one of the greatest songs I've ever heard,' " Phoebe said. "It just killed me."

"Why the hell are you not doing this song," she said to Luther. "Is there a version with you singing it?"

"No," he responded. "I just gave it to Jimmy."

When they finished up the session, Phoebe felt proud that she had done her part in singing such a special song. She thought it might be the tune to establish Jimmy and set him apart from other teen singers. "I felt that he could have a very big career," she said.

As the month of January approached its end, Luther, Jimmy, and Larry grew increasingly excited because they had almost finished recording. The last song they had to do was the lonely ballad

"It's Never Too Late," which they completed on the night of Saturday, January 11. They were all so happy. Another goal that Larry taped to the refrigerator had been accomplished.

The next morning, Luther and the brothers went riding in the R&B singer's 1985 380 SL convertible Mercedes-Benz. They were driving on Los Angeles' winding Laurel Canyon Boulevard, headed to the studio to play Jimmy's just-finished debut album in its entirety. It was a moment the teenager had been waiting for ever since he was a knee-high grade schooler singing in church.

However, what should have been joyous quickly went bad. As Laurel Canyon twisted and turned, nearing Mulholland Drive in the Hollywood Hills, Luther's car crossed the yellow lines of the two-lane street, turned sideways, and smashed into two vehicles headed in the opposite direction. The impact caused injuries that were as brutal as the crash was quick. Among the passengers in the other cars, there was a broken ankle, a broken nose, and two broken legs.

Luther, Jimmy, and Larry were rushed to Ceder-Sinai Medical Center. Doctors first treated Luther for cuts and bruises on his face and scalp. Then they discovered he had broken some ribs. Jimmy fared much worse. He suffered a collapsed lung, and the emergency room personnel watched him closely for signs of other internal injuries.

Meanwhile, Larry lay on an operating table for two hours as doctors struggled to mend the mess that had been made of his body. Their efforts were valiant, but the wounds proved too severe. It wasn't long before his parents had boarded a plane for L.A. and were struggling to find a way to tell their youngest son that his big brother had died.

Luther got the tragic news about Larry while he was still receiving treatment for his own injuries. He told nurses, "He was my best friend."

The next morning, the hospital issued a statement on Luther's health: "His condition has stabilized and there is an excellent prognosis. They are examining him very closely and we're expecting to keep him here for a couple of days."

While Luther was still hospitalized, police began closely investigating the crash. Their analysis of the skid marks from Luther's car revealed that he was doing about fifty mph in a thirty-five mph zone. They recommended to the district attorney that he be charged with felony manslaughter or vehicular homicide. Convictions on these counts would almost surely mean jail time.

The Salvemini family remained supportive of Luther. "We love Luther," said another of the Salvemini brothers, Joe, "and he loves us, and we wish him a speedy recovery." He later added: "While the death of Larry is a tremendous loss for the family, we do not harbor any animosity toward Luther. . . . We know that Luther did not do anything to hurt anybody in the car."

As the police investigation went on, the Salvemini family started making preparations to bury their brother and son. The family's Long Island–based doctor flew out to Los Angeles to see if Jimmy was well enough to attend Larry's funeral.

On January 13, prosecutors decided that they lacked sufficient evidence to charge Luther with either felony manslaughter or vehicular homicide. However, near the end of the month, the city attorney charged Luther with misdemeanor manslaughter and reckless driving. If convicted, Luther faced more than a year in jail and a $1,000 fine.

Amid this flurry of court activity, Larry's memorial service took place at Robertaccio Funeral Home in the Long Island, New York, suburb of Patchogue. Luther attended with his sisters, Ann and Patricia, by his side. Jimmy was also there, saying good-bye to his brother from the seat of a wheelchair.

Some at the funeral described it as "tearful and sorrowful." "This is the most disastrous thing I've ever seen in my life," said the mother of the Salvemini boys. "We're relying on our faith to see us through. Larry had done a lot of things in his young life. . . . Everyone who ever met him loved him. He never had a sad face, always a smile."

When Jimmy's duet partner Phoebe Snow learned what had happened, she thought, "Oh, these poor people." She later received a distressing call from representatives at Jimmy's label, Elekra, who decided in light of the tragedy to shelve the singer's debut album. They felt it would be nearly impossible to launch a potential teen heartthrob out of such horrific circumstances. Phoebe thought, "That's a damn shame!"

Luther was devastated over how circumstances had so quickly and brutally changed. He had loved the brothers and believed in Jimmy's talent. It seemed just days ago they were making music and sharing dreams. Now, Luther was under police investigation and Jimmy was back home in Long Island mourning his brother and trying to heal his broken body.

In addition to dealing with legal matters, Luther also had to confront a whole mess of new rumors stirred up by the accident. There was talk that he was gay and having a relationship with one of the young men in the car. Some thought it was with golden-haired Jimmy; others speculated that he was involved with swarthy, mustached Larry.

Luther never commented on the Salvemini brothers. When asked about the accident later that year, Luther's voice grew soft as he said, "It's a highly personal, painful thing, and I don't want to talk about it."

To stave off the anguish of the accident, the loss of Larry, and all the nasty rumors, Luther dove back into his work. He had a new album scheduled for release, and this time his record label, Epic, promised to do everything in its power to turn him into the mainstream star he always wanted to be.

Luther referred to 1986 as "the crossover year for LV." Reaching this goal was his foremost concern. "It's the main issue of every conversation I have with my management or my record company," he said. "In my mind, my music is not some esoteric thing that appeals to a certain limited crowd of people. It's made for the pop charts; the job of getting it there is a management-record company type of function."

The new album was called *Give Me the Reason,* after the sinewy title track that first appeared on the soundtrack to the Bette Midler film *Ruthless People.* Luther recorded much of the album in Montserrat, then finished the tracks in Los Angeles. The album followed Luther's winning formula, including finger-snapping uptempo numbers (the effervescent "Stop to Love") and an emotive reworking of a pop classic (Dionne Warwick's "Anyone Who Had a Heart"). He also covered one of the tunes that he had previously given to Dionne, "So Amazing." Luther loved the tone of the song, at once plainspoken and boiling over with feeling. He felt it had been lost on Dionne's ill-fated release and he wanted to give it new life.

Marcus Miller remembered that there was a magical vibe when they recorded the powerful ballad. "Can you imagine playing bass and Luther is in the studio right there, and Nat is playing the piano, and Yogi's playing the drums," Miller said. "And you know right then and there that this is a song people will be hearing for the rest of time. This is a classic . . . and it's happening right now."

Another special moment on the album was "There's Nothing Better Than Love," a duet with actor and dancer Gregory Hines.

Give Me the Reason was released in October 1986. Inside on the album's lyric sheet was a special dedication "to Lawrence J. Salvemini—my friend for life . . ."

The cover of *Give Me the Reason* was the first to show the newly slim Luther, the one the public first glimpsed during his appearance on Patti LaBelle's Thanksgiving special the previous year. In the photo, Luther reclined in a black ensemble set off by an open canary-yellow shirt. Like many who lose a lot of weight, Luther seemed to want to show off his new physique. The album came with a color inner sleeve showing two full-page pictures of Luther. In one, he adopted a matinee idol stance, as his dark brown eyes look directly at the camera. The other photo showed him with his head bowed downward, looking like there were so many things on his mind.

With this weight loss, no one could ever say anymore that his size stopped him from making the pop charts. There were no more excuses. He was ready to win. Even critics seemed to be rooting for Luther. "One of pop music's big mysteries in recent years is why Luther Vandross hasn't become a huge crossover star," wrote Paul Green of the *Los Angeles Times*. "His albums consistently sell a million, but that is mostly due to black radio and fan support. After all this time, Vandross has yet to land a top 20 hit." Peter Smith of the *St. Petersburg Times* wrote: "If the pop radio world gives him a fair shake, Vandross could take his rightful place alongside Lionel Richie."

To launch the album, Luther embarked on a ten-city promotional jaunt. Each night he attended a big party, meeting the press, retailers, and all those pop radio programmers who seldom played his records. It seemed that the setup for *Give Me the Reason* was perfect. Everything was building for him to finally score a crossover hit.

Yet, once again, it didn't happen. The first two singles from the album—"Stop to Love" and the duet with Hines, "There's Nothing Better Than Love"—reached the peak of the R&B chart, but they failed to ever make the pop Top 20. Luther had lost the weight and played the game, but he still couldn't cross over.

Luckily, he had his loyal fan base, and was appreciated by fellow musicians. Rock singer/songwriter and all around musical journeyman Paul Simon invited Luther to participate in an all-star gospel tribute that he was staging at the First Presbyterian Church of Hollywood. Luther was uneasy about accepting because, despite his mother's deep beliefs, he never felt much connection to gospel music or even the church. "I never was a big churchgoing person," Luther once revealed. "Suddenly between one and two on Sunday afternoon you turn on all this emotion? I thought it was just a lot of hypocrisy."

Nevertheless, he decided to do the show in part as a way to acknowledge the roots of his music. "Everybody that I loved came straight from the church," he said, listing Dionne, Aretha, and the Sweet Inspirations. Ultimately, he figured: "It doesn't really matter whether or not you've actually sung in a physical church building. If you're of the mind, spirit and gospel bent, you'll be fine."

Looking like a suave black Valentino, Luther chose not to sing a gospel song per se, but to perform "A Change Is Gonna Come," by the late Sam Cooke, who got his start canvassing the country with the gospel quintet the Soul Stirrers. Released after his suspicious shooting death, "A Change Is Gonna Come" found Cooke decrying the evil and hard times that lurked all around him. It even had him wondering, after years of unquestioned faith, if there was a heaven.

When Luther sang this number, he imbued it with passionate old-school fervor. His performance served as a powerful retort to those who said he lacked the emotion of the early soul greats. He proved that he didn't lack the chops to sing gut-bucket soul, but rather that times had changed. Luther was sparkling wine and lobster tails, not fish and grits.

The mostly female fans sitting restlessly in the pews testified to the force of his singing by jumping up and down, waving their arms back and forth, and hollering at his every vocal flourish. This was the same kind of reaction Luther was getting as he embarked on a tour to support the *Give Me the Reason* album. One critic wrote: "Vandross could generate screams reading the Boy Scout Oath."

Now that he had slimmed down, Luther felt looser in concert. He would do a mock moonwalk during "Creepin'," and would also step down from the stage and walk among the fans, touching their damp trembling hands as he passed by.

His costumes now had a tighter fit. He looked fine in tailored black pants and jackets covered in shiny beads.

His weight loss even became the topic of onstage banter.

"You remember lunch this afternoon," he said to his tan, impossibly lean background singer Kevin Owens.

"Yeah, I remember," Kevin answered.

"I remember, too," said Luther. "You were having waffles and pancakes, grits, eggs Benedict, sausage, collard greens, mustard greens, turnip greens, cabbage, ham hocks and cheese, Rice Krispies, a peanut butter and jelly sandwich, two glazed doughnuts with a hamburger in the middle. And I was having a Diet Coke."

"Yeah," said Kevin, "but you look great."

Onstage and in private, Luther openly acknowledged how hard it was to keep the weight off, but he seemed committed to it. "I'm sticking to a low-fat, high-protein diet with lots of fruit," Luther said, "[but] I'm now down to 197 pounds from 326, so there are now certain days when I can eat what I want."

This was particularly impressive given the emotional trauma of the past year. Generally, Luther overate whenever something was bothering him. The food helped still his inner turmoil. Yet even when faced with the AIDS rumors and Larry's death, Luther's diet stayed on course.

Touring with his new slimmed-down physique had other benefits in addition to loosening up his stage manner. As he made his way from Long Beach Arena in Los Angeles to the Omni in Atlanta to the Westbury Music Fair in New York to the Capital Centre near Washington, D.C., he could also indulge in the shopping that each city offered. A stop in Chicago had him dropping by the Gianni Versace store to pick up, as he revealed, "just a few pieces for just a few thousand dollars."

By this point, Luther didn't have to worry about his concerts. Everyone in his organization knew what they were supposed to do, and the band, including such longtime members, associates, and friends as Nat Adderley, Jr., drummer Yogi Horton, and Ava Cherry, was tight. "We really are like a family together," Luther said, "even when we're not onstage."

They picked up raves wherever they went. The *Chicago Tribune* stated that his vocals "border on the miraculous," and *Variety* wrote: "With absolutely no props, gimmicks or vaudeville skits, a very streamlined Vandross enthralled 20,000 attendees with his fantastic voice and sense of humor."

The only issues on this leg of the tour occurred when Luther made the first political move of his career. He canceled two sold-out shows at the Celebrity Theatre in Phoenix, Arizona, to protest the move of the state's governor to rescind Martin Luther King, Jr., Day as an official holiday.

"I feel very strongly about the importance of recognizing Martin Luther King Day as a national holiday," Luther said. "It's important not only to black people but to all Americans to recognize the King holiday and honor one of the world's great human rights leaders."

More controversy came as 1986 began to close and it was time for Luther to face the vehicular manslaughter charges related to Larry's death. Jury selection began, and it was clear that Luther's lack of mainstream success affected him at every level. The judge referred to him dismissively as "an entertainer of some fame," and one juror said to the court, "I don't even know what type of singing this gentleman does." As hard it is to believe, according to a reporter in the courtroom, not one of the forty prospective, mostly white jurors had even heard of him.

The case never proceeded to trial. On December 9, Luther pleaded no contest—like a guilty plea without actually admitting guilt—to reckless driving. He was placed on summary probation for twelve months and ordered to stage a concert in New York or Los Angeles, within the following year, as a benefit for a scholarship in Larry's name. Prosecutors said they made the deal in order to spare the Salveminis an emotionally wrenching trial. Besides, there were such mitigating circumstances as unclear road markings where the accident occurred.

When the plea bargain was announced, the Salveminis sounded less supportive of Luther than they had immediately following the accident. They said they planned to file a wrongful death suit. (Few details ever emerged about this case, but it was quietly settled about one year later for nearly $700,000. The city of Los Angeles contributed $50,000 because of the poor road condition.)

No longer facing an impending trial, Luther felt freer as his road show continued looping its way throughout the country, visiting the same cities over and over again due to feverish demands. He was breaking box-office records and selling more tickets than other acts who had made bigger chart hits.

Perhaps the biggest sign of this success was Luther's series of sold-out shows at Madison Square Garden in the summer of 1987. This was a huge accomplishment made even more special because the New York area was home to Luther and so many members of his band, including drummer Horton and one of his newer background singers, a striking young woman named Lisa Fischer.

Everyone was excited about these shows. Even though the record company hadn't delivered on its promise to make Luther a crossover mega-star, Epic was planning to throw him a huge party to celebrate the Madison Square Garden dates on the night of his fourth show. It was going to be a midnight, post-concert gala for three hundred aboard a Princess yacht. Comedian Eddie Murphy and the hit hip-hop trio Run DMC were invited.

The energy was high as Luther and the gang pulled into town, and the first two shows came off beautifully. By the third night, however, something seemed to be wrong with Luther. He started displaying the same demanding behavior that some of those around him had witnessed in the past. He sharply carped if something wasn't exactly to his liking, if the band wasn't instantly in sync, or someone played a bum note. His behavior terrified some and angered others.

Luther's mood swings were especially troubling because they were so mysterious and unpredictable. He was so intensely private that no one ever really knew if it was the music and work irking him or something in his closely guarded personal life. Sometimes it seemed like the smallest thing could set him on a verbal rampage. At times, Luther could be sweet and extraordinarily generous. Yet he could also be a crooning land mine.

Few know or were willing to discuss exactly what was bothering Luther the night of his third New York City show, but it was so bad that it even spilled over onto the stage. Where Luther normally fawned over the band during a show, taking several minutes to share an anecdote about each musician, that night he didn't even introduce the band members. This was particularly cutting, since it was in a city many of them called home.

Much of the band was furious with Luther following the show. They headed uptown to Mikells, a low-key after-hours getaway spot for the city's top musicians. Everyone seemed to have a gripe about Luther, even drummer Yogi Horton, normally quick with a joke, was particularly agitated. He drank too much and didn't return to his room at the midtown Dumont Hotel until seven in the morning.

His wife waited up for him. She wanted to know what was wrong, why he was so upset. He reeled off a list of complaints as he started undressing, preparing for bed. He said he wasn't making enough money and that he was tired of living in Luther's shadow.

His wife stepped out of the room for a moment to go to the bathroom, and Yogi, clad only in his boxer shorts, walked over to the window of their seventeenth-floor room, forced it open, and thrust himself out onto the hard, unforgiving street, dying upon impact.

When the news started spreading, some of his friends didn't believe it. He was known for saying to people, "If anybody ever tells you I committed suicide, check it out." Others couldn't see how this guy who often made people so happy would make such a desperate choice. If he truly had a problem with Luther, they thought, why didn't he just quit? There seemed to be no answers, nothing to help the tragedy make sense.

That night, Luther went on with the scheduled show, using a substitute drummer, but he canceled plans to attend his grand homecoming party. As the concert began, Luther said, "I'd like to dedicate this performance to the memory of Yogi Horton, the greatest drummer who ever lived." Then, he went into a song whose title had acquired a new poignancy: "Give Me the Reason."

"Any Love" 16

> *"As fabulous as my career has been, I sometimes wonder if my personal life has been compromised by such an uncompromising pursuit of my career. But what am I gonna do, go for balance? You can't put fifty percent of your effort into a career and fifty percent of your effort into a personal life. I think personal lives are chance. If fate wants you to have it, you'll get it. If it doesn't want you to have it, you won't get it."*
>
> —LUTHER, ON FINDING A RELATIONSHIP

Nearly a year had passed since the suicide of Yogi Horton and Luther sat in his car, frozen. He didn't want to be where he was. He wasn't sure if he could go any further. From the parking lot, he could see the building where he was expected by an army of people—managers, publicists, assistants, photographers. Yet he could not go inside. He didn't want to be seen.

A half-hour went by. Then Luther drove away.

Everyone inside was furious. Didn't he know this photo shoot was important? They needed a cover picture for his forthcoming album, *Any Love.* So much time and money was being wasted. They thought, "What's wrong with Luther."

Back at his L.A. home, Luther retreated to his closet, trying to find something that still fit. He needed something that might help mask the 120 pounds he had put back on since he looked so fine on the cover of his 1986 *Give Me the Reason* album, since those heady days when he was in love, and Larry Salvemini and Yogi Horton were still alive.

He finally found a large patterned shirt that he liked, and the photo session was rescheduled. He had one stipulation for the man behind the camera, however: "No photographs below the chest and that's not negotiable."

After the back-to-back lows of the past couple of years—the AIDS rumor, the deaths of friends Larry Salvemini and drummer Yogi Horton—Luther couldn't keep denying himself the cravings that seemed to call out from his very core. He tried to bargain with his hunger. First, he allowed himself to gain five pounds. He could easily lose that, he thought. Then, it was seven, ten, twelve, until it was beyond what he felt he could control. Soon he was pouring hot buttery grits over plates blanketed with cheese, and keeping candy bars on his nightstand. He ate hamburgers sandwiched between two doughnuts.

With this change in eating habits, Luther's blood pressure started to rise, and he was again taking three to four Excedrin so he wouldn't wake up with a pounding headache. When friends called to invite him places, he begged off, feeling—as he once said—like the Elephant Man.

His emotions went into his music. His collaborator Marcus Miller had sent him a tape with an odd shuffling bossa nova–ish instrumental track on it. Luther listened to it one day and a stream of words came to him like coins cascading out of a winning slot machine. The words summed up a desire that had been with him for so many years, a longing for, as he titled the song, "Any Love."

"I was feeling extraordinarily depressed when I wrote that song [in 1988]," Luther explained, "and that's what came out."

Luther sang that he was lucky in so many ways except in matters of the heart. He said that inside him there was a voice screaming and crying for the chance to tell someone "I love you." It was the wish expressed in all of his prayers, and the meaning behind many tears. It neatly summarized the primary lesson Luther had learned since achieving fame. "Success is wonderful," he said, "but it doesn't keep you warm at night."

He ended the song on a hopeful note, telling himself and listeners to keep the faith. "'Any Love' is a song of encouragement," he explained. "It's trying to tell you to hold it together, in spite of what you deem to be the missing piece in your life. That's a song just saying don't think that because one element of your life is missing that your life is totally worthless."

Once released, the song became one of his biggest hits. It continued to prove that Luther had tapped into something that affected so many of his fans, almost as if loneliness had become epidemic.

While "Any Love" pervaded the R&B airwaves, Luther was in the midst of the biggest tour of his career. It was also the most tumultuous. He shared the bill with smoky female R&B singer Anita Baker, who had scored a big hit with her 1986 album, *Rapture.* However, in nearly every way except music, the two were mismatched, like "H_3 Plus O," Luther once joked. Predictably, things started off badly and grew intolerable.

It all began with a proposed duet the two were scheduled to sing at the 1987 Grammys. Luther was up for two awards, Best R&B Male Vocal and Best R&B Song, both for "Give Me the Reason." This was encouraging since he had failed to win twice more since his first devastating loss in the Best New Artist category in 1982.

Anita, on the other hand, was already a Grammy darling, winning two for her album *Rapture*. Though she was a relative newcomer, Anita's career was quickly becoming a model for the kind of success Luther wanted. In addition to her Grammys, Anita had sold five million copies of *Rapture*—more than three million more than the biggest Luther record. These numbers showed that she was a hit with the pop market that Luther still struggled to crack. Her songs like "Sweet Love" showed up on top television shows like the quick-witted romance *Moonlighting*. Luther was both admiring of Anita's success and a bit envious.

Anita, for her part, was an unlikely success story. Standing just over five feet in heels and sporting a short, practical haircut, Anita lacked the glamour of most R&B queens, and she sang with a slurring, eccentric phrasing. Her style and sound shouldn't have worked, but it did.

Like the Queen of Soul, Anita grew up in Detroit and started singing when her grandfather, a traveling minister, would take her around to the city's legion of storefront halls of worship. Anita belted out gospel tunes to approving crowds of old-timers, folks who remembered the way church songs should be sung, how they used to sound down South, back home.

As she grew older, Anita fell for jazz, which she learned while stretching her pipes in local bars. She then joined the established Detroit-area funk outfit Chapter 8. This gave her an opportunity to wail and show off her best Chaka Khan.

It was all fun, but she wasn't making any money. Her family began asking when she was going to get a real job.

She quit music and landed employment as a receptionist in a downtown Detroit law firm. The money wasn't great, but it was steady: $10,000 a year, plus benefits. Things were going along well—she had even been promoted to word processor—when an old business associate called to offer her a solo record deal.

"I told him to drop dead," Baker recalled. "I had my Blue Cross card and my week's vacation."

He sweetened the deal, promising to match her yearly salary and cover all of her expenses—car, apartment—if she would move to Los Angeles to record. That was an offer she couldn't turn down, despite her mother's protests. Being a singer was still her dream.

The album she recorded, *The Songstress,* became a big R&B hit, especially for a record that wasn't on a major label. However, she and the business associate quickly fell out. Legal troubles ensued, and she was tied up in the courts for years.

Finally, she was rescued by Elektra Records, which helped with her legal troubles and put her back in the studio. In just over a year, all of the litigious wrangles were behind her and she had a hit album on the charts and two Grammys on her mantel.

Luther thought that dueting with previous winner Anita on the awards telecast would improve his visibility with the mainstream public and Grammy voters. This could have the double benefit of boosting his sales with the television-watching crossover crowd and increasing his chances to one day take home one of those much-coveted golden gramophones.

Luther pitched Anita on singing the sweet Marvin Gaye/Tammi Terrell classic "Your Precious Love." To rehearse, they met at his Los Angeles mansion. They sat in his dining room and practiced their parts, until they came up with an arrangement that they thought would really knock people out.

Yet on the morning of the show, Anita changed her mind about singing with Luther. Instead, she chose to sing jazz great Billie Holiday's "God Bless the Child" as a tribute to the late gardenia-wearing singer. Producers of the show didn't balk because, in their mind, Anita was the bigger star. Luther suddenly went from being a performer to getting cut from the show. On top of that, the night marked his fourth Grammy loss.

He next saw Anita during the summer at the Kool Jazz Festival in Cincinnati, Ohio. She performed immediately before him and she opened with his hit song "Stop to Love," and then she sang it again to close her set. Luther, of course, felt he would look like a nut if he sang the tune again, even though it was his song. He was furious.

Nevertheless, when his handlers tried to sell him on doing a co-headlining tour with Anita, he couldn't deny that it seemed like a smart business idea. Luther and Anita shared many of the same fans, lovers of smooth R&B, and Anita might also draw some of her pop fans who would then be exposed to Luther.

The two stars signed on for a thirty-city tour that would take them through the end of 1988 and into 1989. Although Anita would go on first, they received equal billing. The concerts soon proved as lucrative as promoters expected. As soon as tickets went on sale for most shows, they immediately sold out.

Fans were overcome with excitement over the pairing of these two beloved talents. "It's like you died and went to heaven," one woman told the *Chicago Sun-Times.*

Luther and Anita both talked up the tour in the press. Anita promised a "night of mushy-mushy, kissy-face love songs," and Luther stated that he wanted the show to leave people saying *"Child, pleeeease, that was fabulous!"*

The months leading up to the tour kickoff were worrisome for Anita. She had yet to finish the follow-up to *Rapture,* and it was critical that she have a new album to promote when she was out on the road. *Rapture* was nearly two years old. Anita, however, would not let go of any of the songs she was recording. She kept mixing and remixing them, trying all new arrangements and then trashing them.

She was so past deadline that her manager took some unfinished tapes to the mastering company, where the album was put together on one reel to get it ready for release. When she discovered what he'd done, she went right to the company, demanded back everything with her name on it, and insisted they destroy the work they'd already done.

Anita was earning a reputation for being difficult, but she didn't care. "People still think I'm temperamental, but it's just that I know what I want and I not only ask for it, I demand it," she said. "Some people have problems with that. And that's too bad. This is my life and my music and it should be done the way I want to do it."

The tour, dubbed *The Heat*, opened on Wednesday, September 28 at the Capital Centre, just outside of Washington, D.C. Things felt weird from the start. Since they had past tensions, the backstage area was coordinated so that the two stars would have very little contact with each other. Whenever Luther entered the venue, security people were under strict orders to seal off Anita's dressing room area. Curtains were placed backstage to separate the two camps. Even their respective guest list tickets were for seats in different sections of the auditorium.

The tensions weren't reserved for backstage, however. At that first show, Luther fired the initial shot in what would be an ongoing feud between these two coheadliners. He took the stage and said, "Let's hear a round of applause for my *opening act*, Anita Baker."

Anita was furious. She was no opening act. She was as much of a headliner on this tour as he was. This wasn't just a question of ego, it was also potentially messing with her money. If promoters thought she was an opening act, her drawing price went down.

Her manager issued a statement: "The contracts clearly state that they are co-headliners, co-stars sharing everything—advertising, billing, facilities, dressing rooms. . . . We agreed that Luther would close every show and Anita was happy to agree to that because she had never worked big arenas. But in every other sense, they are co-headliners."

Luther's manager pointedly responded: "I don't consider her an opening act. [But] she is on before him."

Critics, when reviewing the show, fanned the flames. They scored the show like a fight. Sometimes Anita was the victor; other times it was Luther.

The *Los Angeles Times* wrote: "Anita Baker steals the show from headliner Vandross." In Texas, the *Dallas Morning News Tonight* exclaimed that "Vandross came out the distinct winner" at the Reunion Arena. Then a reviewer for the *Chicago Tribune* offered Luther a stinging bit of backhanded praise when he wrote: "It was beauty and the beast Tuesday night at the Rosemont Horizon. . . . Let's hear it for the beast."

Things degenerated further from there. Luther continuously asked Anita to sing a duet with him. Fans were asking for it. Even critics said it would improve the show. But Anita consistently refused.

As the tour continued, Luther started growing frustrated that while Anita's record was soaring up the pop charts, his *Any Love* album had stalled. This was a shame, because, by and large, it was a polished collection, from the moving title song to his smooth cover of former Delphonics member Major Harris' ballad "Love Won't Make Me Wait," in which Luther explored every nuance of the song's pleading sentiment. The album also included the sensuously insinuating "For You to Love," as well as a resung version of one of the best songs by the group Luther, "The Second Time Around."

"I think that if Anita's album can do so well after the tour, so could mine," Luther reasoned. "I don't know what it will take to get to the next level with my record sales, especially when you have people at the company telling me, after they heard *Any Love*, that it 'doesn't get any better than this.' After this many albums, I do feel

I should be selling five or six million copies and that I really belong in a whole other club as an artist."

As the year came to an end, Anita found herself concerned less with what was going on backstage or even onstage. Her focus was on her personal life. She had been dating handsome real estate developer Walter Bridgforth. On Christmas eve, she donned a $1,500 dress that she'd picked up at Detroit's Jacobson's department store and together she and Walter said their vows and "jumped the broom" into matrimony.

The news got better the following month when she found out that she was pregnant. She and Walter were so happy. She wanted to scream it from the concert stage, but the older women in her family cautioned her. "Just wait," they said, "don't go telling everybody." These wise elders knew that the first few months of pregnancy often brought unexpected tears.

She heeded their warning at first, and even denied being pregnant during a radio interview. "I'm just fat and happy," she told the radio jock.

But she soon found that she couldn't contain her joy. She decided to share it with those around her. Everyone was so pleased for her. It looked like she was well on her way to having it all with a successful career, a loving spouse, and a child on the way. A few weeks later, however, bad news came from her doctor. He could no longer hear the baby's heartbeat.

Just as she had shared her happiness, she now had to reveal her pain. The hard time was made tougher because she was still on tour with Luther. Each night, she had to stand onstage singing love songs while inside she felt so bad.

"Families can suffer their problems and difficulties with each other and it's not easy," Anita said, "but it's multiplied a million times when everyone knows about it."

She was walking through an airport one day when a woman screamed across the terminal: "Sorry about the baby."

When *The Heat* tour concluded in early 1989, both Luther and Anita agreed that it had been disastrous for them personally, but they couldn't deny its success. One run of shows in Chicago took in nearly $2 million, grossing more than tours by Frank Sinatra, Liza Minnelli, and Sammy Davis, Jr., as well as the Grateful Dead.

Around the same time the tour wrapped, two things lifted Luther's spirits. One, he became the first guest on a new late-night talk show hosted by his friend comedian Arsenio Hall. Luther was happy for Arsenio and he also knew that this guest slot would give him increased exposure. But Luther initially had reservations about doing the show. It was his first TV appearance since regaining his weight.

During the show, Arsenio gushed over Luther's *Any Love* album, saying he had the record, the compact disc, and the cassette. Luther then returned the compliment, pointing to Arsenio and asking the audience, "Isn't he fabulous?"

The other thing making Luther happy was that he'd received two more Grammy nominations: Best R&B Male Vocal and Best R&B Song, both for the haunting "Any Love." He told friends that he really thought this could be his year.

"I'd like to finally get a Grammy," he said. "I've been nominated . . . and although that's an acknowledgment in itself, I'd like to *win* one."

Critics around the country agreed that he was long overdue.

USA Today: "Grammyless Luther Vandross is a sure shot."

San Francisco Chronicle: "Look for Luther Vandross to finally win his first Grammy."

Chicago Tribune: "Give this one to the . . . deserving Luther Vandross."

Washington Post: "Luther Vandross' 'Any Love' should win."

Nelson George, then a writer for the music industry trade publication *Billboard,* devoted much of an entire column to questioning why Luther was so overlooked and unappreciated in all areas, from award shows to the pop charts: "Why isn't Vandross a household name? During this same period, such worthy singers as Willie Nelson, Whitney Houston, [Anita] Baker, and Julio Iglesias have been sold to the American public with cover stories, personality profiles, and national TV exposure. Yet Vandross, who I would argue is not just black pop's premier vocalist but ranks as the most expert ballad singer of his generation in any genre of pop, has not been give the attention his talent demands."

With this wellspring of support, Luther felt confident of his chances this time. The night before the awards telecast, he attended a party thrown by Arista Records president Clive Davis. Luther showed up in a bright blue tuxedo trimmed in black.

The next night, Luther attended the Grammys, which was largely swept by acrobatic jazz vocalist Bobby McFerrin, who brought home several awards for his quirky a cappella anthem "Don't Worry Be Happy." Anita Baker's "Giving You the Best That I Got" beat Luther in the R&B Song category, and she also won for Best R&B Female. Luther, on the other hand, left with nothing, losing Best R&B Male to screechy British newcomer Terrence Trent D'Arby.

Luther once again went on an eating binge. "I headed straight to the kitchen," Luther remembered. "It's a knee-jerk reaction to whatever's going on with me."

Luther also continued fiercely promoting *Any Love.* He was still uneasy about the way he looked, but he committed to more television appearances. With a competitiveness generally reserved for Pac-Man, he challenged Dionne Warwick on a celebrity version of *Family Feud*, and he also put in a stop on a show that was hosted by a woman who shared his threadbare roots but had gone on to be hailed as "the queen of talk": Oprah Winfrey.

Oprah, of course, had been very public about her own struggle to lose weight, so she and Luther chatted extensively about the trials of dieting and the stigma—both internal and external—of being overweight. He told her how food and heartache were intertwined for him. It was the only way he knew how to numb the pain of loss and the gnawing hunger of longing.

Luther performed "Any Love" on the show, and you could see Oprah mouthing the words, silently singing along. An audience member later asked Luther if he had found "Any Love" yet. He answered "No," and admitted that he was becoming obsessed with it. "Whatever is missing in your life," he said, "is what you actively pursue."

Shortly after this appearance, Luther went back on tour. This time sans Anita, but he was still selling out shows wherever he played. He broke a box-office record in England, selling out ten nights at London's Wembley Arena, which seats more than 11,000 people. The shows grossed over $3.5 million, besting highs set by rock super groups Fleetwood Mac and Dire Straits.

The show Luther took to England was elegant in its simplicity. The only people on the bare circular stage were the headliner himself, the dashing Kevin Owens, the always eye-catching Ava Cherry, and Lisa Fischer, the newest addition to Luther's camp.

Luther met Lisa several years earlier when he was auditioning background singers at a Brooklyn rehearsal hall. Like him, she had spent much of her early career doing background work, singing on records for people like Billy Ocean and Latina R&B songstress Angela Bofill. Lisa had also lent her lead vocals for studio groups like the minor disco act Shades of Love, and recorded a snappy dance smash, "On the Upside," using the Amazon-like alias Xena. By the time Lisa met Luther, she was primed for a change. Life had been hard growing up the daughter of a teenage mother in the drug-filled environs of Brooklyn's Fort Greene projects. She was ready for a new kind of life and thought Luther might be the one to help her get it.

At the audition, Luther sat at the piano and sang complicated lines for her to sing back to him. She nailed every one. Then he said, "If you can dance, you've got the gig." She broke into a few moves right then and there, and the job was hers.

Luther saw such star potential in Lisa that he featured her in the "Stop to Love" video. She filmed her part standing on a crane, which made it seem like she was flying through the streets of Los Angeles. Lisa looked like she had just stepped out of a fashion magazine with a closed blue trench coat squared by taut shoulder pads, her plume of curls piled high like a royal headdress, and red blush that slashed upward across her honey-toned cheeks.

She became so popular that such acts as the Rolling Stones booked her whenever she wasn't touring with Luther. Not long afterward, she landed her own record deal.

At Wembley, Luther, Kevin, Ava, and Lisa moved around in carefully choreographed sync, using every inch of the round stage. It marked the furthest refinement of Luther's college fantasies: a group of men and women performing onstage while dressed to the nines. Ava and Lisa wore $12,000 gowns and diamond-encrusted boots.

While things looked beautiful onstage, the backstage atmosphere could sometimes be tense. Even after drummer Yogi Horton's suicide, Luther was still an excruciatingly demanding boss. "Luther is indeed the most difficult entertainer I've ever worked with," said his then-manager Billy Bass. "He's so exacting, he's a perfectionist."

As Luther saw it: "I'm paying money for people to be good."

Sometimes he mocked his own backbreaking reputation. Once, onstage, he demanded jokingly: "Where's my water? I gotta get some water. Somebody's gonna get fired if I don't get my water."

When the tour ended, Luther focused his energies on the house he had bought from Rona Barrett. He had made $2.5 million worth of renovations since he purchased it four years earlier, and now it was his prized showpiece. Luther decorated the whole house in warm muted colors: gray in the game room, beige in the living room, and his favorite color, pink, in the master bedroom.

"If I were not a singer," Luther once said, "I'd be an interior designer."

When people complimented his home and his penchant for decorating, he joked that he "was cursed with good taste."

In the foyer, there were several acclaimed pieces of modern art: a Picasso, a Sam Francis, and David Hockney's matter-of-factly erotic "Two Men in a Shower." This fine work had recently returned home after being on loan to the Metropolitan Museum of Art in New York, the Los Angeles County Museum of Art, and the Tate Gallery in London.

The entire house reflected Luther's ornate tastes. The suped-up game room featured a lacquered leather pool table. The sofa in the rotunda was covered in gray lambskin, and framed platinum records hung above it on the wall. In the kitchen, there were no plastic cups. If you wanted water, you had to use crystal.

Luther's favorite room was his office, awash in forest green, where he'd sit on the couch and catch up on all of his favorite television shows.

He explained: "OK, so if I have a day off, here it is: I start out with *Family Feud. The Price Is Right.* Then I turn to Channel 7 and I do *Loving, All My Children,* and *One Life to Live.* Then Sally Jesse, then Oprah, then Geraldo. I could go the whole day. At night, I love *LA Law, Who's the Boss.*"

If there was wrestling on, he'd check up on the exploits of Earth Quake, the Undertaker, Ted Di Biase, and Mr. Fuji. He joked to friends that he wanted to become a wrestler called "Lightning Luther."

When nothing he wanted to watch was on TV, he'd break out old tapes of the controversial but often hysterical *Amos 'n' Andy.*

With the house complete, Luther threw parties and invited people to drop by. Another R&B great Gladys Knight stopped over one night to cook dinner for Luther and his visiting mother, Mary Ida, and sisters, Ann and Pat.

Later, Whitney Houston came by, and they all played the board game Scruples.

"Everybody cheated," Luther remembered, laughing.

Dionne Warwick lived five blocks away and would often join Luther for Pac-Man battles. Indeed, one of those times helped set into motion what would become a career high for Luther, taking him to places and earning him accolades that had previously—frustratingly—seemed beyond his reach.

Luther and Dionne were in the middle of a fierce game. Luther had just gotten the upper hand, gobbling more dots and squiggly ghosts than his boyhood idol, when Dionne's son David Elliott came by to pick her up. Luther remembered, as a teenager, watching Dionne on the Ed Sullivan show, pregnant with David, as she sang the "Battle Hymn of the Republic."

David asked Luther if he wouldn't mind listening to some songs he'd been working on. Luther said, "Of course not," and David proceeded to play a tape of three cuts. Luther wasn't crazy about the first or the last one, but he heard something in the second number. It wasn't perfect, but it had some beautiful moments in it. Luther asked David to play it again, another time, then once more.

It was a song about lifelong commitment, becoming one with another person. What Luther loved most was one moment in the chorus. The vocalist sings the words that provide the song's title, "Here and Now . . . ," and then there's a long pause, a lovely space before the next words, "I'll promise to love faithfully," Luther loved this space, this drop in the song. It literally sounded like *falling* in love.

Luther decided to record it as one of the new songs on his greatest hits package, *The Best of Luther Vandross . . . The Best of Love.* The two-disc set celebrated Luther's nearly ten years as a solo recording artist. Before he laid "Here and Now" down to tape, he had to make some changes to it. He likened it to the way a supermodel might love a dress, but still have to make alterations so that it becomes a perfect fit. "I Lutherized it," he said of his additions to "Here and Now," adding a delicate string arrangement and a soaring bridge to the middle.

To launch the song, which was a perfect marital anthem, the record company, Epic, decided to do a unique promotion with one of New York's Premier R&B Stations WBLS-FM. They put together what was called the "Wedding of a Lifetime" contest. The winner would get Luther to attend their nuptials and serenade them with "Here and Now." Their ceremonial union would also be broadcast live on the radio.

A few weeks after the contest began, the station announced that the winners were Sharyn Gillyard and Michael Haynes, both of Queens, New York. Their exchange of vows took place in early October, and Luther was right there singing in front of them and their gathered family and friends.

This promotion got people talking, and "Here and Now" soon topped the R&B charts. The next time he appeared on Oprah's show, she asked him to sing it at her wedding if she got married.

What's more, it was steadily rising on the pop charts, something few Luther songs had ever done. In order to help its upward momentum, the record company rush-released a video for the song. They used a tactic that had long been employed to help black acts from jazz musicians to Motown groups attain mainstream audiences. While Luther sang the song in the video, two white lovers frolicked in a pastel landscape.

"Here and Now" became Luther's first Top 10 pop hit. The audiences at Luther's concerts started changing immediately. Comedian Sinbad, who was often the opening act at these shows, once looked out at a crowd and said, "Seriously, I've never seen so many white people come out for Luther."

With these new developments in his career, Luther decided it was time to make other changes. He weighed more than three hundred pounds again, and he was tired of it. He wanted to lose weight. The decade was coming to a close. He was about to turn thirty-nine, and his career was heading to places he always had wanted it to go. It was time to kick his weight problem once and for all.

He sent a note to Oprah, who had now become his friend and confidante on weight matters: "Let's end this struggle as soon as we can."

On Thanksgiving 1989, Luther ate dinner with family. He enjoyed the full meal, heaping his plate with large-sized portions of turkey, stuffing, and other holiday dishes. He tried to enjoy every forkful and spoonful. It was the last solid food he would taste for six months.

The day after Thanksgiving he embarked on a liquid protein diet called HMR 500. It was similar to the program Oprah once used when she first lost a lot of weight. Luther would mix a diet powder with six ounces of water and drink it five times a day. Initially it was trying. The first week, he said he felt like Linda Blair from *The Exorcist,* just as evil as he could be, but he grew to enjoy the diet's effects: the way his jacket buttons now fastened so easily, and how his pants hung gracefully down his leg.

He maintained the diet despite temptations. Early in 1990, he threw a bash at his house celebrating the one-year anniversary of his friend Arsenio Hall's television show. The place was full of guests: Arsenio, Sylvester Stallone, his old boss Bette Midler, journalist Ed Bradley, Gregory Hines, Janet Jackson, Pee Wee Herman, Burt Bacharach, and Marsha Warfield of TV's *Night Court.* Neighbor Elton John dropped by and sang with Luther on some 1960s faves like "I Heard It Through the Grapevine" and "There Goes My Baby." Yet while everyone else nibbled on the finest catered goodies, Luther ate nothing.

An even bigger test occurred later that month when Luther was nominated for yet another Grammy. This time it was in the Best R&B Male category for the peppy tune "She Won't Talk to Me." Before the awards were announced, a critic from the *Boston Globe* wrote: "What do the Grammy voters have against Vandross, anyway? His losing streak is taking on a gruesome futility."

The big night came and went. Luther again was awardless, but this time he didn't go on an eating binge. He stuck to his diet. He was determined that he could do this.

By June 1990, he was down to about 221 pounds and his waist decreased from 54 to 34 inches. He was winning the battle.

As planned, he went off the liquid diet and slowly started enjoying whole food in moderation. He carefully watched what he ate, though. Backstage before concerts, he munched on broiled whitefish, and when he went to one of his favorite restaurants, Roscoe's House of Chicken and Waffles in Los Angeles, he pulled the skin from his deep-fried chicken breast.

The problem with this diet, however, was that it addressed what

Luther was eating, but it didn't tackle the question of why Luther overate. He wasn't dealing with trying to change the pattern that had been established since he was a teenager, where he would crave food whenever he was upset about something from career-related disappointment to the profound loneliness that seemed to always be a part of his life.

Sure enough, within months, there were reports that Luther had gained back at least forty of the pounds he had lost. It came at a bad time, too, because Luther was already committed to a new tour. Night after night, he had to show himself in front of thousands of people, revealing how he had failed once again to keep the weight off. This was the hardest part about being heavy.

"The . . . thing that's awful about this," Luther once said, "is that the drug addict, the cokehead, the alcoholic, the cigarette smoker, the child abuser—whatever your thing is, you can use Head and Shoulders, you can use Visine, you can get the earwax out, you can use Crest, Scope, Arid Extra Dry, cologne, you can put on your Giorgio Armani tuxedo and you can enter the room undetected. Okay? This [gesturing to his stomach] you can see the minute you walk through the door, the minute you get out of a car. That's what really sucks about it."

The reason he'd started overeating again was all too familiar. "I shouldn't be," he said, "but I'm still kind of [in love]. It was so promising. I found myself going back to old bad habits." Once again, when Luther talked about love he didn't reveal any specifics about the person involved. It also was seldom clear, when Luther said he was in love, if he was actually involved in a mutual relationship or if he was simply pining away for someone who didn't share his feelings.

The only thing clear about Luther's romantic life was that whenever he felt lonely he turned to food for comfort. It was all about "emotional eating," and pretty soon Luther refused to comment on his weight whatsoever. "It used to not be so touchy with me," he told one reporter. "Now I feel a little on display about it all. The point is, I'm not Superman. I'm tired of discussing it openly. You get what you get when you see me."

The one bit of good news that he got during this dark period came early the next year. The Grammy voters chose to nominate Luther's exuberant performance on "Here and Now" for Best R&B Male vocal. This time, Luther didn't build his hopes up. He tried to enjoy just being acknowledged. "Being nominated is like putting a quarter in the machine to play Pac-Man," Luther said after hearing the news. "Even if you don't win, you get excited."

As in previous years, he attended some of the parties that preceded the show. He dropped by a bash thrown by Sony, the parent company of his record label, Epic, at New York City's Rainbow Room. Nearly two thousand people were there, including folk-rock legend Bob Dylan, actor Jack Nicholson, and Diana Ross, who recently had let Luther produce one song ("It's Hard for Me to Say") on her album *Red Hot Rhythm and Blues.* Also at the posh affair was Sony's newest star, a budding, pretty, and popular singer named Mariah Carey, who came on the arm of her mom.

The next night at the awards, Luther was ready for whatever happened. He was well practiced in controlling his nerves as his category was announced, then keeping a strained smile on his face when it was revealed that someone else was taking home what should have been his Grammy.

At this year's show, some of Luther's friends, associates, and label mates won big. Quincy Jones nabbed six for his album *Back on the Block.* Chaka Khan picked up one for her duet with Ray Charles, "I'll Be Good to You." Anita Baker added yet another to her extensive collection for the album *Compositions.* And Mariah Carey, who made a big entrance on the scene with hits like "Vision of Love" from her self-titled debut album, took honors for Best Female Pop vocalist and Best New Artist.

When it was time to announce the Best Male R&B vocalist award, an odd pair walked out onstage. It was bluesy soul vocalist Regina Belle with Michael Bolton, a blue-eyed soulster who was almost universally hated by black music fans. Luther sat in the audience, anxious and still. His old friend from high school, Fonzi Thornton, was by his side.

Belle and Bolton listed off the nominees: "Here and Now," Luther Vandross; *Johnny Gill*, Johnny Gill; *Misunderstanding*, Al B. Sure!; *Round and Round*, Tevin Campbell; *Whip Appeal*, Babyface.

"And the award goes to," Michael Bolton said, "Luther Vandross."

The whole theater erupted with applause. A smiling Luther, looking sharp in a black velvet tuxedo, rushed down the aisle to the stage and did a line from "Here and Now" that captured how much the moment meant to him and how long he'd been waiting. In perfect pitch and without musical accompaniment he sang, "Your love is all I need."

He went home that night and for once didn't have to eat away his pain and sorrow. He was victorious. Yet despite winning the Grammy, there was something even more important that he still desired. It hit him when he realized that this was one of the greatest moments in his career—ten years in the making—but he had no one to hold close and share it with.

17

"Power of Love"

"You keep working on the various parts of your life to make them whole. It's like having a farm scene with no sky. You got grass, you got farm, you got cow. But no sky. Something is wrong with this picture."

—LUTHER, ON HIS NEEDS AND WANTS

On April 21, 1991, Luther turned forty, and he was ready to make changes in his life. He appreciated what he'd accomplished, but there was so much more that he needed to become more content with his life and career.

He felt he was living a cruel paradox. "I've stood onstage and seen couples hugging and just spiritually bonding to my music," he said. "Then, I can go back to my hotel room and the red messages light on my hotel room? Nothing."

Once again, he put these feelings into his music. He started writing songs that weren't just about holding on to the hope of love. Instead he tried to express the importance of feeling good about yourself while the wait for love was on. He knew that was his only chance of finding true inner happiness. He had to become OK with being by himself. This was a hard thing to do after all the pain and sacrifice he had made in the name of love, putting up with cheating partners (as he sang about on "Busy Body" and "I'll Let You Slide") and letting the pursuit or loss of romance impact his weight and his health. He felt he was too grown to let things go down like that anymore. He penned a song called "Don't Want to Be a Fool."

It had a pretty, lilting melody, but the message was stern. Luther, who called the song "autobiographical," revealed there was only so much he was willing to risk in the pursuit of love. He still wanted it, desperately, but there were limits. As he sang so movingly, "I've decided I can't let nobody fool me again."

This signaled a change in his whole approach to songwriting. "My music's about finding a place; it's about liking yourself; it's about feeling good in your own skin," Luther explained. "A lot of times I'm singing about how people view themselves before they enter a relationship, how they see themselves when they're in a room alone. I'm trying to explore what bothers me and what might bother other people."

Luther recorded "Don't Want to Be a Fool" for an album he was working on called *Power of Love*. It had been nearly three years since Luther's last album of new material, 1988's *Any Love*, but he felt the hiatus was necessary.

"I was just over the top with fatigue," he said. "This voice isn't a trumpet you can take out of a case and play. It's a muscle. I'm not an assemblage of parts. My voice gives out, it wears thin when I work too hard. And I was battling with my diet, losing weight and gaining it back, losing it again. I needed a rest."

Having all this time to think made him reconsider a lot of things about his life. He didn't want to carry around a lot of old wounds and gripes anymore. He was ready to be free of all that stuff. He decided to try to reconcile with people who he'd become estranged from in the past, starting with Anita Baker.

Both of them had cooled off significantly since the inflamma-
tory *Heat* tour a couple of years earlier. They talked one-on-one
and came to terms with their former grievances. Luther told her
that it always bothered him that she wouldn't sing a duet with him
on the tour. Anita explained that the reason she didn't want to sing
with him is that she was pregnant and didn't want to have to hang
around for at least two hours after her own set in order to do a
duet. She apologized for not explaining things to him then, but she
didn't feel comfortable because the atmosphere had been so tense.
"I ended up losing the baby, anyway," she told him.

Luther understood and felt that what they needed to do was
record a duet to squash all the talk that they hated each other. He
suggested they pair their voices on a cover of Ben E. King's darkly
yearning "I (Who Have Nothing)." Anita thought it was a good
idea and agreed to do it. However, on the day they were scheduled
to record in L.A., she was nowhere to be found.

"She simply didn't show up," Luther said. Their up-and-down
relationship had once again taken a fall.

Instead, he recorded the duet with dance music diva Martha
Wash, who, like Luther, had experienced her share of troubles
being overweight in an image-obsessed industry.

Luther recorded much of the new album in New York and Los
Angeles since Hurricane Hugo had demolished his beloved studio
in Montserrat just a few years earlier. It was horrible to think
about: all that beauty violently blown away.

Nevertheless, even without retreating to that island locale,
making the album was pricey. Ultimately, it cost nearly
$900,000, but Luther wanted to ensure that his new release
sounded state-of-the-art.

He had issued a mandate to his record label, Epic, and executives at the parent company, Sony Music. He wanted a number-
one pop record. It seemed like everyone he knew—Dionne,

Aretha, Whitney—had one. Now that he had a Grammy, he felt it was the next step to cementing his mainstream success.

"My career cannot continue until I can claim that I've had a number-one record. I'm ravenous for one. I don't think it's unreasonable or self-serving to ask for. Somebody has it every week."

The weapon he had for achieving this goal was a medley he'd devised that paired a new tune, "Power of Love," with a somewhat obscure number he remembered from his teenage years, "Love Power," a hand-clapping, gospel-flavored track by the New York trio the Sandpebbles. By putting the songs together, Luther crafted an upbeat anthem that, like many of his other cuts, had an old-school, good-time, street-corner feel with a thoroughly modern polish.

Luther's mother heard the song and felt it reflected all the values that she tried to instill in her sons and daughters. "The Lord knows that the only thing my children and I had when they were growing up was our love," she said. "I would always tell them, 'Love wins out; don't care about how bad things get. If you love strong enough, you don't fear bad things because you just keep on keeping on. Because in the final analysis, if you love strong enough, you win.'"

When the album, called *Power of Love*, was released, the title track got instant praise. "Vandross has never sounded better than on the 'Power of Love/Love Power' medley," chimed one reviewer.

Radio programmers were also enamored with the song. Pop stations added it to their play lists because of the success they had with Luther's "Here and Now."

"We had no more proving to do with the pop marketplace," said a Sony executive. "It's an acknowledgment of him as an artist that between adult contemporary, pop, and urban radio, we have over three hundred stations playing his record now."

Things were going perfectly. MTV, which had never been supportive, was even showing the song's rousing video, featuring Luther surrounded by a wailing gospel choir.

In order to ensure that the song reached the top of the pop charts, Sony hired an independent promotion firm to get the song more radio spins. All of these efforts worked beautifully. On June 22, 1991, "Power of Love/Love Power" entered the pop Top 10, only the second single in Luther's decade-long career to do so, following the earlier success of "Here and Now." It started at number seven, and by the next week had bolted to number four. The only songs keeping it from the top spot were "Unbelievable" by the British electronic rock outfit EMF at number three, "I Wanna Sex You Up" by the pop/R&B foursome Color Me Badd at number two, and the charming ballad "Rush Rush" by chirpy, former choreographer Paula Abdul at number one.

The following week, Luther held at number four. A rise to the top was still within his reach. However, seven days later he fell to number five. The week after that, he dropped out of the Top 10.

The anger Luther felt was profound. After a tense meeting with his management, Luther told a reporter that he had just done his best "Darth Vader imitation." He simply couldn't understand what went wrong: "I make the best pizza in town. Why does the delivery truck keep getting flat tires?"

Luther filed suit against Sony to be released from his contract.

"This case is not about money," said Luther's lawyer. "It's about artistic freedom. It's about Luther's career. He feels that Sony has pigeonholed him and . . . not done all it could to expand his audience."

Sony contested these claims. "Mr. Vandross is seeking to end his relationship with the company, betraying the spirit and good faith of his contract and leaving Sony Music no choice but to enforce its legal rights," said a label representative.

It was a hard time, but there were some things making Luther smile. His sister Ann, a sometimes actor, was racking up raves for her portrayal of an abused wife in young director Matty Rich's biting, low-budget drama about hard life in the projects, *Straight Out of Brooklyn*. The *Washington Post* called her performance "particularly fine," and the *Hartford Courant* wrote that she brought "warm, all-sacrificing nobility" to her role. The whole family, including mother Mary Ida, sister Patricia, and little brother "Ronnie," was proud.

Also making Luther happy was that he had shed more than one hundred pounds, dropping to a thirty-four-inch waist, and in February 1992, he picked up another Grammy—this time for "Power of Love/Love Power." When accepting the award, he walked onstage and said, "I'd like to thank my diet doctor."

Perhaps fearing the loss of one of its key artists, Sony chose to settle with Luther. There were rumors that other record companies were basically willing to offer Luther a blank check if he joined their roster. After all, he had eight albums in a row that, while not producing many pop hits, each sold more than a million copies. The only other male artists to do that were white rockers Bruce Springsteen, Neil Diamond, and Billy Joel.

As part of the new agreement, Sony gave Luther his own imprint, LV Records, and committed to increasing its promotion efforts like never before. In 1993, Luther completed a new album, *Never Let Me Go*, and to herald its release Sony placed six-by-fourteen-foot murals of the album cover in the country's fifty largest malls. They also developed large three-dimensional panoramas to put up in music shops.

With all of this promotion, the success of *Never Let Me Go* seemed assured. But there was another problem this time: the music. Critics panned the album, which stuck perhaps too close to the model of his past efforts. One writer charged that Luther "has turned out almost the same album eight times before." Another wrote: "It's almost as though someone stole the soul."

Listeners seemed to agree. The devotion of Luther's faithfuls ensured that the album sold at least one million copies, but not one song from it even reached the pop Top 40.

Still, Luther believed in the album and went on tour to support it. Around the same time, a concert promoter approached him with what he thought was a grand idea for a tour package, pairing Luther with that hot new girl group En Vogue, which was all over the radio. With their hip-hop beats and high-fashion image, they would bring a certain edge to the tour.

The reality was that Luther had been touring regularly for over ten years now. Although he always pulled a crowd, it wouldn't hurt to add something a little different this time around. Luther agreed, reluctantly. He wasn't convinced that his mature audience would enjoy the women who were calling themselves "the funky divas," but he went along with it under certain conditions.

He invited the four members of the group over to his palatial L.A. home to discuss the terms. They would be paid $55,000 each performance, but they had to agree not to do anything that would lessen the effect of Luther's own show. This included not wearing the colors blue or red as well as any clothing that was mirrored or sequined.

"It was in their contract that they couldn't wear certain colors and outfits," Luther explained, "because that would diffuse the impact of what my backup singers wore. After all, those [colorful, beaded] gowns that Lisa and Ava wear onstage cost me $20,000 each, and they have several of them. And since they were designed to get maximum response from the audience, I don't think it was unreasonable to ask En Vogue not to wear the same colors or styles we did. Look, people who buy tickets to my show expect to see and hear something new and different every time. Impressing them with the fabulous clothes my singers wear is almost as important as the performance itself."

The four women of En Vogue listened and accepted these provisions. They had to. What most people didn't know, and what their glamorous image belied, was that they were broke and desperately needed money.

En Vogue started in 1988 in Oakland, California, as the vision of two music producers, Denzil Foster and Thomas McElroy. The two held auditions for singers to make up a girl group that could combine old school Supremes-like glamour with an ear-to-the-street hip-hop vibe. The women who made the cut each came with a distinct and identifiable image and attitude. There was beauty queen Cindy Herron, a onetime Miss Black California; Dawn Robinson, the rock-loving hippie chick; Maxine Jones, a miniature Earth momma; and the endearingly unpretentious Southern gal, Terry Ellis. This prefab foursome shouldn't have worked, but somehow the singers' gutsy vocals and slick image connected with listeners. Soon they were seen as more than just musical paper dolls.

"We were created with someone else's dream in mind," Dawn once explained. "We were forced into a situation, and we made it work."

The only problem was that as they sold millions of records because of songs like the thumping "Hold On" and "My Lovin' (You're Never Gonna Get It)," almost all the money was going back to their producers. The four singers made almost nothing from record sales, so touring meant survival.

Rehearsals for the tour began in late August at the Target Center in downtown Minneapolis. (Artists often choose venues far from the hotbeds of New York or L.A. to rehearse and try out their new shows.) Workers tooled with Luther's glitzy Art Deco set and twirling circular stage literally around the clock. Luther inspected every detail of the production, which cost more than one million dollars to mount.

"There is not a single staircase on that stage that has not been approved by me," Luther said. "Not a single step. If a drawing shows eleven steps and I have agreed to eleven and there are twelve or ten, they are rebuilding."

The wardrobe bill alone came to nearly $200,000 because Luther had multicolored glass-beaded suits made for him in various sizes to fit his fluctuating weight.

While the construction workers and technicians labored on the stage, Luther, Kevin, Ava, and Lisa practiced a series of elaborate dance steps that would allow them to make full use of the round stage. During the last seventy-two hours of rehearsal, Luther's group and En Vogue ran through the entire show twice a day.

After the Anita Baker fiasco, Luther's people were pleased that he seemed to be getting along with the four young women of En Vogue. There had only been one disagreement thus far, and it was relatively minor. Luther had asked them to appear on the *Arsenio Hall Show* to spread the word about the tour. But they refused, saying that they were becoming overexposed. According to En Vogue Luther said he understood.

The situation certainly didn't affect the show, which was starting to look good. Ticket sales were strong, and it seemed the tour would be a big hit. Personally, however, it came at a bad time for Luther. He was dealing with the flop album and he had regained all the weight he lost the previous year.

Again, he blamed it on bad love, but he offered no details on who his relationship had been with. There were no pictures, no trail of juicy newspaper gossip items, and no scorned lovers threatening to "tell all." It was all very quiet, very cloaked, very typically Luther.

"I've just been through a devastating breakup," Luther explained, still secretive about the details of his private life. "Aretha says she sings better when she's sad, but that's not the case for me. I think I sing best when I'm happy, or at least I feel best about it."

Then, during the first days of the tour, tragedy struck. Luther's beloved sister Patricia, who had just turned fifty, died of complications from diabetes. She was the one who used to harmonize so sweetly with her doo-wop group the Crests as her little brother "Ronnie" watched on. She was the one who bought him 45's when his allowance ran thin and sometimes, when their momma wasn't home, had to tell him to get out from underneath those stereo headphones and do his homework.

At Larry Salvemini's funeral, one of the lowest points of Luther's life, Patricia and his other sister Ann were by his side supporting him as he had to face the Salvemini family, sit among them, and grieve with them. Luther and his two sisters were like a three-person team, sharing bad times and good ones. They all had so much fun enjoying Luther's blessed fortune, as they clowned around on the set of his video or broke bread with legends like Gladys Knight. It sometimes seemed like this astonishing ride would never stop. Now, however, the joyful trio had become a sad party of two.

Luther felt for his mother during this time. Once again, he saw life bring the wrenching pain of loss to her soft brown face. The first time he watched her mourn was when his father, her beloved husband, slipped away so suddenly. Then, just a year before Patricia's death, Luther's brother, Charles, died at age forty-two, also from diabetes.

Many people didn't even know this had happened because Luther seldom spoke of Charles. As a child his brother would be outside playing football while Luther was in the house watching TV and listening to Dionne Warwick. Nevertheless, the loss must have exacted a toll. He could see how painful it was for his mother to say good-bye to her oldest son. He could feel the foundations of his family slowly crumbling away.

After Patricia's death, it was clear that diabetes was like a storm cloud shadowing those he loved. The disease had now taken his father, his brother, and his sister. This tragic chain of circumstances had to make him consider his own life and mortality, had to make him wonder if some force was numbering his days.

Sadly, there wasn't much time for quiet or contemplation following Patricia's death. Luther needed to get right back onstage. Tickets had already been sold for the tour, and the livelihoods of dozens of people solely depended on him. It was moments like this when he grasped the bittersweet totality of what it meant to be a star.

He performed at the Target Center two days after his sister's death, and then flew to the funeral at 6:00 A.M. the next morning. He came back to the tour without ever missing a show.

For most of this time, work was Luther's life and he gave himself over to it fully. That's what made it especially frustrating when more things started to go wrong on the tour. Reviews came in and they weren't always pleasing. Often, they focused on Luther's size. In Houston, a writer opened his critique with: "There's no point in beating around the bush. The first thing you noticed when Luther Vandross took the stage Wednesday at The Summit was that he's put on weight again."

Most of the worst comments, however, targeted En Vogue. In Minneapolis, they were called "a major disappointment," and in Milwaukee, the videogenic quartet was said to come off "smaller than life." A journalist for USA Today wrote: "The carefully scripted show seemed cold and impersonal. Even their stage patter sounded rehearsed. . . . You get the feeling En Vogue wouldn't drink unless it was scripted in." He added: "It didn't help that they shared the stage with a seven-piece band, greatly reducing the quartet's visibility. (Vandross smartly kept his musicians offstage.)"

These comments incensed the group, who took their concerns to Luther. They complained that they weren't able to wear their best, sexiest outfits because of the contract restrictions. Then they balked at having their band onstage with them. Luther, however, maintained that their band needed to be set up onstage to ease the transition between the two acts. That way, during En Vogue's set, his musicians could be getting ready offstage.

As the conversation concluded, Luther confronted them once again about not doing *Arsenio*.

"Why do you keep bringing this up," En Vogue's Dawn asked him.

"I have the right, as a forty-two-year-old man, to bring this up," Luther responded, officially starting what became a full-out war. Behind Luther's back, En Vogue called him "Lucifer."

Soon, as on the tour with Anita, roadies draped curtains backstage so that Luther would never have to see En Vogue. This was a momentary solution, until En Vogue did something that made Luther, in the words of his spokesman, "hit the wall." They decided to remove their band from the stage without telling him and instead chose to sing along to prerecorded backing tapes. This went against everything Luther felt his shows and musicianship represented.

"He wants his fans to be entertained by live singers," his spokesman detailed, "not by singers singing to a tape. He [does] not want a reoccurrence of a Milli Vanilli type of [thing]."

The next month of the tour brought changes for both of the touring—and warring—parties. En Vogue's Cindy privately married her fiancé, baseball player Glenn Bragg. She also discovered she was pregnant.

In Luther's camp, his longtime manager Billy Bass abruptly

quit. "Luther's a great artist," he explained at the time. "No question he's the Frank Sinatra of our time. But I've been with him three years, and frankly the road isn't the fun it used to be. I'm fifty-two."

Later, he elaborated. Luther, he said, "is a very successful guy in his professional life, but a guy who's often very unhappy off the stage. And when Luther is miserable, he tends to make the lives of those around him miserable."

Bass didn't offer more details, but really none were needed at this point. After spats with Aretha and Anita, as well as difficulties with people like sound engineer Michael Brauer and the late drummer Yogi Horton, Luther's reputation for sometimes being difficult was a well-established fact. His testiness, if in the wrong mood, was as much a part of him as his soothing voice.

Luther seemed to be in an especially bad mood when the tour arrived in Miami in early November. Upon reaching a backstage doorknob, he refused to touch it until an assistant wiped it off for him. Shortly thereafter, he saw that a member of En Vogue had wandered over to his side of the drawn curtain. His temper hit full-tilt, and he called the Miami police to demand that the group be charged with trespassing.

A few days later, En Vogue left the tour, giving Cindy's pregnancy as their official reason for dropping out. "We feel sorry for him," Cindy said. "This reflects an unhappy person."

Luther replaced the group with smooth R&B singer Oleta Adams, but that didn't end the feud. It was inflamed again when Luther saw the cover of the April 1994 *VIBE* magazine, which pictured Dawn, Maxine, Terry, and a very-pregnant Cindy, and read: "En Vogue Delivers: The Funky Four (Soon to Be Five) Talk About Fame, Fashion, and the Biggest Diva of All, Luther Vandross."

Inside, the group commiserated about their time touring with the singer.

"Luther was nasty," Cindy said. "That's just the kind of person he is. It was so intense, but as a Christian I had to try to understand that we're all people, and we have our own lives, and things that have affected us and our weaknesses."

Luther called them "spoiled, non-truth-telling contract breakers," and said that the whole experience made him appreciate Anita Baker more: "She's above taking the tabloid route that En Vogue did because Anita is a real woman, a genuine diva."

After the nightmarish experience of this tour—with the fights with En Vogue, the departure of his manager, and the sad death of his sister—Luther turned his attention to trying to revive his recording career, which was dragging due to the ho-hum response to *Never Let Me Go.* Luther increasingly felt angry, offended even, that his label couldn't firmly establish him as a pop artist. To him, they acted like he should be satisfied with whatever success he had.

"It's a racist perspective," he said. "You're talking to the person who sang for Juicy Fruit, Pepsi, and 7-Up. Suddenly I get to Sony and I'm [only] an R&B singer."

He called up Tommy Mottola, who had recently become both head of Sony Music and husband to its biggest rising star, Mariah Carey. The newly ensconced president could tell Luther was agitated.

"What's the matter," he asked.

"What's the matter," Luther responded, "is that a lot has not been accomplished here. I've had nine platinum [more than one million sold] albums in a row. I sell out arenas. But I have not had a number-one single yet. There's no reason that shouldn't happen. . . . I want a number-one just like Lionel Richie and Natalie Cole and Whitney Houston and all of my friends who come to my house. I don't think that's unreasonable. I think my record company should know this is something I aspire to. . . . The missing link is the performance of the company to get that for me."

Some executives would have been thrown by such demands, but Mottola had a plan. He wanted to pair Luther with producer Walter Afanasieff, who had overseen Mariah's stream of number-ones, and let them do an album of covers, focusing on easily recognizable songs that the mainstream public was familiar with.

"You do what I say," Mottola assured Luther, "and I guarantee I will get you what you want."

The plan intrigued Luther. He had never let anyone else produce one of his albums before. In fact, it was even something he fiercely fought against. It was the stipulation that kept him waiting so long for a record deal in the first place. Yet he couldn't deny that Mottola's idea sounded appealing. Mottola had a well-established reputation for making things happen. He had helped turn Mariah from a background singer to a multimillion-selling international mega-force in just a few short years. Luther decided to go along with the plan.

They immediately got to work selecting songs. There were so many choices. The initial list included nearly twelve hundred songs, but they slowly narrowed it down. Many of the selections were songs made famous by Luther's teenage favorites: the Supremes' "Reflections," the Temptations' "The Impossible Dream," Dionne Warwick's "What the World Needs Now Is Love," and Aretha Franklin's "Since You've Been Gone."

Other cuts were by people he had worked with in the past. He did Barbra Streisand's sentimental "Evergreen." (She later sent him a note saying she loved the way he sang it.) He also recorded Roberta Flack's melancholy "Killing Me Softly." This song was special, because it was what he was singing when she watched him onstage all those years ago in Merrillville, Indiana. It was that performance that inspired her to forcibly nudge him to pursue a solo career. Luther might not have been in the position to be selecting songs if it weren't for that number.

He decided to be faithful to the original and rendered the lyrics as they were written, directed to a guitar-playing male singer.

"It would have been stupid to do a gender change of the lyrics," Luther explained. "Anyone who would do this clearly does not understand what the lyrics are about. The song is about being affected by someone's performance." (Still, once the song was released, people made jokes about it. One Atlanta radio DJ got in trouble for suggesting Luther was serenading up-and-coming hip-hop/R&B singer R. Kelly.)

One song he really wanted to do was the classic Philly Soul slow jam "Love Don't Love Nobody" by the Spinners. Luther loved that record, how tender and vulnerably lead vocalist Phillipe Wynne had sung the lyrics. Wynne had died several years earlier at an Oakland, California, nightclub while performing that very song. He was in the middle of his third encore of the night when he clutched his chest and slowly crumbled to the floor. By the time he reached a nearby hospital, there was nothing doctors could do. Wynne was dead at age forty-three.

Luther was halfway through recording his version when he abruptly stopped. "I don't want to do it," he told the producer. "I don't want to hear myself or anybody else do it. I want to remember Philippe Wynne singing this song."

Throughout the recording process, Mottola and producer Afanasieff constantly tried to think of different songs that Luther could do. This occurred whenever they heard a song playing from a radio, over a store's P.A. system, or even in an elevator. Afanasieff insisted that they do a gospel-styled update of folk-rocker Stephen Sills' "Love the One You're With." Luther consented even though he thought the song offered "questionable advice."

Mottola's wife and Afanasieff's frequent collaborator Mariah would also get in on the act. One day, she thought of the Lionel

Richie/Diana Ross showpiece "Endless Love," which stayed at number-one on the pop charts for nine weeks in 1981. It also picked up a Grammy for best collaboration. This felt like an ideal selection.

"Oh, and I can sing it with him," Mariah said.

This made the idea seem even more special. While Mariah was then largely known as a sugary Top 40 princess, her R&B roots went deep. She had always loved Luther's music.

"Luther, to me," Mariah said, "is one of the best male vocalists in the world."

Luther also admired Mariah.

"She has one of the greatest voices on the planet," he offered. "So when we went into the studio, the chemistry between us was almost perfect. Our voices blended so well that the song instantly took on a life of its own."

The results pleased everyone, and it was decided that the duet would be the lead single for the new album, now called *Songs*. The label planned to go all out to promote it.

During the months Luther spent in the studio, he was also losing weight again. This time his diet plan consisted of mostly juices and small food portions five days a week, but on weekends he could indulge, stopping by his favorite restaurant, Roscoe's House of Chicken and Waffles, whenever he was at home in L.A.

"By Saturday, after not having my Roscoe's fix all week, I'm not someone you'd want to be around," Luther joked. "When I'm finally on my way there, get out of my way because I'll knock you down to get in there."

Since he was thin again, Sony chose to make the promotional campaign very visual, running ads and putting up posters that showed full-body shots of Luther looking dapper in suits, trench coats, open-collared shirts, and a fedora. Many of the photos were glossy or sepia-tinted, making Luther look like a classic crooner of yore, someone who could go head-to-head against Frank Sinatra, Nat King Cole, and Johnny Mathis combined.

The label also arranged for Luther to record his first television special to launch the project. They taped it for PBS at London's Royal Albert Hall. Mariah came by to sing "Endless Love," and Luther went through extreme lengths to ensure that one of his favorite background singers, Lisa Fischer, would take part in this special event. She was then on tour with the Rolling Stones and, for a time, it seemed like she would be stuck in the United States. She had a concert in Chicago the night before Luther's show, and she had to be in Denver three days later. Luther, however, chartered a private plane to whisk her from Chicago to London and then back to Denver at a cost of $60,000. He also paid her a full week's salary.

In early September 1994, "Endless Love" went to radio stations, and its success was immediate. Pop radio loved the song. It was a pretty ballad, and it featured current darling Mariah, who had notched eight number-one hits in her four-year career. *Billboard* magazine wrote: "Button-pushing as it can be, the single is destined to rocket to the top of the Hot 100. Any bets on how many weeks it will take?"

Finally, Luther thought, he would have a number-one pop record like all his friends and peers. He would be a member of that club.

"I feel it in my bones," he said. "This is gonna be the Big One."

The song rocketed into the pop Top 10, entering at number six just two weeks after its release. This marked an astounding climb. The next week, it vaulted to number three, then two, with the only song ahead of it being "I'll Make Love to You" by the hip-hop/doo-wop quartet Boyz II Men. A space at the top spot seemed certain.

One week later, however, "Endless Love" unexpectedly slipped back to number three. Rocker Sheryl Crow's catchy "All I Wanna

Do" bumped ahead of it. "Endless Love" held just two spaces from Luther's much-desired apex for three more weeks. Then it fell to nine, and two weeks later, it was out of the Top 10.

Making matters worse, *Songs* was panned by critics who accused Luther of watering down his sound to appease the pop market. They felt that on his previous albums, Luther dramatically reinterpreted classic tunes, where on this album, he blandly kept as close to the originals as possible.

Geoffrey Hines of the *Washington Post* wrote: "Even if one ignores the complicated racial politics of black singers trying to accommodate white audiences, knotty artistic questions remain. The move from R&B . . . to mainstream pop inevitably involves a softening of both rhythms and attitudes. Not only do the beats become more regular and restrained, but the stories grow more sentimental. On his best recordings, Vandross creates a crackling tension between his romantic yearnings and nagging reality, but on these pandering pop fantasies the tether to reality is often cut loose and the music drifts off into meaninglessness."

Mario Tarradell put it more simply in the *Dallas Morning News*: "Will Luther Vandross, once renowned for spreading his creamy tenor all over soulful love songs, ever return to the stirring romanticism that made his first three albums—*Never Too Much*; *Forever, For Always, For Love*; and *Busy Body*—soundtracks for nights of dinner, dancing and . . . well, you get the idea?"

Songs still sold more than one million copies, like all of Luther's other albums, but few of his longtime fans seemed to like it very much. The lackluster response to the project even impacted Luther where he'd always been invulnerable: touring.

Sales were so bad for an Atlanta show the following summer that promoters gave away five thousand tickets just days before the concert. Other dates in Cincinnati, Ohio; Hampton, Virginia; and Devore, California, were canceled outright.

Crowds weren't the only things missing on the *Songs* tour. Ava and Lisa, after more than a decade on the road with Luther, had left to chase after some of their own dreams. Ava signed a new solo deal, and Lisa was increasingly in heated demand. Not only had she scored a Grammy-winning solo hit with the blistering ballad "How Can I Ease the Pain," but she also made big money on tour with the Rolling Stones, where she'd pile her hair high, squeeze into some hot pants, and go note for note with the group's lead singer, Mick Jagger.

It was the end of an age. "It's a well-known fact, no women in show business were as well-dressed as Luther's girls, Lisa and Ava," the singer reminisced. "Now that Lisa is making her own album and pursuing her own career and Ava is doing the same, it sort of brings to a really nice close that chapter of my presentation."

By the fall of 1995, there had been so many unfortunate developments in Luther's life. He had lost hold of his recording career, the thing he had fought so hard to establish. He had let someone else produce his album, something he had never before wanted to do. He thought it would reap him greater rewards, but it added nothing to his sales and ended up alienating longtime fans.

Later, Luther distanced himself from the *Songs* project.

"[The idea] came from the record company," Luther said. "I did it to keep the peace and as an experiment. I have no complaints about it. I have been doing cover songs all along. On each album, I do one. I thought the *Songs* album was a little bit more standard."

After that, Luther felt more than ever that he needed to reconnect with core fans. He released a wonderfully fun and moving holiday album, *This Is Christmas,* at the end of 1995, and the next year he returned with another set, *Your Secret Love*. He called this one "a return home"—"a real Luther album."

The sound of *Your Secret Love* was smooth and familiar. The title track sported a sensuous, polished groove like many of Luther's early hits, and Luther covered two songs: Stevie Wonder's "Knocks Me Off My Feet" and Little Anthony and the Imperials' "Goin' Out of My Head." However, unlike the conservatively arranged cuts on *Songs,* these numbers marked a return to Luther's flourishing reinterpretations.

One of the more touching moments on the album was a duet with Lisa Fischer, "Whether or Not the World Gets Better." This was the special ballad that Luther had written for Jimmy Salvemini and recorded with Phoebe Snow exactly ten years earlier. It came off like a tribute of sorts, a way to transcend all the pain that had been caused and endured since that time. Luther even kept much of the song's original backing music intact, including the drums performed by the late Yogi Horton.

The album's title track made it into the Top 10 of the R&B charts, but at this point the sound of black radio was rapidly changing. It was becoming dominated by rap and R&B laced with booming hip-hop beats. The cool, never-break-a-sweat vibe of folks like Luther and Anita Baker seemed more dated every day. In an *Entertainment Weekly* review, critic David Browne wrote: "Unrequited passion will always be in style, but Vandross needs to seduce some new sounds as desperately as he does the partners in his songs."

Unintentionally, the album's title also stoked old rumors about Luther's carefully cloaked sexuality. Gossip columnist Michael Musto of the *Villlage Voice* quipped: "Shouldn't it be *My* Secret Love."

Still, through all the changes in music and the critic-thrown darts, Luther could always be assured of one thing. Each of his solo records had sold more than one million copies and *Your Secret Love* kept up the winning streak.

After the release of this album, Luther spent some time away from the business. For Christmas of 1996, he flew his whole family, including his mother and sister Ann as well as his many nieces and nephews, to Los Angles to celebrate. They were happy to be with "Ronnie," and he affectionately joked that the whole gang was like the Beverly Hillbillies.

The death of his father, brother, and sister had kept him constantly aware that time was always a precious commodity when it came to loved ones. He knew no one was promised tomorrow.

Early the next year, he relocated to the East Coast. The January 1994 earthquake near Los Angeles, which killed fifty-seven people and seriously injuring fifteen hundred, had scared him from California. The day after the disaster he put his lavish mansion up for sale.

"If the [real estate] office had been open at five-thirty in the morning when it happened, I would have sold it then," Luther said.

He took a huge loss on the house, selling it for a paltry $3 million, when he had bought it for $6 million and later added $2.5 million in renovations. Yet, money aside, he was simply ready for a change.

He settled in Greenwich, Connecticut, about thirty miles from New York City. The new house sat on thirteen acres with an outdoor swimming pool and tennis court. The grand estate measured 19,659 square feet, with four stories and a six-car garage. It came with twenty-five rooms, including nine bedrooms and a surprising eleven bathrooms. There was also a nearby guesthouse on the grounds.

Luther paid $8.5 million for the place. He made a $4.7 million cash down payment and financed the rest.

Even though Luther's records and tours weren't as successful as they had been, he still raked in a lot of money. Since he wrote the bulk of the songs on most of his albums, his publishing checks for songwriting were huge. A few years earlier, he had been listed as one of the Top 20 wealthiest African-Americans with an estimated net worth of $12 million.

After purchasing the house, Luther got around to one of his favorite pastimes: decorating. He wanted this new pad to be just as lavish as his Beverly Hills home. In the entrance foyer, he placed a table made from imported Lalique crystal. The living room had chairs covered in Scalamandre silk and tables adorned with Tiffany lamps. In the family room, he dug out the fireplace and installed an inset television.

The thing that got every visitor talking, however, was one room where the walls were covered in cashmere. Once, Oprah stopped over for a cookout where Luther served coconut shrimp and peach cobbler, and she joked that you could take the cashmere off the walls and make yourself a nice dress.

When he wasn't testing out fabrics and different furniture pieces, Luther indulged in some of his favorite pastimes.

"My idea of a perfect, relaxing day is to wake up, watch *Leeza* then *The Price Is Right*, the midday news, *Oprah* of course, then both shows of *Married with Children, Martin,* and whatever else comes on," he admitted. "Sometimes, I need the mindless entertainment."

Publicly, Luther declared himself ready for a fulfilling relationship. He was eager to embrace the long-awaited love of his life. As usual, he didn't discuss it with any specificity. "I'm in the perfect place to find happiness," he said. "I'm ready. When you're in love, there is nothing to cope with—like feelings of loneliness and isolation. And somehow the food is no longer as important. Besides," he added, "I'm drug-free, rich, and fabulous."

Other than his lingering loneliness, the only other major problem in his life involved the continued struggles with his record label, Sony. After twelve albums, his contract with the company was nearly complete. He only had to deliver a couple of songs that could be used on a new greatest hits album. At this point, Luther was tired of fighting over who should write and produce the cuts. Sony, in his opinion, had never liked the tunes he wrote. Label executives said that he had never given them a song that could go to number one on the pop charts. They maintained that so much of his music sounded the same. Luther was ready to cry uncle.

He told label executives, "OK, fine, show me the songs I should've been recording all along. Show me where I was deficient in my whole career."

For one of the new cuts, they put Luther with one of the hottest new acts around, the man who was singularly refashioning contemporary R&B, R. Kelly. What was so awesome about R. Kelly's talents was that his songs had such breadth and range. He could do a tawdry sex-you-up romp like his smash "Bump and Grind," then switch up and deliver an uplifting gospel-inspired anthem like "I Believe I Can Fly." A song he did for Michael Jackson, "You Are Not Alone," topped both the pop and R&B charts. Kelly seemed like the perfect person to help freshen Luther's sound.

Luther met R. Kelly on the night of the recording session. Kelly hadn't sent Luther a tape of the song before then. He wanted Luther to learn it fresh in the studio. He played the song titled "When You Call on Me (Baby That's When I Come Runnin')," once for Luther, who thought, "Hmmm, that has a pretty melody."

Then Luther said, "Let's go. Point me to the mic."

The song turned out beautifully. Not only was it one of Luther's most evocative performances, some of the lyrics also encapsulated what had been one of Luther's strongest appeals over the years.

"It doesn't take much for me to know when a woman's lonely," Luther sang, "especially when I'm all alone myself."

Though it was an artistic triumph, the tune failed to even break the R&B Top 30. Luther left his record label of more than ten years on a downbeat note rather than a high. Now it truly was the end of an era.

He didn't spend much time thinking about his years at Sony, however. He had soon moved on to a new label, Virgin Records, home to the Rolling Stones, the Spice Girls, David Bowie, George Michael, and Janet Jackson, with whom Luther once recorded the duet "The Best Things in Life Are Free" for the soundtrack to the movie *Mo' Money*. Luther liked the way the careers of these acts had been handled so he was pleased to be there.

Virgin offered him complete creative freedom, and Luther felt relieved that his artistic instincts were being trusted again, that he didn't have to fight anymore.

"I am thrilled to have an association with Virgin Records, a company which I have long admired," Luther stated. "Their track record both internationally and domestically excites me and fills me with passion. They love their artists and that's that! I'm glad to be a part of their family."

He also reiterated his primary career goals: "I see my peers—Whitney [Houston], Mariah [Carey], Richard Marx, and they've all had number-one records and I want one, too. It's that simple," Luther said. "My eyes are really wide open now for my career proceeding. What I have to do is make the music I have faith in, and after that, someone has to serve as the carrier of that music to the most people who potentially will hear it."

Luther titled his first Virgin album *I Know*. It contained the most diverse blend of music that he had made in years. He seemed to be trying to please all the different types of listeners he had picked up throughout his career. It featured everything from a faithful cover of Leo Sayer's adult contemporary staple "When I

Need You" to a soaring dance track, "Are You Using Me," produced with the underground club gurus Masters at Work. This marked a glorious return to the dance floor.

He explained: "I started out, you know, [with] 'Never Too Much' and 'Glow of Love' and 'Searching'—all big club hits at the time. And I really enjoyed that."

He invited Stevie Wonder and acclaimed jazz singer Cassandra Wilson to guest on a couple of tracks, and for the first single, "Nights in Harlem," he revisited his youthful days hanging out near the Apollo.

"I wanted to write about that in a celebratory way," Luther said, "and state what it was like when I grew up."

I Know hit stores in July 1998, and shortly after its release, Luther suspected that something was wrong with the way it was being promoted. He'd be in airports or walking down the street when people would come up to him and say, "Hey, Luther, when are you gonna put a new album out?"

By November, *I Know* had only sold a couple hundred thousand copies, becoming Luther's least successful album in the history of his career. It broke his record of having consistent million-sellers. He was devastated. This was supposed to have been a new beginning, after leaving Sony, but now he had dipped to an unprecedented career low.

He responded to this disappointment the same way he had dealt with troubles ever since he was a teen. He felt that eating was the only thing that could soothe his pain. He knew he shouldn't. He was well aware that as he got older carrying such excess weight became more and more dangerous. Most perilously, it inflamed his diabetes, the condition that had already taken his father, brother, and sister. Yet Luther couldn't stop himself.

"On a rational level it should have been scary," Luther later explained, "and it should have been enough to deter me from doing the things I was doing, but the food had its clutches on me strong enough that it . . . it sort of demanded that I ignore reason."

That Thanksgiving he ate "enough for a family of six." The food didn't make him feel better, though. If anything, he felt worse than ever. "I was just disgusted with my lack of self-control," he recalled. "So, I said, 'That's it.' That was my last hurrah."

"I'm Only Human"

> *"Luther Vandross the artist was well nurtured, well fed, [but] Luther the person was dehydrated and suffering from drought."*
>
> —LUTHER, AFTER THE FLOP OF
> HIS 1998 ALBUM *I KNOW*

After things went wrong for Luther at Virgin Records, he and the label mutually agreed to split. It was his first time without a record deal in nearly twenty years, but Luther was happy about it. He needed a break, time to focus on his life, something he had been neglecting in his fierce pursuit of awards and chart-topping hits.

One of the first things he did was start spending more time with his family. He recognized the need for this when he was over at his sister Ann's house and one of his grandnephews pointed at him and said, "Isn't that Luther Vandross."

"That is it," Luther said. "I am taking time off. I won't have that. I'm Uncle Ronnie."

Luther also recommitted himself to losing weight after his Thanksgiving 1998 eating binge. He was determined to get control of his overeating. He also knew that he couldn't continue abusing his body this way. His blood pressure was high again, causing such extreme headaches that he downed aspirin until he was sick to his stomach. Physicians were warning him about the severity of his diabetes.

"One of my doctors said my sugar reading, my diabetic reading was higher than anyone he's ever treated," Luther remembered. "I was on the exit ramp."

This time, instead of initially depriving his body of food, he tried to first change his eating habits, drastically reducing the carbohydrates he consumed. He would go to Kentucky Fried Chicken twice a day and each time order a whole roasted chicken and a diet Pepsi. He did this for weeks until he no longer craved the carbohydrates.

He then slowly began to modify his eating plan, lessening his portions, removing the chicken's skin, and adding vegetables to his diet. By early 1999, he could feel his pants loosening around the waistline. The diet was working.

A short time later, a personal tragedy tested Luther's resolve to keep his emotions from impacting his weight. His sister Ann, the one who made such a memorable showing in the film *Straight Out of Brooklyn,* died from an asthma attack. She was fifty-two. The mixture of sadness, loss, and grief hit Luther and his mother like the blunt end of a gun. It had all become too painfully familiar: the funeral arrangements, the saying good-bye, and the lingering trail of melancholy memories, questions, and fears.

The already tight bond between Luther and his mother became stronger. He was now her last remaining child. He felt for her, watching each of her loved ones being slowly pulled away, but he felt helpless to ease her pain.

The course of Luther's mourning surprised him. He found himself growing distant from his sisters' daughters, the very ones he wanted to reach out to. "There was a little while, a little window of time there, when I couldn't look at my nieces," Luther recalled.

"They had grown up. They were women now, and they looked just like my sisters."

His nieces would call him up and ask, "Uncle Ronnie, when you gonna come and visit us?" He'd make up excuses saying, "Oh, you know, I'm gonna come soon. I'm on the road." He wanted to be there for them, but he didn't have the strength after all he had lost. "I just couldn't see them," he remembered. "I just couldn't."

However, as weeks passed, Luther felt that he could no longer be apart from these young women who had lost their mothers. He forced himself to be a part of their lives. He tapped into the same determination that enabled him to continue touring after his sister Patricia died. "It's just something you have to get through," Luther observed. "I can't be absent from their lives. I have to be there for them."

In these emotionally trying days, it would have been easy for Luther to slip back into his old habits, eating until the pain subsided. Luther, however, stuck to his diet plan. He had made a promise to himself.

"If there was any time I might have fallen off the wagon [it was then]," Luther explained after Ann's death. "But what would that solve? None of that was going to bring anything back to the way it was."

Luther became ever more committed to losing weight and improving his health. It was his first thought when he opened his eyes each morning. Instead of whole roasted chickens from KFC, he used a George Foreman grill to cook chicken breasts and fish for dinner. He stocked his refrigerator with V8, turkey burgers, diet sodas, and frozen fish fillets. He nixed such snacks as Peanut Butter Cap'n Crunch, which he once likened to a "religious experience," and replaced them with dried, air-popped "Just Blueberries" that came in eighty-calorie bags.

When he toured, he brought along two George Foreman grills

and cooked his own food, mostly Chilean sea bass, salmon, or swordfish. His favorite on-the-road snacks were sugar-free Popsicles.

These frozen treats caused a minor crisis during a Boston tour stop when caterer Al Brown couldn't locate them at any of the local grocery stores. Brown reported this news to Luther's road manager, who promptly freaked out. Luther had once fired someone for failing to find these Popsicles.

"Oh, no, Al," the road manager told the caterer. "You have to find these Popsicles."

"We looked all over the city and could not find them," Brown replied.

"All right, then you tell Luther," he said.

When Luther got offstage that evening and returned to the backstage food area, probably looking for one of those icy treats, Brown stopped him and told him that the food staff was unable to locate the Popsicles. Luther simply said "All right" and let the matter pass.

Not wanting to press his good fortune, Brown bought fifteen boxes of the sugar-free Popsicles at the next stop so that they would never run out again.

As his weight loss became more noticeable, Luther began joking about it onstage. "I know I'm very private about my private life," he told a New York audience, "but I recently got a divorce. That's right, Mrs. Fields and I no longer see each other." Then he opened his jacket revealing his newly thin frame.

Luther largely focused on relaxing and enjoying life when he wasn't on tour. He made a lot of changes, including putting his lavish Connecticut estate on the market. He wanted to be back in Manhattan, so he rented an Upper East Side penthouse for $30,000 a month. His Connecticut home sold for $10.75 million.

With no immediate need to spend long evening hours in the

recording studio, Luther immersed himself in the city's nightlife. On April 21, 1999, he celebrated his forty-eighth birthday at the intimate Sugar Bar, owned by Ashford and Simpson. Cissy Houston, Diana Ross, Natalie Cole, Vanessa Williams, and many others attended the festive event and helped Luther eat his custom-made fat-free birthday cake.

Throughout the year, Luther seemed to pop up everywhere. Aretha Franklin played a private concert at the restaurant/ballroom Cipriani Wall Street, and Luther was in the front row. The queen sang a lyric about wanting a wedding ring, and Luther spontaneously slipped a band off of his hand, reached onstage, and placed it on her finger to the applause of the exclusive attendees. As soon as the song was over, however, Luther humorously demanded his ring back.

Two months later, Luther sat in the audience of one of Whitney Houston's sold-out Madison Square Garden shows. Whitney pulled him onstage to add some harmonies when she sang her hit "Exhale (Shoop Shoop)."

By the time Luther attended Ashford and Simpson's quarter-century wedding anniversary at Tavern on the Green in December 1999, it was clear to everyone how well his diet was working. He had lost about 140 pounds, weighing in at just under 200 pounds. The more he lost, the more comfortable he felt going out on the town having fun. He still didn't smoke or drink, but he loved taking in the energy of the city. He missed it after all those years in Los Angeles and miles away in Connecticut.

With his newly thin physique, Luther could also once again indulge his love for fashion. "I guess I like Gucci better than McDonald's now," he said to a friend. He bought things he never would've dared wear in the past, like a skintight pair of python pants, and he donated all of his extra large clothes to his mother's church.

Luther also indulged in shoes. He ordered customized footwear by the dozens from designer Warren Edwards' shop on East Sixtieth Street. His favorites, which took nearly six weeks to make and could cost as much as $3,000, were satin lace-ups accented with bits of patent leather. He was also partial to black handcrafted footgear by Italian shoemaker Silvano Lattanzi.

He felt so much freer without the excess weight. He surprised a bunch of his traveling companions when he showed up to meet them for a trip to Hawaii with his hair a shocking shade of red. He explained that, a few days earlier, he had been sitting in his hairdresser's chair, thinking, "Now, how do I show up at the airport and turn the mutha out?"

Once he returned from his Hawaiian vacation, Luther continued enjoying his new city life. He watched jugglers and stilt walkers at a March 2000 party for the boy band 'N Sync at the Laura Belle ballroom in midtown. That same month, he sauntered over to the Waldorf-Astoria hotel for a Democratic National Committee fund-raising dinner. He sang the Barbra Streisand staple "Evergreen" and received a compliment from President Bill Clinton.

"I want to thank Luther Vandross," the president said in his opening remarks. "We've never had a conversation about 'Evergreen,' but I think it's the best love song of the last twenty-five years, and so I was very happy when he sang it tonight."

The entire spring of 2000 seemed like a nonstop bash for Luther. In April, he went to the Metropolitan Pavilion to help his friend Oprah Winfrey launch her much-anticipated O magazine. Luther was among one thousand invitees, including Sean "Puffy" Combs, Diana Ross, Martha Stewart, Rosie O'Donnell, Eartha Kitt, and Ivana Trump. The ever-youthful rock-and-roll goddess Tina Turner performed for Oprah's guests and at the close of her set, she invited Luther, Oprah, Diana, and Rosie onstage to dance.

Luther was so happy, going out, hanging with his friends, and enjoying himself. There were even hints that something romantic was going on with him. Although he never discussed it, a *New York Post* gossip item from this time read: "[F]inding love at the Red Cat [restaurant] was hip crooner Luther Vandross, who canoodled at a corner table with a friend." As was typical with things involving Luther, there was no mention of whether the "friend" was male or female.

Everything was going well for Luther, until he began receiving a string of disturbing phone calls in late June. He was at home in New York, sitting on the couch watching TV when the telephone rang. He picked it up.

"Hey, baby," said the voice on the other end of the line. It was Valerie Simpson of Ashford and Simpson. "How are you doing?"

"I'm fine," Luther responded. "How are you doing?"

"I'm great," answered Valerie, then she quickly got off the phone. Usually, she and Luther tied up the lines for hours.

Shortly thereafter, Luther's Pac-Man buddy Dionne Warwick called. "How are you feeling?" she asked.

"I'm feeling fine," he said. "I'm just sitting here watching *The Price Is Right*."

"Okay, then," she said. "I'll let you go." Again, Luther and Dionne often chatted for hours. After a few more similar calls, he wondered what was up.

What Luther didn't know was that many radio stations and Internet sites were reporting that he had died of AIDS. Again, people tried to link his dramatic weight loss to the deadly disease.

His close friends felt devastated when they heard the rumors. "I was hysterical," said Cissy Houston. "I tried to get his mom on the phone to ask her, 'Where's Luther? How is he?' But I couldn't get her. I couldn't get anybody."

He finally heard about the false death reports while en route to the Essence Music Festival in New Orleans, where he was scheduled to perform. As his set began, the band played the whirling opening strains of "The Glow of Love." Luther walked onstage at the cavernous New Orleans Superdome looking splendorous in a white tuxedo with long tails. He didn't address the rumors immediately, but right before singing "If Only for One Night," he said, "It makes me feel good when I sing this song." He paused. "And I sound real good for somebody who's dead." The whole crowd cheered.

Before launching into his marital anthem "Here and Now," he joked, "I'm going to use this song in my own wedding. Since I'm not dead, I can find myself a bride."

For the most part, Luther denied he was bothered by the recurrence of these rumors. He said he mostly laughed them off. Other times, however, he'd admit to harboring anger toward those who continued to spread the lies, saying, "I pity how boring their fucking lives are."

Luther returned from New Orleans to the relatively leisured pace of his New York City life. There were dinners with friends at his favorite Italian restaurant Trattoria Dell'Arte, across from Carnegie Hall. He went to see the comedy *Scary Movie* five times and checked out the WWF at Madison Square Garden whenever his favorite wrestler Chris Jericho was there. "I saw him hit a referee with a chair," Luther gushed, "and it was like art."

When he wasn't running the streets, Luther spent many hours sitting in front of the TV. He watched the Discovery Channel when he felt like being "educated," as he put it, but for a laugh he turned on reruns of *The Jeffersons* or *Married with Children*. He played along with contestants on *Jeopardy* and *Wheel of Fortune,* and he never missed the legal drama *The Practice.*

"It's the only show that shows you that good is not always good," he said, "and evil is not always evil."

With no recording obligations on the horizon, Luther also spent more time reading. He kept up with Oprah's Book Club, especially enjoying Wally Lamb's *I Know This Much Is True* and *She's Come Undone*, about a young woman who struggles with obesity. He also made his way through a biography of one his favorite artists, Picasso, Arthur Golden's *Memoirs of a Geisha*, and the first four books chronicling the adventures of that young wizard Harry Potter. Some of his other selections suggested that Luther was still trying to make peace with the recent loss of his sister. He read Neale Donald Walsch's *Conversations with God* and John Gunther's memoir of losing his son to a brain tumor, *Death Be Not Proud*.

Luther was living the kind of life that some enjoy once they retire. He had more time for friends, family, books, dinner parties, movies, and anything else he could think of to fill the hours of the day. He had never known this kind of relaxed freedom before. Ever since he was a teenager, he'd been performing and trying to make it as a musician. However, after two years of this slowed down pace, Luther was getting a bit antsy. There were still so many things he wanted to accomplish, like getting a number-one pop record and winning more Grammys. By the end of 2000, he had made a decision. He wanted back in the game.

"Take You Out"

*"People have told me I'm not worth the time of day /
Said I was over-the-hill."*

—LUTHER, FROM "YOU STOPPED LOVING ME"

*Author's Note: In May 2001, on Mother's Day weekend, I traveled
to Kingston, Jamaica, to write an article on Luther for* VIBE *magazine.
This is what I saw.*

Luther closed his eyes, deep in concentration, as he rehearsed on
an outdoor stage. Behind him were towering green mountains
topped by plush ivory clouds. He and his small fleet of background
singers were intently practicing their exquisite harmonies for a performance later that evening. Yet standing there underneath the
aquamarine sky, they seemed to transform from professionals running through their paces to joyful children of God serenading the
heavens.

"Oooh oooh oooh . . . oooh oooh oooh," they crooned in perfect pitch. Luther was teaching them the background parts to his
new single "Take You Out." The song sounded fresh, but also like

vintage Luther. It wasn't some steamy romp but a classy invitation to a night out on the town.

"Oooh oooh oooh . . . oooh oooh oooh," repeated the background singers, all facing forward, their eyes keenly focused on Luther. "Again," he'd say, and they would run through the same sequence of notes with even more precision, moving closer to the ideal sound that Luther heard in his head. When he was finally satisfied with this part of the song, he began teaching them the chorus: "Can I take you out tonight / to a movie / to the park . . ."

They ran through the lines again and again, as Luther listened closely, his head facing downward, pushing for perfection. Finally, when he was satisfied with the way things sounded, the band kicked in and they did a full run-through of the song.

After all of that practice, the music was coming together. Even the workers setting up the chairs in the field were grooving to the beat. "Is that Luther's new song?" one woman asked another. "That sounds good!" The band finished the number and it seemed like everyone within earshot started clapping their hands together and yelling out, "Yeeeeeeah." However, onstage you could tell that everything wasn't right. There was something Luther didn't like, and as soon as the applause subsided, he let it be known: "Um, somebody sang 'to the movies,' but it's only one movie."

Luther had always been a perfectionist, but he was overseeing this new phase of his career more closely than ever. After the dismal failure of his last album, he was getting ready to launch a comeback, and as a fifty-year-old singer, he knew he couldn't take any chances this time. This could be his last shot.

The comeback plan began in August 2000. Luther became the first act signed to J Records, the new venture of industry legend Clive Davis, the former president of Arista Records. Luther had worked with Davis before when producing albums for Dionne Warwick and Aretha Franklin.

That was partly why Davis seemed the perfect person to help bring new energy to Luther's career. He had already done the same thing for Dionne and Aretha when their careers were waning. More recently, Davis oversaw the transformation of Carlos Santana from esteemed but low-selling classic rocker to bona fide pop phenomenon. Santana's 2000 Davis-helmed album *Supernatural* sold fourteen million copies, earned nine Grammy awards, and twice spawned something Luther has always longed for, a number-one pop single.

This new deal with Davis gave Luther renewed energy. Shortly after the announcement, Luther was asked, "What do you see in your future?"

He answered, "Luther Vandross, age seventy, still singing his butt off."

Luther and Davis soon started work on the project. The goal was to find songs that sounded contemporary but also got at the essence of what made Luther so great. They agreed that Luther would do some songs himself and have outside producers work on others.

One song Luther chose to oversee was a cover of the plaintive "Any Day Now," originally recorded by suave 1960s soul crooner Chuck Jackson. "I wanted to soften it and make it sadder," Luther explained. "I used to go to the Apollo every time Chuck Jackson and the Shirelles were there."

The songs that came in from outside producers had to be tailored to Luther's style. On the ballad "Can Heaven Wait," written by hip-hop-influenced R&B singer Joe, there was a lyric that referred to "all the shorties that I tasted." Davis insisted that the hip-hop slang "shorties" be changed to the more mature and discreet "flavors."

Luther liked a lot of what the young producers were coming up with. "Take You Out" was a favorite, because he could imagine it playing on the radio alongside current hit-makers Britney Spears,

'N Sync, and Christina Aguilera. The song made him feel modern, not, as he once said, "like a Flintstone in the middle of a bunch of Jetsons."

In addition to rethinking the music, Davis also felt that Luther needed an updated image. The label enlisted a hot new stylist to put Luther in trendy leather coats and shiny fabrics. After they shot the video for "Take You Out," which featured *NYPD Blue* actress Garcelle Beauvais, the label shelled out big bucks to digitally erase Luther's facial wrinkles. Davis wanted Luther to look as fresh as he sounded.

Luther focused on the album almost exclusively throughout early 2001. The longest break he took was in February, when he attended fashion shows by John Bartlett, Hugo Boss, and Tommy Hilfiger, among others.

Wearing a black shirt with chiffon sleeves, Luther was a special guest at the fashion show for Sean Jean, the clothing line overseen by hip-hop mogul Sean "Puffy" or "P Diddy" Combs. He was seated in the front row near comedienne Sandra Bernhard, rap temptress Lil' Kim, and NBA star Patrick Ewing. Puffy invited Luther, because he had always loved his music. "Nobody has a voice like Luther," Puffy once remarked. "His voice, his charisma, his energy, and his karma [are] . . . just so positive."

A few days after the fashion show, Puffy asked a favor of Luther. The flashy rap star, then in midst of a high-profile gun possession trial, was having an on-again, off-again relationship with Latina actor/pop starlet Jennifer Lopez, also a devoted Luther fan. Puffy arranged for Luther to do something very special for her.

Just before Valentine's Day, Lopez entered a recording studio to do some work on an upcoming album. The lights were dimmed, and she noticed a man sitting on a stool in the middle of the studio. It was Luther, and he gestured for her to come close to him. Music started playing, the opening strains of "A House Is Not a

Home." Luther then sang the entire song to her, with their faces just inches apart. She swooned. "It was the most amazing thing that ever happened to me," she later said.

Contrary to Puffy's intentions, however, it did little to improve things with Lopez. They broke up within days of Luther's serenade. Puffy and Lopez nursed their relationship wounds; Luther got back to work.

One of the key goals of the new album was to introduce Luther to younger listeners, people who may well have been conceived to his most romantic numbers. That was the reason why the record label remixed some of the songs to give them more of a hip-hop feel, and also why he was doing an interview with *VIBE*, a magazine whose readership was precisely the demographic they were targeting.

The interview was initially scheduled for Friday morning. But I got a call from Luther's assistant canceling it. Luther, he said, was a little out of it, since he had just arrived on the island. Before boarding a plane, Luther always did two things: call his mother and take a Valium, and the drug's effects hadn't worn off yet. The assistant told me that the interview would happen later, but then he called again and said it wasn't going to work for that day at all.

The next morning I got a call inviting me to attend Luther's morning step class, something that had become a daily routine as part of his ongoing struggle to lose weight and maintain it at a healthy level. Luther was still managing to keep off most of the weight that he had lost since 1998. He ate 1,200 calories a day, mostly fish, fruit, and vegetables, and was exercising regularly. He was determined that the disease that befell his father, brother, and sister would not also claim him.

"I reversed my health," he said. "I'm proud that I had a hand in determining my own fate."

At the Kingston hotel, his trainer set up for step class in an empty suite. Even before Luther arrived, the room was pretty full because he had invited his band members and background singers to the class. They were all assembled in their assorted workout gear, stretching and catching up with each other since months had passed since their last show.

The conversations continued until a tall, lanky man appeared in the doorway. His skin was the color of rich garden soil, and he sported his hair in short, tight-to-the-head curls. He wore a white long-sleeved athletic shirt and trimly cut black sweatpants. It was Luther. And he looked good.

Soon, the room was all smiles, hugs, and handshakes. A beaming Luther seemed happy to be back among his touring family, asking one background singer, Cindy Mizelle, about her baby and talking up his latest songs to one of the musicians.

As class began, Luther took his place at the front of the room the same way that he commands the center of a stage. The instructor yelled out step commands while a soundtrack of up-tempo R&B oldies played in the background: Kool and the Gang's "Celebration," LaBelle's "Lady Marmalade." When Sam and Dave's "Soul Man" came on, Luther started singing along: "I'm a soooul man . . . I'm a soooul man." However, toward the middle of the song, he changed the lyrics to "I'm a tiiired man . . . I'm a tiiired man," making the whole room laugh.

After class, Luther and his band showered, changed, and headed straight to the outdoor stage for rehearsal. They ran through Luther's new songs while a rush of preparations took place in two white tents behind the stage. In one tent, a woman with long braids ran steam across the background singers' flowing black garments. And in another, food was being prepared and laid out according to strict specifications detailed in Luther's "rider"— the litany of edibles and other things that a concert promoter is contractually obligated to provide at each show.

The document stated explicitly:

All name-brand items must be exactly those listed. If any of the items are not available, please advise the production manager. All food items should remain unopened and in original packaging.

- 1 pound of fresh ground turkey and fresh ground chicken (ask the meat department to grind fresh chicken breast if necessary)

- Jane's Krazy Mixed Up Seasonings (original, sweet lime pepper, and lemon pepper)

- Mrs. Dash Salt-free (original and table blend)

- McCormick ground ginger, ground pepper, and Grill Mates Montreal chicken seasoning

- Lawry's seasoned salt-free

- Nu-salt salt substitute

- Knorr Aromat Seasoning, all-purpose for table or kitchen and for meat

- Large box of Equal packets

- Three Parkay 0 calories sprays

- Three "I Can't Believe It's Not Butter" 0 calories sprays

- Two cases of Evian water (small bottles)

In the dressing room:

- Six small bottles of assorted decaffeinated unsweetened sodas (Coke, 7-Up, Shasta root beer, cherry, peach)

- Six small bottles of Evian (room temperature)

- Four boxes of Celestial Seasoning's "Apple Orchard" (apple cinnamon and cranberry cove) tea bags

- One first-class tea service with four China teacups and saucers, plain white or off-white, a teakettle or Thermos with hot water. No coffee needed.

- Bottles of assorted Gatorade

- Six 16-ounce bottles of Crystal Light or Ice

- Six large drinking glasses

- One bus tray of clean ice

- One fresh fruit tray to include watermelon, honeydew or cantaloupe melon, red seedless grapes, strawberries, pineapple, etc.

- Tray of condiments to include Equal (no Sweet'N Low or any other sugar substitutes), lemon wedges, swirl sticks, etc.

- Two fresh floral arrangements

- Grilled fish with plenty of steamed vegetables

The folks working the food tent looked deadly serious as they went about laying out platters of food, lining up water bottles, and making little hills of condiments.

The music stopped onstage, and Luther and the band members began making their way toward the tents. Now that he was done with the sound check, Luther was ready to talk. We left the commotion of the tent area and retreated to a grassy mound outside of his relatively modest dressing room trailer, sitting down in a couple of white lawn chairs. Behind us was a wire fence, and on the other side of it, a few shirtless elbow-high local boys were running around and playing, only occasionally glancing over, never seeming to notice the superstar in their midst.

It was a good time in Luther's life. He had lost weight and managed to keep it off, and he had big expectations for his new record. ("Truth be told, I want it to do what none of the other ones have done," he said. "I want a number-one pop record.") Sitting there just hours before a near sold-out show, he was also proud that he could still fill a venue. ("I've been putting asses in seats for twenty-two years now," he boasted.)

Indeed, it had been an incredible career, not just rags to riches, but from conceiving a dream to living it. Yet even with so much accomplished, there were still obstacles, those nagging stumbling blocks that never seem to wear away. In addition to his ongoing struggle with weight, there was his personal life, which he never felt comfortable discussing. It was sad in a way, because as he sang on one of his hits from 1996: "Secret loves never last as long."

"Would you say you've spent more time being in love or waiting for love?" I asked him, delicately broaching what I knew could've been an explosive topic.

"Waiting," he said, without reservation. "Waiting. And the time that was spent being in love was largely, unfortunately, always unrequited or unreciprocated, whatever the word is. Those were just the circumstances. So I'm still waiting. Next question."

"Have you had an interesting love life?"

"Yeah, I've had an interesting, but not satisfying love life," he answered. "You know, a lot of times you find yourself trying to fit your big, enormous life into someone else's small box of a life because they don't have ambition of their own and that never works out. I don't want nobody riding on me, you know. Because it just doesn't feel good."

"What kind of love are you looking for?"

"I want to play house, you know," Luther responded. "I want someone waiting with the light on when I come back from the concert. I want someone to say, 'Well, I talked to the road manager and he said your last song finished at ten. Now, it's a quarter to one. Why are you coming in this room so late?' "

"You *want* somebody to do that?"

"Hell, yeah," he said. "I want to know that somebody is looking out for me, somebody who's not on the payroll."

"So why has it been so hard to find love?"

"You know, I found myself a lot of times with people who want to be platonic friends. I mean they want to be real, genuine friends, because I'm really good friendship material. But after that I've had problems moving it into that romantic phase."

"But, Luther, everybody feels that way," I tried to reassure him.

"I don't care about what everybody feels," he snapped. "We're talking about me, okay? We're talking about me and the songs I write and why they're written that way. Plus, everybody isn't under the same scrutiny that I am under, you know what I'm saying? Everybody doesn't have people going, 'Well, why is Luther talking to that person?' and 'I wonder if Luther is this or that.' Enough said."

"So, how come we know so little about your love life?"

"Because it is simply none of your . . ." he started, paused, then changed course. "Because you're not entitled to. Based on me making records, no one's entitled to know any more than I tell them. That's just my position on that."

There was a long pause. We were looking into each other's eyes, neither breaking the gaze.

"You're trying to zero in on something that you are never ever gonna get," he said.

"What am I trying to zero in on?" I asked.

"You know what you're trying to zero in on," he said. "You know . . ."

"Why you trying to read my mind?"

"You've been trying to read my mind all afternoon and trying to zero in," he said with a smile. "You're just circling the airport. Look at you, just circling the airport. You ain't never gonna land."

We stopped talking for a moment as someone with Luther's crew passed by and asked how he was doing. "Oh, I'm fine," he said, laughing. "This writer from *VIBE* magazine is trying to pump me for all this information, *which he ain't gonna get*. So, I'm just sitting here enjoying myself."

The man moved on and I asked, "Does being so secretive make it hard to find a relationship?"

"Yeah, it does."

"So is it worth it?"

"I wonder," he said. "You have come up with the question of the recent days. I really wonder if it's worth it."

At one point, my tape recorder stopped abruptly and Luther leaned toward the microphone, laughed, and said, "I'm this! I'm that! I'm this! I'm that!"

Shortly after this exchange, Luther retired to his trailer to prepare for his performance. As night began taking over the sky and the opening acts started to play, I moved to my seat in a special cordoned-off area to the left of the stage. I watched as the sharply dressed Jamaican crowd grooved to hometown reggae favorites Stevie Face, Judy Mowatt, and Richie Stephens. Just before Luther took the stage, more members of his entourage started filling this small section. I stood up as two older women passed by me. Then Luther's assistant introduced me to one of them, a short woman with a soft face and an easy smile. It was Luther's mother.

Earlier, Luther had explained why it was so important for him to be with her on this Mother's Day weekend. "I'm her only remaining child," Luther said. "They say that the worst pain in the world is when your children predecease you, and it's happened to her three times." As his mother walked by slowly because of her chronic arthritis, she firmly grasped my hand and thanked me for writing about her son.

Moments later, the concert began, opening with the joyful whirl of the "Glow of Love," which Luther originally performed with the disco outfit Change. Luther and his singers strolled out onstage in their sparkling, understated but glamorous gear, waving and smiling while the crowd cheered. Soon, the band ripped into "Never Too Much," the tune that made Luther a solo star, and he sang it like it was still 1981 and he was still a background singer struggling to be taken seriously as an artist in his own right. He delivered the tune's rapid lyrics with the rhythmic intensity of a rapper. It was as if his words were being fired from a machine gun aimed at all those who ever doubted him.

He ended the song with a long croon, "Oh, my love."

He sang it again, one note lower: "My love."

Then again, lower still: "My love," easing perfectly into the opening note of his ballad "Wait for Love." It was a virtuoso transition and further proof that he remained a stylist without peer. His yearning delivery matched perfectly with the song's sentiment. "Wait for love and you're going to get the chance to love," he sang, like it was a daily affirmation, a mantra.

It reminded me of something he had said as we sat behind his trailer, when I asked if he'd trade his talent and success for true love. "Oh Lord," he chuckled. "You have asked the question that I've asked myself for the last five years. But the answer is no. It's no, because I feel that my talent is a gift and I'm not trading a gift like this. I also feel that love, when it happens, will be an additional gift, and I feel that when it happens right, it will obscure some of the pain of the past fifty years."

The show finished about an hour and a half later, and I joined Luther for his ride back to the hotel. His face was covered with droplets of sweat, and he had white towels wrapped around his head and neck. The car moved bumpily through the dark, unlit streets of Kingston. I asked Luther if he was pleased with the show, particularly with the way the new song "Take You Out" sounded. "Oh, I was totally pleased," he answered. "But the tape will tell the tale." He explained that each night after a show he reviews audio recordings of the concert. "See, these are very proud musicians," Luther said. "So if there's anything to correct, it's not an attack on their ego or anything. They want to get it right."

The car pulled into the rounded driveway of the hotel. We got out and a throng of handlers, friends, band members, and assistants awaited Luther, filled with smiles and compliments about the show. Though he was surrounded by people now, Luther was certain he would wind up doing what he does most nights, retiring to his room alone, the consummate singer of love songs ever waiting for love.

Epilogue

"Can Heaven Wait?"

"When I say good-bye,
it's never for long . . ."

—LUTHER, ON THE
2004 GRAMMY AWARDS

Luther's first thought was about his mother. It was the morning of September 11, 2001. Comfortable in his Park Avenue apartment, Luther had been watching TV and talking on the phone with a friend. Suddenly, on his TV screen, the inexplicable happened. A plane slammed into one of the World Trade Center towers. Luther, long afraid of flying, wondered how the plane could have gone so far off course.

Then another plane rammed into the other tower, and—in a period of time that was too short for far too many—the whole site was a crater of gray powder and twisted steel. Luther felt his body fill with terror, not just for those trapped inside the rubble, but for his mother, who lived in lower Manhattan very near those fallen towers.

He rushed to be with her. Police refused to let cars go past Fourteenth Street, so he had to walk to his mother's home, block by block, the amount of dust and debris increasing as the numbers on the streets decreased. As he steadily made his way through this mess, he couldn't help thinking that much of what made up the thick, particle-filled air had once lived and breathed.

He reached his mother, saw that she was safe, and quickly started making plans for her to move from Manhattan to Philadelphia, where she had friends and relatives. It no longer felt safe for her to be in New York.

Over the next several weeks, Luther did what he could to help his crippled hometown. He joined Ashford and Simpson, Roberta Flack, Patti LaBelle, Stephanie Mills, Diana Ross, Dionne Warwick, Martha Wash, and a host of others for a remake of Sister Sledge's disco classic "We Are Family" to benefit survivors and others affected by the 9/11 terrorist attacks. Working on this project brought back warm memories, since Luther sang background on the original.

A couple of weeks later, before a football game between the New York Jets and the San Francisco 49ers, Luther was on the field at New Jersey's Meadowlands Arena, which sits about thirty minutes from where the Twin Towers once stood. Surrounded by U.S. Marines, as well as New York City Police and Fire Department personnel, he movingly sang the national anthem and brought many in the nearly 80,000-strong crowd to tears.

The months that followed found Luther decorating his mother's new luxury apartment in one of Philadelphia's historic buildings. He did the place in a tasteful blend of muted brown tones mixed with an occasional splashy animal print. One wall hosted a massive backlit cabinet, while another was covered with personal photographs. There was a picture of Mrs. Vandross meeting former president Bill Clinton, who was a big fan of her son's music. There was also a photo of Luther surrounded by his nephews. If anyone dropped by her place and complimented the decor, she'd say proudly, "Ronnie did that."

When Luther wasn't fixing up his mother's apartment, he continued to focus on his music career. His first album for J Records had done very well, selling more than a million copies like most of his other releases. He felt victorious after the dismal flop of 1998's *I Know*. The whole industry knew that Luther was back.

To celebrate the album's impressive sales, J Records threw him a party at the luminous Hudson Hotel near Central Park. Luther greeted guests, industry executives, and the press in the building's cozy twenty-fourth-floor penthouse. He adored all the attention. He had been so long without it.

Early in 2002, he set off on a tour to promote the album. Since it was a hit, Luther once again played to full houses. Sounding great, he liked being back out on the road singing new songs. It made him seem more like a contemporary artist and less of an oldies act.

The tour brought some memorable moments. There was a lavish shopping spree at the Versace shop in Toronto, and some fabulous antiquing at various stops along the itinerary. One of his favorite finds was a pair of chairs that he had reupholstered in silk.

At Atlanta's Fox Theatre, both Luther and the audience got a big surprise. Luther was singing one of his lovely new ballads, "I'd Rather," when someone's cell phone rang in the second row. Annoyed, Luther looked over at the offending seat holder and saw a man wildly gesturing toward him.

Luther examined the person more closely and realized it wasn't any old crazy man, it was R&B singer Bobby Brown. He was trying to signal that his wife and Luther's longtime buddy, Whitney Houston, was on the phone. Luther, without stopping his song, walked over and grabbed the phone from Bobby. Then, he asked the whole theater to yell "Hi Whitney!"

All of this was great fun. There was nothing better than playing to enthusiastic crowds each night, and at the same time knowing that he had an album steadily rising up the charts. The only thing bothering him was that much of his onstage apparel no longer fit at all. He had put on about forty pounds.

As usual, it started innocently with a cheat day here and there. Maybe he was eating from all of the stress associated with promoting a hit record, or helping his mother leave the city. Then, perhaps he was craving food for some inexplicable emotional reason that he didn't yet fully understand. Whichever was the case, by the middle of 2002 he was well over 250 pounds, and it wouldn't be long before he would be nearing 300.

The tour wrapped and Luther jumped into making a second record for his new label. There were so many goals he wanted to attain now that he was with a record company that believed in him and could deliver on its promises. He still desired a number-one pop record, and when it came to awards, he wanted his music recognized outside of just the black music categories.

"I want to attain crossover success," he said as he worked on the new album. "I don't want to be nominated only for an R&B Grammy. I want to be nominated for a pop Grammy as well."

The song he felt could make this happen was the autobiographical "Dance with My Father," which he wrote with his friend, pop-rock balladeer Richard Marx. Luther told everyone who would listen that this song, about losing his dad at an early age, was going to take him places that had been closed to him for too long.

He called Clive Davis, the president of his label, and said, "I've written my 'career song,' my Grammy 'Song of the Year' song!"

The tracks he chose to surround this moving centerpiece offered the same contemporary spin on his trademark sound as the last album. Busta Rhymes, Queen Latifah, and Foxy Brown rapped on a few cuts, and he invited Beyoncé Knowles, lead singer of the girl group Destiny's Child, to sing a duet with him.

Luther adored Beyoncé because, even as a relative newcomer, she exhibited traits of all Luther's favorite artists. She dazzled with the shimmering glamour of Diana Ross, the somewhat detached poise of Dionne Warwick, and the melismatic gusto of Aretha Franklin. The song he recorded with her was one that another of Luther's favorite singers had first done with a dear, late friend. It was "The Closer I Get to You," originally by Roberta Flack and Donny Hathaway.

When Beyoncé entered the recording studio, she was struck at how hot and humid it was. Luther explained that he kept the temperature warm in order to protect his throat. "Don't you let those people have you messing up your voice," he told the talented young woman, "because that's your instrument."

Beyoncé was initially nervous about working with someone so revered, someone her parents listened to while she was growing up, but Luther soon disarmed her. He started cracking jokes and yelled, "Go on girl, *sang* that" as she ran through her part.

"It was a dream come true," she said. "He has so much soul he makes your heart hurt."

In March 2003, samplers of the "Dance with My Father" album went out to the press and influential radio DJ's in order to create a buzz for its June release. The response to the album was enthusiastic, and Luther's calendar began filling up with commitments. The record company had months of setup promotion planned in advance of the album's release. They really wanted this to be a big one.

It all rolled according to plan, until April came around and changed everything. The month began innocuously enough. On Monday, April 7, Luther was at the New Orleans Superdome belting the uplifting "One Shining Moment" before thousands of sports fans gathered for the final game of the NCAA basketball tournament.

Luther was back in New York three days later, attending the opening of the Broadway musical *Nine,* starring Hollywood sex symbol Antonio Banderas. Wearing a fully-buttoned black leather trench coat, a heavy-looking Luther walked the celebrity red carpet. Camera flashes popped, sending off bright blasts of light. Luther tightly winced his eyes and gritted his teeth.

On Sunday, April 13, Luther and two friends got a manicure at the Liza Healthy Nail Center on Madison Avenue. He and his pals joked about how exhausted they were from the weekend. "You know how coconut cream pie can make you tired," one of them said, laughing, as they all dried their nails under the salon's fans.

About seventy-two hours later Luther's assistant showed up at his door and got no answer. That day—and on the many uncertain ones that followed—Luther faced challenges far greater than winning Grammys, topping the charts, or even finding someone to love.

He might never remember all the details of those harrowing hours after collapsing on his apartment floor, barely conscious but scared, alone, thirsty, and longing to hear his mother's voice. He might never truly know the worry of family, friends, and fans as he slipped into a coma, just like his father more than forty years earlier, and languished in that state for weeks. He might never fully realize how a bout with pneumonia almost robbed him of one of his greatest treasures, the ability to sing.

In the weeks following his horrific stroke, many of Luther's famous friends and colleagues offered support. Roberta Flack, during a May interview on *Good Morning America*, looked into the camera and said: "Hi Luther. I love you. I hope you are getting up soon."

Anita Baker also offered her thoughts on her former tour mate. "Maaannn, Luther and I have had at least two or three more fights and subsequent makeups since that tour together," Baker told a reporter. "We've been there and someplace else a couple of times over. But I was paralyzed by the news. I'm still paralyzed. The *People* magazine with his picture on it is right here in my kitchen, and I walk by it and look at him and talk to him. Look, he has to get better because we need him. I need him. There is no other but Luther. . . . So he's going to pull through for his sake and ours. Please, God."

Some singers offered tributes to the stricken singer in their concerts. Stephanie Mills, once that pigtailed teenager who sang so boldly in *The Wiz*, would often dedicate a song to the man who contributed to the show that made her a star.

Aretha Franklin, in her semi-retirement tour that summer, projected pictures of Luther on an onstage screen. The audience responded with cheers.

In July 2003, at the Essence Music Festival in New Orleans, organizers staged an all-star salute to Luther, who has played the event five times in its eight-year existence. Planners wanted to make sure that even though Luther couldn't be there, his music would be heard. They corralled Patti LaBelle, Ronald Isley, Gerald Levert, Usher, Faith Evans, and Kelly Price to perform Luther's songs. They even used Luther's accomplished band, still led by Nat Adderly, Jr., to back these guest artists.

When Luther's musicians arrived at rehearsal, it was the first time many of them had seen each other since the singer's stroke. No one knew, as they ran through all those familiar songs, if this would be the last time they'd ever perform together as a group.

The tribute performances were magical. Usher brought a polished showman's flair to "A House Is Not a Home." Faith Evans was deeply wrenching on "Wait for Love," then quickly transformed herself into a glistening disco princess for Change's "The Glow of Love." Ronald Isley turned in a tenderly emotive "If This World Were Mine," and Patti LaBelle stirred up the house singing with Kelly Price on "Stop to Love." Later she joined Gerald Levert for a steamy "If Only for One Night."

Her performance was thrilling, but behind the scenes she'd been having a hard time thinking about her sick friend, the boy who used to run behind her at the Apollo, who started her first fan club. She called up one of the organizers, a close friend, at three A.M. the morning before the show just to talk. Then she missed afternoon rehearsal, because she had just fallen asleep from the night before.

Onstage, Patti, who has been performing for most of her life, never let on that she was having such a hard time. The only hint she gave was saying, "I'm happy to be here, but not for the reasons I'm here."

Gerald Levert, the awesomely talented son of the O'Jay's lead singer Eddie Levert, also had a lot on his mind. The thirty-six-year-old Gerald, who also has struggled with his weight, had just toured with Luther in 2002. The two singers used to talk about the hardships of dieting whenever they saw each other backstage. "We'd be like, 'OK, what did you eat today?'" Gerald remembered. "'Are you watching your blood sugar? How's your blood pressure?'"

On the last night of the tour, Luther gave Gerald a pricey sweater as a gift. The catch was that it was a few sizes too small. Luther wanted it to serve as an incentive for the younger vocalist.

"Man, I think this would look good on you," Luther said to Gerald, "but first you're going to have to lose some weight in order to fit in it."

By the time Gerald played the Essence festival, the sweater was still a little too tight, but he planned to lose enough weight for it to fit by the next time he sees Luther.

"When Luther gets all the way right," Gerald said, "I'm going to come up to him in that sweater and go, 'You didn't think I could do it, did you?'"

By the time of the Essence Music Festival in July, Luther had been moved from the hospital to a New Jersey rehabilitation center, and his *Dance with My Father* album had been released. It achieved one of Luther's longtime career goals by debuting at number one on the pop charts, selling nearly a half million copies in its first week. The sad irony was that it had taken a near-death experience to get him there.

To promote the album, Luther's seventy-nine-year-old mother did a grueling string of back-to-back interviews, from the *Today* show to *Good Morning America* to *Entertainment Tonight*. "These interviews are the least I can do for him," she said, "considering he has been taking care of me."

For the "Dance with My Father" video, the record company called on a bunch of celebrities to make appearances. Stevie Wonder signed on and showed up with his two sons.

"It is an expression of love and appreciation that I have for him," Stevie said, explaining his participation after the video shoot. "It is just an honor to know him and for us to be friends."

Quincy Jones offered a picture of himself with one of his daughters, and Whitney Houston and Patti LaBelle sent in photos of themselves with their fathers.

Beyoncé and her dad danced together in the video, and the daughters of Marvin Gaye and Donny Hathaway posed holding framed photos of their late fathers, making the video both joyful and bittersweet.

With the album a success, the next concern was the Grammys. Everyone around Luther and at his label was rooting for him to fulfill his wishes and snag some notices in the big mainstream categories.

When the nominations were announced in December, Luther

received five nods: R&B male vocalist, R&B song ("Dance with My Father"), R&B album (*Dance with My Father*), R&B duet ("The Closer I Get to You" with Beyoncé), and—what he'd been waiting for his entire career—song of the year ("Dance with My Father").

Luther's business manager, Carmen Romano, drove out to the rehabilitation center to tell Luther the good Grammy news in person. He stopped at a bakery to pick up some treats for Luther on the way. When Carmen arrived, Luther was in the midst of a physical therapy session. Yet he looked up from what he was doing to see Carmen standing there smiling with an armful of fresh baked goods.

"You look like you have something to tell me," Luther said.

"Yes, actually I do," Carmen replied. "Today was the day of the Grammy nominations."

"Did we get any?" Luther asked.

"Do you know what this is," Carmen said, holding up five fingers.

"Your hand," Luther remarked dryly.

Carmen chuckled, and then said, "You got five nominations!"

"Get out," Luther yelled, before asking the nurses if they could sneak in some champagne. "We need to celebrate."

Over the next few days, nurses would sometimes talk to Luther about the awards show in order to test his short-term memory.

"Luther, do you know when the Grammys are?" they'd ask.

"Yes," he'd say, "they're in February."

That same month, Clive Davis, president of J Records, came to the rehabilitation center to visit Luther and present him with a platinum plaque commemorating the 1.5 million copies that the *Dance with My Father* album had sold. Luther was elated.

"That's fabulous," he said. "Let's get a cake."

J Records later released photos of Luther from this visit with Davis. To many, the singer, dressed in a tan turtleneck and chocolate suede jacket, looked better than they expected. But there were signs of the struggles his mind and body had been through. His head tilted strongly to the side, dark glasses covered his eyes, and his fingers were balled into loose fists. Control over the more than sixty muscles in the hand is one of the last things that many stroke victims recover.

After his December visit, Davis told the press that there was a possibility Luther could attend the Grammys. This raised hopes of some fans, but longtime industry observers saw this as a way to trump up sympathy votes since ballots were then in Grammy voters' hands. It didn't seem likely that someone who experienced such a debilitating ailment would be able to take part in a glitzy award show less than one year later.

Meanwhile, as December started winding down, Luther and his mother had other things to think about. Christmas was coming. This had always been a time the family spent together.

She asked if he'd like to come home for the holidays. His face lit up. "Yes," he exclaimed like a happy child.

Mary Ida talked it over with his doctors, but they felt it was far too risky. There was the chance that he could have another stroke or contract pneumonia. In the end, her practicality outweighed her deeply felt wishes. "[Luther] is the only one I have left," she said, ". . . so I'm going to be patient."

On the chilly afternoon of December 25, 2003, mother and son were together at the rehabilitation facility. They were happy to be with each other and glad that Luther was still able to enjoy the holidays, but it was so unlike the lively times they used to have when Ann and Patricia were still alive and they all used to gather at one of Luther's mansions. The rehab center was nice and comfortable, but it was no place like home.

"Sometimes I feel like, 'Will my tears ever stop falling,'" Mary Ida said.

Still, her spirits lifted several days later when she saw Luther, assisted by two therapists, take his first tentative steps toward walking again. "Prayer does work," she said. "I am living proof that it works. And [Luther] is living proof, too."

Once the holidays were over, everyone's attention turned to the Grammys again. Doctors quickly nixed any notion that Luther would be able to attend the show in Los Angeles. One of the main problems was Luther's intense fear of flying. They didn't want anything to upset him, and they didn't want him taking Valium as he had when he flew in the past. A long road trip was also out of the question.

Sure enough, just days before the February 8 show, a spokesperson announced that Luther would not be attending after all. Nevertheless, a televised tribute was planned for Luther. Janet Jackson was originally intended to host the special segment, but that changed due to controversy from her breast-baring incident at the Super Bowl the previous week. Patti LaBelle stepped in for her, first introducing Luther's piano-playing label mate Alicia Keys, who delivered an assured "A House Is Not a Home." Next, Canadian pop behemoth Celine Dion, despite some early technical difficulties, put a softly moving touch on "Dance with My Father." Accompanying her on piano was the song's cowriter, Richard Marx.

The biggest surprise of the evening came after Dion's performance. Suddenly, on several video monitors placed throughout the theater, Luther himself appeared. He wore a buttoned black suede jacket and a peach turtleneck. As in the early pictures from the rehab center, his body tilted sharply to one side.

"Hello everybody," he said with a pronounced slur. "I wish I could be with you there tonight. I want to thank everyone for your love and support."

Then, he did something completely unexpected. He sang a bit of his hit song "Power of Love/Love Power," sounding very near, if not exactly, like the Luther everyone remembered. It was the first utterance that most people had heard him make in nearly a year.

About an hour later on the show, it was time to present the coveted award for Song of the Year, the one Luther desired most. Songwriters Carole King and Babyface walked onstage to present the award. The nominees were Christina Aguilera's "Beautiful," Avril Lavigne's "I'm with You," Warren Zevon's "Keep Me in Your Heart," Eminem's "Lose Yourself," and Luther's "Dance with My Father."

King read the winner. It was "Dance with My Father," and the award went to both songwriters Luther and Richard Marx. This added to the other three awards Luther had won that night for R&B male vocalist, R&B album, and R&B duo, which he shared with Beyoncé.

Since Luther couldn't attend, business manager Carmen Romano accepted the Song of the Year award on his behalf. He read a statement from Luther thanking various record company people, doctors, nurses, therapists, and most especially the woman who raised him and continued trying to lift his burdened spirit.

"To my mother," the statement read, "whose shared sentiments I expressed in this song, who tirelessly promoted my music for me while I could not, I share this award with you. I love you, Momma."

Richard Marx then came to receive his award, and while he seemed close to tears, his words lightened the mood and helped bring some of Luther's essence to the proceedings. He called Luther "my friend who I love, [and] who I wish was here with me because he'd be whispering to me about what everyone was wearing."

Luther might well have been talking about the clothes people donned that night, but he was doing it from the rehab center. His mother was by his side.

In addition to her Philadelphia apartment, Luther's mother

now keeps a place near the rehab center. She visits two or three times a week, spending much of the day with him. Yet no matter how long she stays, it is always hard leaving. Luther begs her not to go. "Momma, I want to go home with you," he says. This was sometimes the hardest thing for her to bear.

She tries to stay positive and productive. Now that she's an experienced interview subject, after helping promote Luther's album, Mary Ida serves as a spokeswoman for diabetes.

"Seeing Luther struck down by a stroke caused largely by diabetes was the last straw for me," Mary Ida said in a statement. "I knew I could stay silent no more about this disease that has literally stolen away members of my family. No one can understand the sadness I feel. That's why I'm urging people to take diabetes very seriously and to go get tested."

As for Luther, he spends the bulk of his time, nearly six hours daily, in therapy. The physical therapists help with his strength and coordination. They teach him how to easily move from the bed to his specialized wheelchair. They also assist him as he goes down the long, tough road toward walking again.

The occupational therapists guide him in relearning the basic skills of everyday life, things most people take for granted as they rush to get ready for work, grab something to eat, or quickly throw their clothes off and jump into bed at the end of a hard day. Luther undergoes excruciating hours just trying to accomplish tasks like brushing his teeth, putting on a shirt, and sipping from a cup.

When he isn't in therapy, he spends time with visitors. Luther still gets attention from his closest celebrity friends, who Mary Ida affectionately calls "his mother hens." Cissy Houston and Gladys Knight regularly drop by. Aretha Franklin sends flowers and teddy bears when she can't make it in person.

Sometimes Dionne Warwick comes over and sings her hit "Alfie" with him, and Patti LaBelle also tries to make it to the rehab center whenever she can. Once she showed up with a basket of cornbread and watermelon, two of Luther's favorite snacks.

"Do you recognize me?" she asked tentatively upon entering the room.

"Yes, I recognize you," he said. "Now would you please hurry up and give me that cornbread?"

Later, they started singing together, and Luther showed that he is still a perfectionist. Patti flubbed a lyric, and he said, "You know that was wrong, don't you?"

When others aren't around, Luther passes the time doing fifth grade–level crossword puzzles and reading *People* magazine and the industry trade *Billboard*. He also loves to joke with the nurses, who are responsible for making sure he rests and eats properly. Excessive weight is one of the foremost factors that can contribute to another stroke, but in the rehab center, Luther has been successful on a slow and steady diet. He's lost more than sixty pounds since his stroke.

The next step in Luther's recovery is to move to an assisted living facility, though that seems several months down the line. The giant leaps in his abilities are likely behind him. Now, it's simply a slow process, not to get him back to the person he once was, but to allow him to adjust to the person he has become.

At first, Luther was testy and impatient with the speed of his progress, but increasingly he seems calmer. He now realizes that things are not going to change overnight.

Mary Ida hurts watching her son struggle so much, but she believes that it's all according to God's plan. "The Lord always has an answer: Yes, no, and wait," she explains. "You have to wait on the Lord. Whatever your problems are, prepare to wait for His answer."

On April 21, 2004, it was clear that patience was paying off. Luther turned fifty-three, older than any of his siblings, or even his father, got the chance to be.

As his recovery continues and his memory slowly returns, Luther will have much to think about as he begins to recollect his life and career. He has certainly known many triumphs. Though mainstream audiences have sometimes overlooked or discounted him, his R&B following has used several opportunities to let him know he was appreciated.

In 1999, the TV show *Soul Train* honored him with an award, recognizing his career achievements. When accepting, Luther laid out the ethos that ruled his life: "I never drank, never did drugs, never smoked, and I am here to tell the story. People always ask me what to tell young people, and I say, 'Do it right. Do it straight, and do it because you love it.' "

The following year, Black Entertainment Television honored him with a star on their Walk of Fame, and in the accompanying ceremony, Chaka Khan and Patti LaBelle—two women who Luther long admired—helped celebrate *him.*

In addition to receiving such honors, Luther also has seen first-hand how his songs helped people change their lives. He was walking through an airport in Hawaii when a woman walked up to him and said the song "Don't Want to Be a Fool" helped her leave an abusive husband. Like Luther, who called the song one of the most autobiographical he's ever written, she still wanted love, but there was a limit to what she would risk in pursuit of it.

Moments like these were so much more meaningful to him than when people said that they had "made babies" to his music. Luther disliked it when people called him "Dr. Love" and other such titles that even some of his closest celebrity friends used for him.

"I think it trivializes the musical contribution that I'm trying to make," Luther said, "and the musical career that I'm trying to have and how I'm trying to be remembered. I don't want to be remembered in the context of the bedroom. I don't want to be in that bag. I want to be in the bag that includes the best singers of our time, not in the bag with those who are bumping and grinding and talking about people's thighs and booties and stuff. That's unfair to what I've tried so hard to work for. The music is about romance, yes. But it's not about booties."

He refused to let fans treat him like some crooning lothario. When a woman tossed a pair of panties onstage during one of his concerts, he chastised her in front of the whole audience. "I am not flattered by that," he said into the microphone. "Come and pick up your drawers."

Later, he commented on the incident. "I thought it was nasty," he said. "I mean, unidentified drawers? I want to be remembered as one of the premier singers of our time, period, and I feel that throwing your drawers at me compromises and trivializes my effort to do that. I appreciate attention from fans, but not to the degree that your drawers come on stage with me. If that makes me a prude, then I'm King Prude."

Perhaps these "Dr. Love"–like titles uncomfortably amplified the cruel paradox of his life, that he inspired feelings of love among others but rarely found any to call his own. This unquenched thirst for love, and how it so completely infused his music, placed Luther among that small group of artists, including Billie Holiday, Frank Sinatra, Tammy Wynette, and Roy Orbison, for whom longing becomes almost a genre unto itself.

But romance was just one of the many things Luther has seemed to constantly be striving for. There were the Grammys, and the number-one hits, the crossover recognition, and the million-selling albums. For as much as he's achieved, there always seems to be another goal taunting him in the distance. There is nothing wrong with seeking excellence in a field, and to the extent that Luther's continued yearning has pushed him artistically, then it's been a good thing. However, to the extent that it sometimes kept him from enjoying all he already accomplished, then it's been a damn shame.

Luther, after all, has lived a life that few are able to. He's seldom had to compromise his dreams. With patience and consistent work, he's seen most of them flourish. He became a solo recording star. He stood onstage surrounded by singing and dancing men and women, looking fine and sounding smooth.

The women he admired as a teenager, Dionne, Diana, and Aretha, later became his friends. He produced their records and shared numerous intimacies with them. He played Ms. Pac-Man with Dionne, talked soaps with Aretha, and once enjoyed a re- markable moment with Diana at Madison Square Garden. During a New York stop on her 2000 *Return to Love* tour, she called him up from the audience and invited him to sit on the stage steps with her. Diana then sang one of her sweet, reflective slow songs, while Luther held her hand, occasionally offered some harmonies, and played with the golden fringe on her floor-length gown.

In his fifty-three years, Luther has seen and accomplished things that would seem nearly impossible for a chubby, brown- skinned boy from New York's Lower East Side projects. He's trav- eled a path that, by any measure, can be summed up in the title of one of his most enduring songs: "So Amazing."

Discography

LUTHER VANDROSS—ALBUMS AS GROUP LUTHER

1976

Luther (Cotillion)
Producer and writer on album. Tracks: "Funky Music (Is a Part of Me)," "The 2nd Time Around," "I'll Get Along Fine," "Everybody Rejoice," "Emotion Eyes," "This Strange Feeling," and "It's Good for the Soul (Parts I and II)."

Funky Christmas (compilation) (Cotillion)
Tracks: "May Christmas Bring You Happiness" and "At Christmas Time."

1977

This Close to You (Cotillion)
Producer and writer on album. Tracks: "This Is for Real," "A Lover's Change," "Don't Take the Time," "Jealousy Is in Me," "I'm Not Satisfied," "This Close to You," "Don't Wanna Be a Fool," "Come Back to Love," and "Follow My Love."

LUTHER VANDROSS—SOLO ALBUMS

1981

Never Too Much (Epic)
Tracks: "Never Too Much," "Sugar and Spice (I Found Me a Girl)," "Don't

You Know That?" "I've Been Working," "She's a Super Lady," "You Stopped Loving Me," and "A House Is Not a Home."

1982

Forever, For Always, For Love (Epic)
Tracks: "Bad Boy/Having a Party," "You're the Sweetest One," "Since I Lost My Baby," "Forever, For Always, For Love," "Better Love," "Promise Me," "She Loves Me Back," and "Once You Know How."

1983

Busy Body (Epic)
Tracks: "I Wanted Your Love," "Busy Body," "I'll Let You Slide," "Make Me a Believer," "For the Sweetness of Your Love," "How Many Times Can We Say Goodbye," and "Superstar/Until You Come Back to Me (That's What I'm Gonna Do)."

1985

The Night I Fell in Love (Epic)
Tracks: " 'Til My Baby Comes Home," "The Night I Fell in Love," "If Only for One Night," "Creepin'," "It's Over Now," "Wait for Love," "My Sensitivity (Gets in the Way)," and "Other Side of the World."

The Goonies (Original Motion Picture Soundtrack) (Epic)
Track: "She's So Good to Me."

Ruthless People (Original Motion Picture Soundtrack) (Epic)
Track: "Give Me the Reason."

1988

Any Love (Epic)
Tracks: "I Wonder," "She Won't Talk to Me," "I Know You Want To," "Come Back," "Any Love," "Love Won't Let Me Wait," "Are You Gonna Love Me," "For You to Love," and "The Second Time Around."

1989

The Best of Luther Vandross: The Best of Love (Epic)
Tracks: "Searching," "The Glow of Love," "Never Too Much," "If This World Were Mine (Duet with Cheryl Lynn)," "A House Is Not a Home," "Bad

Boy/Having a Party," "Since I Lost My Baby," "Promise Me," " 'Til My Baby Comes Home," "If Only for One Night," "Superstar/Until You Come Back to Me," "Stop to Love," "So Amazing," "There's Nothing Better Than Love (Duet with Gregory Hines)," "Give Me the Reason," "Any Love," "I Really Didn't Mean It," "Love Won't Let Me Wait," "Treat You Right," and "Here and Now."

1991

Power of Love (Epic)
Tracks: "She Doesn't Mind," "Power of Love/Love Power," "I'm Gonna Start Today," "The Rush," "I Want the Night to Stay," "Don't Want to Be a Fool," "I Can Tell You That," "Sometimes It's Only Love," "Emotional Love," and "I (Who Have Nothing)."

1992

Hero (Original Motion Picture Soundtrack) (Sony)
Track: "Heart of a Hero."

Mo' Money (Original Motion Picture Soundtrack) (A&M)
Track: "The Best Things in Life Are Free."

1993

Never Let Me Go (Epic)
Tracks: "Little Miracles (Happen Every Day)," "Heaven Knows," "Love Me Again," "Can't Be Doin' That Now," "Too Far Down," "Love Is on the Way (Real Love)," "Hustle," "Emotion Eyes," "Lady, Lady," "Medley: How Deep Is Your Love/Love Don't . . . ," and "Never Let Me Go."

1994

Songs (Epic)
Tracks: "Love the One You're With," "Killing Me Softly," "Endless Love (Duet with Mariah Carey)," "Evergreen," "Reflections," "Hello," "Ain't No Stoppin' Us Now," "Always and Forever," "Going in Circles," "Since You've Been Gone," "All the Woman I Need," "What the World Needs Now Is Love," and "Impossible Dream."

1995

This Is Christmas (Sony)

Tracks: "With a Christmas Heart," "This Is Christmas," "The Mistletoe Jam (Everybody Kiss)," "Every Year, Every Christmas," "My Favorite Things," "Have Yourself a Merry Little Christmas," "I Listen to the Bells," "Please Come Home for Christmas," "A Kiss for Christmas," and "O Come All Ye Faithful."

1996

Your Secret Love (Sony)
Tracks: "Your Secret Love," "Love Don't Love You Anymore," "It's Hard for Me to Say," "Crazy Love," "I Can Make It Better," "Too Proud to Beg," "I Can't Wait No Longer (Let's Do This)," "Nobody to Love," "Whether or Not the World Gets Better," "This Time I'm Right," "Knocks Me Off My Feet," and "Goin' Out of My Head."

1997

One Night with You: Luther Vandross: The Best of Love, Volume 2 (Sony)
Tracks: "One Night with You (Everyday of Your Life)," "When You Call on Me/Baby That's When I Come Runnin'," "It's All About You," "I Won't Let You Do That to Me," "Power of Love/Love Power," "Don't Want to Be a Fool," "The Best Things in Life Are Free (Classic Club Edit)," "Little Miracles (Happen Every Day)," "Endless Love (Duet with Mariah Carey)," "Always and Forever," "Love the One You're With," "Your Secret Love," "I Can Make It Better," "Love Don't Love You Anymore (TM's Urban Mix)," and "My Favorite Things."

1998

I Know (Virgin)
Tracks: "Keeping My Faith in You," "Isn't There Someone," "Religion," "Get It Right," "I Know," "I'm Only Human," "Nights in Harlem," "Dream Lover," "When I Need You," "Are You Using Me?," "Are You Mad at Me?" "Now That I Have You," and "Nights in Harlem (A Darkchild Extended Remix)."

1999

Luther Vandross Greatest Hits (Epic)
Tracks: "Never Too Much," "Don't Want to Be a Fool," "Here and Now," "Love the One You're With," "Any Love," "Superstar/Until You Come Back to Me (That's What I'm Gonna Do)," "A House Is Not a Home," "Give Me the Reason," "There's Nothing Better Than Love (Duet with Gregory Hines),"

"Creepin'," "So Amazing," "Stop to Love," "Power of Love/Love Power," and "How Many Times Can We Say Goodbye (Duet with Dionne Warwick)."

2001

Luther Vandross (J)
Tracks: "Take You Out," "Grown Things," "Bring Your Heart to Mine," "Can Heaven Wait," "Say It Now," "Hearts Get Broken All the Time (But the . . .)," "I'd Rather," "How Do I Tell Her," "Any Day Now," "If I Was the One," "Let's Make Tonight the Night," "Like I'm Invisible," "Are You There (with Another Guy)," and "Love Forgot."

Dr. Dolittle 2 (Original Soundtrack) (J)
Track: "If I Was the One."

2003

Dance with My Father (J)
Tracks: "If I Didn't Know Better," "Think About You," "If It Ain't One Thing," "Buy Me a Rose," "The Closer I Get to You," "Lovely Day," "Dance with My Father," "She Saw You," "Apologize," "Hit It Again," "Right in the Middle," "Once We're Lovers," "Lovely Day, Part 2," and "They Said You Needed Me."

The Essential Luther Vandross (Epic)
Tracks: "Any Love," "So Amazing," "Wait for Love," "Power of Love/Love Power," "For You to Love," "I (Who Have Nothing) (Duet with Martha Wash)," "Anyone Who Had a Heart," "A House Is Not a Home," "Never Too Much," "Since I Lost My Baby," "Stop to Love," "It's Over Now," "Your Secret Love," "Superstar," "Here and Now," "Knocks Me Off My Feet," "Goin' Out of My Head," "If Only for One Night," "Creepin'," "She's So Good to Me," "Give Me the Reason," "She Loves Me Back," "The Night I Fell in Love," "If This World Were Mine (Duet with Cheryl Lynn)," "Don't Want to Be a Fool," "There's Nothing Better Than Love (Duet with Gregory Hines)," "How Many Times Can We Say Goodbye (Duet with Dionne Warwick)," "Love the One You're With," "Endless Love (Duet with Mariah Carey)," and "I Want the Night to Stay."

Live 2003 at Radio City Music Hall (J)
Tracks: "Never Too Much," "Here and Now," "Take You Out," "Love Won't Let Me Wait," "Superstar," "Stop to Love," "If Only for One Night," "Creepin'," "I'd Rather," "A House Is Not a Home," and "The Glow of Love."

LUTHER VANDROSS—ON OTHER ALBUMS

1973
Delores Hall, *Hall-Mark* (RCA)
>   Male vocalist and writer on "Who's Gonna Make It Easier for Me."

1974
Maggie Bell, *Queen of the Night* (Atlantic)
>   Uncredited background vocals on album.

1975
David Bowie, *Young Americans* (Virgin)
>   Background vocals on "Young Americans," "Win," "Fascination,"
>   "Right," "Somebody Up There Likes Me," and "Can You Hear Me."
>   Cowriter on "Fascination."
Gary Glitter, *Gary Glitter* (Bell)
>   Uncredited background vocals on album.
Stephanie Mills, *Movin' in the Right Direction* (ABC)
>   Background vocals on album.

1976
The Brecker Brothers Band, *Back to Back*
>   Background vocals and arrangement on album.
Roy Buchanan, *A Street Called Straight* (Atlantic)
>   Background vocals on album.
Judy Collins, *Bread & Roses* (Elektra)
>   Background vocals on "Everything Must Change" and "Come Down in
>   Time."
Bette Midler, *Songs for the New Depression* (Atlantic)
>   Background vocals on "Strangers in the Night."
Andy Pratt, *Resolution* (Nemperor)
>   Background vocals on "Can't Stop My Love."
Todd Rundgren/Utopia, *Nimbus Thitherward: Finally on the Beach in London,
>   1976* (live recording not released until 1996) (Takrl)
>   Background vocals on album.

1977
Average White Band & Ben E. King, *Benny and Us* (Atlantic)
>   Background vocals on "Get It Up for Love," "Fool for You Anyway," "A

Star in the Ghetto," "What Is Soul," "Someday We'll All Be Free,"
"Imagine," and "Keepin' It to Myself."
Chic, *Chic* (Atlantic)
    Background vocals on album.
The J. Geils Band, *Monkey Island* (Atlantic)
    Background vocals on "Surrender" and "Monkey Island."
Nils Lofgren, *I Came to Dance* (A&M)
    Background vocals and arrangement on album.
Andy Pratt, *Shiver in the Night* (Nemperor)
    Background vocals on album.
Ringo Starr, *Ringo the 4th* (Atlantic)
    Background vocals on album.

1978
The Atlantic Family Live at Montreux (Atlantic)
    Co-lead vocals on "Everything Must Change."
Chic, *C'est Chic* (Atlantic)
    Vocals ("special guest artist") on album.
Sean Delaney, *Highway* (Casablanca)
    Background vocals on album.
Gregg Diamond/Bionic Boogie, *Hot Butterfly* (Polydor)
    Lead vocal on "Hot Butterfly."
Roy Buchanan, *You're Not Alone* (Atlantic)
    Co-lead vocal on "Down by the River."
Roberta Flack, *Roberta Flack* (Atlantic)
    Background vocals on album.
The Good Vibrations, *I Get Around* (Millennium)
    Vocals on album.
Garland Jeffreys, *One-Eyed Jack* (A&M)
    Background vocals on album.
Quincy Jones, *Sounds . . .* (A&M)
    Co-lead vocal on "Takin' It to the Streets" and "I'm Gonna Miss You in
    the Morning."
Lemon, *A-Freak-A* (Prelude)
    Background vocals on album.
Odyssey, *Hollywood Party Tonight* (RCA)
    Guest vocalist on album.
Roundtree, *Get on Up (Get On Down)* (12" single) (Island)
    Uncredited vocal.

Carole Bayer Sager, . . . *Two* (Elektra)
    Background vocals on "One Star Shining."
Carly Simon, *Boys in the Trees* (Elektra)
    Background vocals on "De Bat (Fly in Me Face)."
David Spinozza, *Spinozza* (A&M)
    Background vocals on "Superstar," "Doesn't She Know by Now."
Cat Stevens, *Back to Earth* (A&M)
    Background vocals on "New York Times."
T-Life, *That's Life* (RCA)
    Background vocals on album.
The Wiz (Original Soundtrack) (MCA)
    Writer on "A Brand New Day (Everybody Rejoice)." Member of adult
    choir on album.

1979

Average White Band, *Feel No Fret* (RCA)
    Background vocals on "Too Late to Cry."
The Charlie Calello Orchestra, *Calello Serenade* (Midsong International)
    Background vocals on album.
Charme, *Let It In* (RCA)
    Background vocals on album. Uncredited lead vocal for "Georgy Porgy."
Cher, *Prisoner* (Casablanca)
    Background vocals on "Shoppin'."
Roberta Flack, *Featuring Donny Hathaway* (Atlantic)
    Background vocals on album. Co-background vocal arrangement on
    "God Don't Like Ugly" and "Back Together Again."
Delores Hall, *Delores Hall* (Capitol/EMI)
    Background vocals and arrangement on album.
Jay Hoggard, *Days Like These* (Arista)
    Background vocals on album.
Evelyn "Champagne" King, *Music Box*(RCA)
    Background vocals on album.
Bette Midler, *Thighs and Whispers* (Atlantic)
    Background vocals on "Cradle Days," "My Knight in Black Leather,"
    "Hang on in There Baby," "Hurricane," and "Married Men."
New York City Band, *Sunnyside (Original Music from the Motion Picture)*
    (Casablanca)
    Vocal solo for "Ride That Wave" and "Sunnyside." Uncredited vocal
    solo on "Got to Have Your Body."

Revelation, *Get in Touch* (RCA)
>   Background vocals on album.

Ben Sidran, *The Cat and the Hat* (Horizon)
>   Uncredited background vocals on "Hi-Fly."

Sister Sledge, *We Are Family* (Cotillion)
>   Background vocals ("special guest artist") on album.

Soirée, *Soirée* (RCA)
>   Background vocals on album. Vocal arrangement on "You Keep Me Hanging On" and "Do You Love Me."

John Tropea, *To Touch You Again* (Marlin)
>   Background vocals on "Livin in the Jungle," "Look What They've Done to My Song."

The Warriors (Original Motion Picture Soundtrack) (A&M)
>   Background vocals on "Echoes in My Mind" by Mandrill.

1980

The Brecker Brothers, *Détente* (Arista)
>   Background vocals and arrangement on "You Left Something Behind," "Don't Get Funny with My Money," "You Ga(Ta Give It)." Additional lyrics on "Don't Get Funny with My Money."

Change, *The Glow of Love* (Warner Brothers)
>   Lead vocal on "The Glow of Love" and "Searching."

Fame (Original Motion Picture Soundtrack) (Polydor)
>   Background vocals on "Fame" by Irene Cara.

Roberta Flack and Peabo Bryson, *Live & More* (Atlantic)
>   Background vocals and arrangement on Roberta's band on album.

Terumasa Hino, *Daydream* (Inner City)
>   Background vocals on album.

Cissy Houston, *Step Aside for a Lady* (Columbia)
>   Background vocals on album.

Chaka Khan, *Naughty* (Warner Brothers)
>   Background vocals on "Papillon (a.k.a. Hot Butterfly)" and "Our Love's in Danger."

Jimmy Maelen, *Beats Workin'* (CBS)
>   Background vocals on "Two Good Reasons," "If It Wasn't You," "Sympathy for the Devil," "Turn the Music Up," and "Squeeze Play."

Bette Midler, *Divine Madness* (Atlantic)
>   Background vocals on album.

Mtume, *In Search of the Rainbow Seekers* (Epic)
    "Frontground vocals" on album.
Jess Roden, *Stonechaser* (Island)
    Background vocals on album.
Michael Zager Band, *Zager* (Columbia)
    Background vocals on "Don't Sneak on Me," "Zorba," "Call Me," "Your
    Love," "I'd Love to Make Up with You," "Rasputin," and "I'm Afraid to
    Let You Know."

1981

The Brooklyn, Bronx, & Queens Band, *The Brooklyn, Bronx, & Queens Band*
    (EMI)
    Background vocals on album.
Change, *Miracles* (Atlantic)
    Background vocals on album.
Roberta Flack, *Bustin' Loose (Music from the Original Motion Picture Soundtrack)*
    (MCA)
    Background vocals and arrangement on album. Writer on "You
    Stopped Loving Me."
Hi-Gloss, *You'll Never Know* (Epic)
    Background vocals on album.
The J. Geils Band, *Freeze-Frame* (EMI)
    Background vocals on "Angel in Blue," "River Blindness," and "Flame
    Thrower."
Stephanie Mills, *Stephanie* (20th Century Fox)
    Background vocals on album.
The Spinners, *Can't Shake This Feelin'* (Atlantic)
    Background vocals on album.
Bernard Wright, *'Nard* (BMG)
    Background vocals on "Music Is the Key."

1982

Irene Cara, *Anyone Can See* (Epic)
    Background vocals on album.
Linda Clifford, *I'll Keep on Loving You* (Capitol/EMI)
    Vocal arrangement on album. Background vocals on "Ain't You Glad,"
    "Only the Angels Know," "All the Man I Need," "I Lied," and "Don't
    Come Crying to Me."
Aretha Franklin, *Jump to It* (Arista)
    Producer on album. Background vocals and arrangement on "Jump to

It," "(It's Just) Your Love," "Love Me Right." Rhythm arrangement for
"It's Your Thing." Vocal arrangement for "If She Don't Want Your
Lovin' " and "Just My Daydream."

Bob James, *Hands Down* (Warner Bros.)
   Vocals on "Macumba."

Kleer, *Taste the Music* (Atlantic)
   Background vocals on "Swann."

Cheryl Lynn, *Instant Love* (CBS)
   Producer on album. Writer and background vocals on "Instant Love"
   and "Sleep Walkin'." Background vocals on "I Just Wanna Be Your
   Fantasy." Vocal arrangement for "Instant Love" and "If This World
   Were Mine." Co-lead vocal on "If This World Were Mine."

Ullanda McCullough, *Ullanda* (Atlantic)
   Background vocals on album. Vocal arrangement on "Men Kiss and
   Tell," "Getting Ready for Love," "Watching You Watching Me," and
   "What's It All About."

1983

Aretha Franklin, *Get It Right* (Arista)
   Producer on album. Writer, background vocals, and arranger on "Get It
   Right," "Pretender," "When You Love Me Like That," and "I Got Your
   Love." Writer and arranger on "Every Girl (Wants My Guy)."

James Ingram, *It's Your Night* (Qwest)
   Background vocals on "Party Animal."

Linda Lewis, *A Tear and a Smile* (Epic)
   Co-lead vocal on "Why Can't I Be the Other Woman."

Stephanie Mills, *Merciless* (PolyGram)
   Writer on "My Body."

David Sanborn, *Backstreet* (Warner Bros.)
   Background vocals on "Neither One of Us."

Fonzi Thornton, *The Leader* (RCA)
   Background vocals on "Be My Baby" and "Sayin' Goodbye (To Lonely
   Nites)."

Dionne Warwick, *How Many Times Can We Say Goodbye* (Arista)
   Producer on album. Writer, background vocals, and arrangement on
   "Got a Date," "So Amazing," and "How Many Times Can We Say
   Goodbye." Writer and arrangement on "I Do It 'Cause I Like It."
   Writer on "What Can a Miracle Do."

Betty Wright, *Back at You* (Epic)
   Background vocals on "Burning Desire" and "She's Older Now."

1984

Teddy Pendergrass, *Love Language* (Elektra/Asylum)
> Producer, writer, background vocals, and arrangement on "You're My Choice Tonight (Choose Me)."

1985

Carly Simon, *Spoiled Girl* (Epic)
> Background vocals on "Can't Give It Up."

The Temptations, *Touch Me* (Motown)
> Writer and background vocals on "Do You Really Love Your Baby."

Stevie Wonder, *In Square Circle* (Tamla/Motown)
> Uncredited scatting on "Part-Time Lover."

1986

Labyrinth (Music from the Original Motion Picture Soundtrack) (EMI)
> Background vocals on "Underground" by David Bowie.

Jimmy Salvemini, *Roll It* (Elektra)
> Producer on album. Background vocals and writer on "Roll It." Writer on "Whether or Not the World Gets Better," "Gloria My Love," "She's Fascinating."

1987

Irene Cara, *Carasmatic* (Elektra)
> Background vocals and arrangement on "Get a Grip."

Ava Cherry, *Picture Me* (Capitol)
> Background vocals on "Picture Me," "Good Intentions," and "For Your Pleasure."

Nick Kamen, *Nick Kamen* (Warner Bros.)
> Background vocals on "Help Me Baby."

Cheryl Lynn, *Start Over* (Manhattan)
> Background vocals on "Don't Bury Me."

Doc Powell, *Love Is Where It's At* (PolyGram)
> Background vocals on "Give It Up," "What's Going On," and "Bad Times."

Diana Ross, *Red Hot Rhythm and Blues* (RCA)
> Background vocals and writer on "It's Hard for Me to Say."

1988
Gregory Hines, *Gregory Hines* (Epic)
> Producer, writer, and background vocals on album. Co-lead vocal on "There's Nothing Better Than Love."

1990
Whitney Houston, *I'm Your Baby Tonight* (Arista)
> Producer and writer on "Who Do You Love."

1991
Lisa Fischer, *So Intense* (Elektra)
> Background vocals, arrangement, and production on "Get Back to Love," "Wildflower," and "Send the Message of Love." Arrangement and production on "Some Girls."

Aretha Franklin, *What You See Is What You Sweat* (Arista)
> Producer and co-lead vocal on "Doctor's Orders."

Patti LaBelle, *Burnin'* (MCA)
> Background vocals on "When You Love Somebody (I'm Saving My Love for You)."

Richard Marx, *Rush Street* (Capitol)
> Background vocals on "Love Unemotional."

Kevin Owens, *That Time Again* (JBR)
> Background vocals and arrangement on "You're My Everything."

1993
Richard Marx, *Paid Vacation* (Capitol)
> Background vocals on "The Way She Loves Me."

Frank Sinatra, *Duets* (Capitol)
> Co-lead vocals on "The Lady Is a Tramp."

1994
Naomi Campbell, *Babywoman* (Epic)
> Background vocals on "All Through the Night."

Cindy Mizelle, *Cindy Mizelle* (EastWest)
> Background vocals on "Love Talk to Me."

1995
Yvonne Lewis, *No Strangers in Paradise* (Glorious)
> Background vocals on "It's Gonna Be All Right."

1997

Richard Marx, *Flesh and Bone* (Capitol)
> Background vocals on "What's the Story" and "Can't Lie to My Heart."

BeBe Winans, *BeBe Winans* (Atlantic)
> Background vocals and arrangement on "Thank You."

1999

Natalie Cole, *Snowfall on the Sahara* (Elektra)
> Background vocals on "Say You Love Me."

Bibliography

American Diabetes Association Complete Guide to Diabetes, 2nd ed. Foreword, Bruce R. Zimmermann and Elizabeth A. Walker (New York: Bantam, 1999).

Andriote, John-Manuel. *Hot Stuff: A Brief History of Disco* (New York: Harper-Entertainment, 2001).

Barnes, Ken. Liner notes for *Sister Sledge: We Are Family*, Reissue/Compilation (Atlantic Recording Corporation, 1995).

——. Liner notes for *The Best of Chic, Volume 2* (Atlantic Recording Corporation, 1992).

Baumgart, Malcolm. Liner notes for *Patti LaBelle and the Blue Belles: The Early Years* (Ace Records, Ltd., 1993).

Bego, Mark. *Bette Midler: Still Divine*. Introduction by Rita Coolidge (New York: Cooper Square, 2002).

——. *Aretha Franklin: The Queen of Soul*, 2nd ed. (New York: Da Capo, 2001).

Bessman, Jim. Liner notes for *The Very Best of Ashford & Simpson* (Warner Brothers Records, 2002).

Bowie, Angela, with Patrick Carr. *Backstage Passes: Life on the Wild Side with David Bowie* (New York: Cooper Square, 2000).

Bowman, Jeffery. *Diva: The Totally Unauthorized Biography of Whitney Houston*. Introduction by J. Randy Taraborrelli (New York: HarperPaperbacks, 1995).

Bronson, Fred. *Billboard's Hottest Hot 100 Hits*, updated and expanded, 3rd ed. (New York: Watson-Guptill, 2003).

———. *The Billboard Book of Number One Hits*, revised and updated, 4th ed. (New York: Watson-Guptill, 1997).

Brown, William F. Liner notes for *The Wiz: The Super Soul Musical "Wonderful Wizard of Oz"* (Atlantic Recording Corporation, 1975).

Buckley, David. *Strange Fascination: David Bowie: The Definitive Story*, revised and updated ed. (London: Virgin, 2000).

Bull, Chris, ed. *While the World Sleeps: Writing from the First Twenty Years of the Global AIDS Plague*. Foreword by Larry Kramer (New York: Thunder's Mouth, 2003).

Cann, Kevin. *David Bowie: A Chronology* (New York: Fireside, 1983).

Caplan, Louis R., Mark L. Dyken, and J. Donald Easton. *American Heart Association: Family Guide to Stroke Treatment, Recovery, and Prevention* (New York: Times Books, 1994).

Chin, Brian. "All The Right Reasons." Liner notes for *Luther Vandross: Give Me the Reason*, remastered ed. (Sony Music Entertainment, 2002).

———. "Never Enough Luther." Liner notes for *Luther Vandross: Never Too Much*, remastered ed. (Sony Music Entertainment, 2002).

———. "Gwen Guthrie, 1950–1999: singer-songwriter." Liner notes for *Gwen Guthrie: Ultimate Collection* (Universal Music Company, 1999).

———. "Luther's Intimate Portraits." Liner notes for *Luther Vandross: Greatest Hits* (Sony Music Entertainment, 1999).

Christgau, Robert. *Christgau's Consumer Guide: Albums of the '90s* (New York: St. Martin's Griffin, 2000).

———. *Record Guide: The '80s* (New York: Da Capo, 1994).

———. *Rock Albums of the '70s: A Critical Guide* (New York: De Capo, 1981).

Considine, Shaun. *Barbra Streisand: The Woman, The Myth, The Music* (New York: Dell, 1986).

Costa, Jean-Charles. Liner notes for *Dance, Dance, Dance: The Best of Chic* (Atlantic Recording Corporation, 1991).

Coveney, Janine. Liner notes for *The Best of Anita Baker* (Rhino Entertainment Corporation, 2002).

Crimp, Douglas, ed. *AIDS: Cultural Analysis, Cultural Activism* (Cambridge, Mass.: MIT, 1988).

Davis, Clive, with James Willwerth. *Clive: Inside the Record Business* (New York: Ballantine, 1974).

Diebold, David. *Tribal Rites: San Francisco's Dance Music Phenomenon: 1978–1988*, 2nd ed. (Northridge, Calif.: Time Warp, 1986).

Dyson, Michael Eric. *Reflecting Black: African-American Cultural Criticism* (Minneapolis: University of Minnesota Press, 1987).

Edwards, Henry, and Tony Zanetta. *Stardust: The David Bowie Story* (New York: Bantam, 1987).

Fox, Ted. *Showtime at the Apollo* (New York: Holt, Rinehart and Winston, 1983).

Franklin, Aretha, and David Ritz. *Aretha: From These Roots* (New York: Villard, 1999).

Galloway, A. Scott. "Celestial Butterfly." Liner notes for *Got to Be Real: The Best of Cheryl Lynn* (Sony Music Entertainment, 1996).

———. Liner notes to *Odyssey: Native New Yorker: A Golden Classic Edition* (Collectables Recording Corporation, 1991).

George, Nelson. *Buppies, B-Boys, Baps, & Bohos: Notes on Post-Soul Black Culture*, updated and expanded ed. (New York: Da Capo, 2001).

———. *The Death of Rhythm & Blues* (New York: Plume, 1988).

George-Warren, Holly, and Patricia Romanowski, eds. *The Rolling Stone Encyclopedia of Rock & Roll: Revised and Updated for the 21st Century*, 3rd ed. Consulting ed. Jon Pareles (New York: Fireside, 2001).

Gorman, David. "Why the World Needs a Spinners Box (a.k.a.: What Took Us So Damned Long?)" Liner notes for *Spinners: The Chrome Collection* (Atlantic Recording Corporation, 2003).

Hachinski, Vladimir, and Larissa Hachinski. *Stroke: A Comprehensive Guide to "Brian Attacks"* (Toronto: Key Porter, 2003).

Harley, Sharon. *The Timetables of African-American History: A Chronology of the Most Important People and Events in African-American History* (New York: Simon and Schuster, 1995).

Hirshey, Gerri. *Nowhere to Run: The Story of Soul Music* (New York: Times Books, 1984).

Houston, Cissy, with Jonathan Singer. *How Sweet the Sound: My Life with God and Gospel*. Foreword by Whitney Houston (New York: Doubleday, 1998).

Jones, Quincy. *The Autobiography of Quincy Jones* (New York: Doubleday, 2001).

Journeys in Black: Luther Vandross. Directors Stephanie Frederic and Lyle Mason (UrbanWorks Entertainment, 2002).

Kelley, Norman, ed. *Rhythm and Business: The Political Economy of Black Music* (New York: Akashic, 2002).

Khan, Chaka, with Tonya Bolden. *Chaka!: Through the Fire* (New York: Rodale, 2003).

LaBelle, Patti, with Laura B. Randolph. *Don't Block the Blessings: Revelations of a Lifetime* (New York: Riverhead, 1996).

Lima, O. J. Liner notes for *The Essential Luther Vandross* (Sony Music Entertainment, 2003).

Love, Darlene, with Rob Hoerburger. *My Name Is Love: The Darlene Love Story* (New York: William Morrow, 1998).

Mair, George. *Bette: An Intimate Biography of Bette Midler* (New York: Birch Lane, 1995).

Marymont, Mark. "The Crests—For Collectors Only." Liner notes for *Johnny Maestro & The Crests: For Collectors Only* (Collectables Records, 1994).

Matlock, Mark. Liner notes for *The Very Best of Kleeer* (Atlantic Recording Corporation, 1998).

Midler, Bette. *A View from a Broad* (New York: Simon and Schuster, 1980).

Nathan, David. Liner notes for *The Sweet Inspirations: Sweets for My Sweet and Sweet Sweet Soul* (Atlantic Recording Corporation, 2002).

——. *The Soulful Divas: Personal Portraits of Over a Dozen Divine Divas, from Nina Simone, Aretha Franklin, & Diana Ross, to Patti LaBelle, Whitney Houston, & Janet Jackson*. Foreword by Luther Vandross (New York: Watson-Guptill, 1999).

——. Liner notes for *Patti LaBelle & the Bluebelles: Over the Rainbow: The Atlantic Years* (Ichiban Records, 1994).

——. Liner notes for *The Sweet Inspirations: The Best of the Sweet Inspirations* (Ichiban Records, 1994).

Nazar, George. Liner notes for *The Very Best of Change* (Rhino Entertainment Company, 1998).

Neal, Mark Anthony. *Songs in the Key of Black Life: A Rhythm and Blues Nation* (New York: Routledge, 2003).

——. *What the Music Said: Black Popular Music and Black Public Culture* (New York: Routledge, 1999).

O'Brien, Lucy. *She Bop: The Definitive History of Women in Rock, Pop, and Soul* (New York: Penguin, 1996).

O'Dair, Barbara, ed. *Trouble Girls: The Rolling Stone Book of Women in Rock* (New York: Random House, 1997).

O'Dowd, George, with Spencer Bright. *Take It Like a Man: The Autobiography of Boy George* (London: Sidgwick and Jackson, 1995).

Patrick, Mick, and Malcolm Baumgart. Liner notes for *The Sandpebbles: We Got Love Power: The Complete Calla Recordings, 1967–1969* (The Demon Music Group, Ltd., 2000).

Pegg, Nicholas. *The Complete David Bowie*, revised and updated, 2nd ed. (London: Reynolds and Hearn, 2002).

Robinson, Matthew S. Liner notes for *Luther Vandross: Forever, For Always, For Love*, remastered ed. (Sony Music Entertainment, 2002).

——. "The Most Powerful Thing." Liner notes for *Luther Vandross: Power of Love*, remastered ed. (Sony Music Entertainment, 2002).

Sandford, Christopher. *Bowie: Loving the Alien* (New York: Da Capo, 1997).

Schulman, Bruce J. *The Seventies: The Great Shift in American Culture, Society, and Politics* (New York: Da Capo, 2001).

Shilts, Randy. *And the Band Played On: Politics, People, and the AIDS Epidemic* (New York: Penguin, 1987).

Spada, James. *The Divine Bette Midler* (New York: Collier, 1984).

Summer, Donna, with Marc Eliot. *Ordinary Girl: The Journey* (New York: Villard, 2003).

Taraborrelli, J. Randy. *Call Her Miss Ross: The Unauthorized Biography of Diana Ross* (New York: Birch Lane, 1989).

Thomson, Elizabeth, and David Gutman, eds. *The Bowie Companion* (New York: Da Capo, 1996).

Trager, James. *The New York Chronology: The Ultimate Compendium of Events, People, and Anecdotes from the Dutch to the Present* (New York: HarperResource, 2003).

Turner, Steve. *Trouble Man: The Life and Death of Marvin Gaye* (New York: Ecco, 1998).

Ward, Brian. *Just My Soul Responding: Rhythm and Blues, Black Consciousness, and Race Relations* (Berkeley: University of California Press 1998).

Werner, Craig. *A Change Is Gonna Come: Music, Race & the Soul of America* (New York: Plume, 1999).

Whitall, Susan. "Where It Starts: Hubcaps in Hitsville, U.S.A." Liner notes for *Spinners: The Chrome Collection* (Atlantic Recording Corporation, 2003).

Whitburn, Joel. *Joel Whitburn Presents Billboard Top 10 Singles Charts: 1955–2000* (Menomonee Falls, Wis.: Record Research, 2001).

——. *Joel Whitburn Presents Billboard Top R&B Singles Charts: 1942–1999* (Menomonee Falls, Wis.: Record Research, 2001).

——. *Joel Whitburn's Rhythm & Blues Top R&B Albums: 1965–1998* (Menomonee Falls, Wis.: Record Research, 1999).

White, Adam, and Fred Bronson. *The Billboard Book of Number One Rhythm & Blues Hits* (New York: Watson-Guptill, 1993).

Wild, David. *The Official Melrose Place Companion.* Introduction by Aaron Spelling (New York: HarperPerennial, 1995).

Wilson, Mary. *Dreamgirl & Supreme Faith: My Life as a Supreme,* updated ed. (New York: Cooper Square, 1999).

ARTICLES ORGANIZED BY YEAR

1976
Articles include: "Luther," Press kit for *Luther* album. Cotillion Records; David Nathan, "Luther are good for the Soul . . ." *Blues & Soul*, July 31, 1976.

1981
Articles include: J.A., "Luther Vandross: The man most likely . . ." *Melody Maker*, November 3–16, 1981; Stephen Holden, "Luther Vandross: The soul man of all trades," *Rolling Stone*; Stephen Holden, "The Pop-Soul Baritone of Luther Vandross," *New York Times*, November 16, 1981; Herschel Johnson, "The Secret World of Studio Musicians: Even some of the best-known musicians surrender their star status to make big money behind the scenes," *Black Enterprise*, December 1981; Gerrie E. Summers, Review of *Luther Vandross: Never Too Much*, *Sepia*.

1982
Articles include: Cloe Crispin, "Luther Vandross: The Jingle of Success," *High Fidelity*, March 1982; Robert Elms, "Soul for Hire," *The Face*, November 1982; Mike Garner, "Luther—the ladies session man," *Record Mirror*, November 27, 1982; Nelson George, "Too Much Luther Vandross," *Village Voice*, November 23, 1982; Paul Grein, "Vandross Cooks Up a Storm: Grammy Nominee Has Broad-Based Aspirations," *Billboard*; Stephen Holden, "Pop Divas with High-Tech Gloss," *New York Times*; Liam Lacey, "Inside the Sleeve Pop: Anyone Can See Irene Cara," *Globe and Mail*, February 13, 1982; Liam Lacey, "Inside the Sleeve Pop: Jump to It: Aretha Franklin," *Globe and Mail*, September 11, 1982; Liam Lacey, "Yoko surprises at Grammies," *Globe and Mail*, February 26, 1982; "Luther Vandross (11), Cheryl Lynn (9)," *Variety*, December 15, 1982; Darryl Minger, "Luther Vandross: From Background to Center Stage," *Essence*, October 1982; "Quincy Jones leads Grammy nominees," *Globe and Mail*, January 13, 1982; Review of *Luther Vandross: Forever, For Always, For Love*, *Variety*, October 1982; Gregory Seay, "Kool, Gang concert reason to 'Celebrate,'" *Oklahoma City Times*, February 19, 1982; Gerrie E. Summers, "Luther Vandross: His voice is no stranger to you," *Sepia*, January 1982.

1983
Articles include: "Album Sales 'Thrill' Local Record Stores," *Omaha World-Herald*, December 20, 1983; Liam Lacey, "Inside the Sleeve Pop: Get It Right: Aretha Franklin," *Globe and Mail*, July 16, 1983; Liam Lacey, "Inside the

Sleeve Pop: Leader Fonzi Thorton," *Globe and Mail*, April 30, 1983; "New Voices of the Eighties: Luther Vandross," *Ebony,* March 1983.

1984

Articles include: "Around the Region: Concert Backup Has V. Drivers Singing Blues," *Washington Post*, June 12, 1984; Robert Hilburn, "The Top Pop Performers of '84," *The Record, Northern New Jersey*, December 30, 1984; Geoffrey Himes, "DeBarge: All in the Family," *Washington Post*, March 16, 1984; Geoffrey Himes, "Recordings: Williams, Pendergrass, O'Jays: Real Soul," *Washington Post*, July 29, 1984; Geoffrey Himes, "Records: Rock 'n' Soul for the '80s," *Washington Post*, August 23, 1984; Geoffrey Himes, "Vandross' Misguided Love Songs," *Washington Post*, January 29, 1984; Dennis Hunt, "Vandross: Big Man with a Small Ego," *Calendar*, May 6, 1984; Dennis Hunt, "Vandross' 'Body' Language," *Calendar*, January 1, 1984; Connie Johnson, "Vandross Weighs in as a Heavyweight of Soul," *Los Angeles Times*, February 25, 1984; "Lives: Stephen Tyner, Crooner Growing Up in Northeast, Wishing on Becoming a Superstar," *Washington Post*, March 25, 1984; "Luther Vandross (12), DeBarge (10)," Review of concert, *Variety*, February 29, 1984; Review of *Luther Vandross: Busy Body*, *Variety*, March 7, 1984; Sheila Rule, "Harlem's Apollo shines again with new talents," *Globe and Mail*, February 25, 1984.

1985

Articles include: "1985's Top Money Making Concerts," *San Francisco Chronicle*, September 17, 1985; Sheila Benson, "Oscar Bids: The Academy Has Spoken," *Los Angeles Times*, February 10, 1985; Mary Campbell, "Singer Luther Vandross Wraps Himself Up in Successful Work," *Houston Chronicle*, May 28, 1985; Judy Cantor, "Music Makers: Marilyn Is More Than Boy George's 'Best Friend,'" *Associated Press*, March 13, 1985; David Casstevens, "Cowboy's Odd Couple: Hill, Renfro," *Dallas Morning News*, July 25, 1985; Roger Catlin, "British Guitarist Jeff Beck Is Back with Solidly Commercial LP," *Omaha World-Herald*, July 14, 1985; Roger Catlin, "Some Big-Name Rockers Turn Up on a 'Porky's' Soundtrack," *Omaha World-Herald*, March 31, 1985; Stanley Bennett Clay, "Stanley Bennett Clay's Hollwood," *Blues & Soul*, December 10–23, 1985; "Critic's Picks Art," *Washington Post*, August 25, 1985; Richard Cromelin, "Pop Beat: Smiths Forge a New Rock Crusade," *Los Angeles Times*, June 29, 1985; Steve Dale, "Newcomer Houston Just Loves Love Songs," *Chicago Tribune*, August 9, 1985; Matt Damsker, "Pop Music Review a Feast of Hot R&B at Kool Fest," *Los Angeles Times*, June 10, 1985; Patrice Gaines-Carter, "Quick-Change Artists Transform Convention Center Between Shows: Work Crews Can Swiftly Convert Buildings for Different Events," *Washington Post*, July 1, 1985; Michael Geczi, "Music Returns to the Apollo: Legendary Harlem Theatre Reopens with Sounds from Its Stars," *Dallas Morning News*, May 7, 1985; Calvin Gilbert, " 'In Square Circle' Proves to Be Musical Wonder," *Baton Rouge Morning Advocate*, October 11, 1985; Calvin Gilbert, "Fogelberg Album Serves as a Salute to Bluegrass," *Baton Rouge Morning Advocate*, May 3, 1985; Richard Harrington, "One More Time: The Top Pop of '85," *Washington Post*, December 27, 1985; Richard Harrington, "Records Wonder Struck, Again Stevie's Meloid New 'In Square Circle,' " *Washington Post*, September 10, 1985; Richard Harrington, "Rodk: The Year the Music Tried New Ventures and Budget Blues," *Washington Post*, December 29, 1985; Karen Harris, "Luther Vandross: Leaping to Stardom," *Dallas Morning News*, August 16, 1985; Robert Hilburn, ". . . And What About?" *Los Angeles Times*, December 15, 1985; Robert Hilburn, "Crown Heads of Pop: Robert Hilburn Honoring Heads That Wear the Pop Crowns," *Los Angeles Times*, December 28, 1985; Robert Hilburn, "Imposing Debut by Chris Isaak," *Los Angeles Times*, June 15, 1985; Geoffrey Himes, "Vandross: Heart and Soul," *Washington Post*, August 30, 1985; Stephen Holden, "The Pop Life: Disco Revival May Be in the Making," *New York Times*, May 22, 1985; "Houston Gives Good Love Songs," *Houston Chronicle*, August 15, 1985; Dennis Hunt, "Red-hot Debarge Starts to Realize Its Potential," *Los Angeles Times*, July 13, 1985; Dennis Hunt, "Freddy Jackson—A Rookie to Be Reckoned With," *Los Angeles Times*, September 15, 1985; Dennis Hunt, "Ready for the world / 'Sheila's' No Prince Clone; It's Just Sexy, That's All," *Los Angeles Times*, November 3, 1985; Dennis Hunt, "Young Band Ready for World to See," *Los Angeles Times*, October 18, 1985; Dennis Hunt, "Faces El Debarge: Pop Music's Newest Mr. Nice Guy," *Los Angeles Times*, April 21, 1985; Dennis Hunt, "Pop Beat Lennon Bio Stays Out of the Closets," *Los Angeles Times*, May 18, 1985; "In the Groove: Record Review," *Associated Press*, October 21, 1985; Dana Jackson, "Michigan Band Is 'Ready for the World,' " *Houston Chronicle*, November 15, 1985; Dana Jackson, "This Group's Finally Ready for the World," *Chicago Tribune*, December 5, 1985; Rick Kogan, "Luther Vandross: Songs Outshine the Spectacle," *Chicago Tribune*, August 9, 1985; Ann Kolson, "Whitney Houston Hits a High Note," *Houston Chronicle*, August 3, 1985; Liam Lacey, "Inside the Sleeve Pop: The Night I Fell in Love: Luther Vandross," *Globe and Mail*, April 4, 1985; Tom LaMarre, "Off the Raider Field, It's Just Sing, Baby, for Henry Lawrence," *Los Angeles Times*, September 1, 1985; Dee Lyons, "The Music: Let's See What These Dallasites Listen to at Home," *Dallas Morning News*, November 18, 1985; Carolyn McGuire, "Patti LaBelle After the Feast," *Chicago Tribune*, November 28, 1985; Don McLeese,

"Stevie Wonder Back in Tune," *Chicago Sun-Times*, September 22, 1985; Don McLeese, "Security to Show Fans Who's the Boss Friday," *Chicago Sun-Times*, August 5, 1985; Steve Millburg, "Temptations' Hits Stir Orpheum Crowd," *Omaha World-Herald*, November 28, 1985; Chris Mondics, "People," *The Record*, Northern New Jersey, December 10, 1985; "NAACP Image Awards Honor USA for Africa, 'Cosby Show,'" *Associated Press*, December 9, 1985; Lynn Norment, "Luther Vandross: The Voice That Seduces Millions," *Ebony*, December 1985; "The Oak Ridge Boys," *Washington Post*, September 3, 1985; Bob Olmstead, "Big Days: Boss, boats, Billiken," *Chicago Sun-Times*, August 9, 1985; "People," *Dallas Morning News*, December 10, 1985; "People," *Dallas Morning News*, October 26, 1985; Shirley E. Perlman, "Singing His Way to Hollywood," *Newsday*, December 26, 1985; Roger Piantadosi, "Nightlife: After-School Work a Nightlife Study Program to Round Out Your Education," *Washington Post*, August 30, 1985; "Prince's Imprints," *Washington Post*, September 6, 1985; Marty Racine, "Live Music Concerts Are an Expensive Form of Entertainment," *Houston Chronicle*, July 11, 1985; Review of *Luther Vandross: The Night I Fell in Love*, *Variety*, March 27, 1985; Wayne Robins, "On Music; Green and Womack Bare Their Souls," *Newsday*, December 6, 1985; Lennox Samuels, "Tears for Fears Relax on Second Album," *Dallas Morning News*, April 14, 1985; "Singer Vandross Hot Stuff—Really," *Chicago Sun-Times*, August 7, 1985; Patricia Smith, "Vandross Gimmicks Hamper His Artistry," *Chicago Sun-Times*, August 8, 1985; Patricia Smith, "It's Vandross, the Hot Ticket," *Chicago Sun-Times*, August 5, 1985; Russell Smith, "Vandross Croons, Fans Swoon," *Dallas Morning News*, August 20, 1985; Michael Sneed, Cheryl Lavin, and Kathleen O'Malley, "The McCormick Mess . . ." *Chicago Tribune*, August 8, 1985; Paula Span, "The Rebirth of the Boos: Amateur Night Lives on at a Renovated Apollo," *Washington Post*, June 16, 1985; Michael Spies, "Temptations Still Rolling," *Houston Chronicle*, December 12, 1985; Michael Spies, "Records," *Houston Chronicle*, April 21, 1985; Jacqueline Trescott, "The Voice of the Evening: Deejay Melvin Lindsey, Taking 'the Quiet Storm' to WKYS," *Washington Post*, September 5, 1985; Jacqueline Trescott, "Radio Lindsey to Join WKYS," *Washington Post*, August 16, 1985; Ken Tucker, "Black Ballad Singers Thrive in Era of Rockers," *Knight-Ridder Newspapers*, April 8, 1985; Lynn Van Matre, "Black Soul Artists Crossing Over to Success," *Seattle Times*, October 6, 1985; Lynn Van Matre, "Has Black Music . . . Lost Its Soul?," *Chicago Tribune*, September 22, 1985; Andy Warhol, "Thursday, September 5, 1985," *Andy Warhol Diaries*, ed. Pat Hackett (New York: Warner Books, 1991, 674).

1986

Articles include: Lynden Barber, "The Boss Bares His Soul to the World," *Sydney Morning Herald*, November 17, 1986; "Briefly: Judge Orders Singer to Do Benefit Concert," *Associated Press*, December 11, 1986; "Briefly: Vandross Charged with Manslaughter," *Globe and Mail*, January 23, 1986; Joe Brown, "Jackson: Nice, but Not Twice," *Washington Post*, November 14, 1986; Angela Bryant, "Luther Vandross: Music, Clothes and Other Weighty Issues," *Dallas Morning News*, March 14, 1986; Niki Cervantes, "Houston Leads in Music Awards Nominations," *Houston Chronicle*, January 6, 1986; "Charges Pending in Probe of Vandross Car Wreck Death," *Houston Chronicle*, January 14, 1986; Greta Cherenfant, "Brookhaven Almanac: A Song in His Heart," *Newsday*, August 14, 1986; Chuck Conconi, "Personalities," *Washington Post*, January 13, 1986; Russ DeVault, "Cover Story Same Ol' Whitney Houston Her Success Is Astronomical, but Her Feet Are on the Ground," *Atlanta Journal and Constitution*, August 9, 1986; Russ DeVault, "Isleys, Jasper Form a Trio That Aims to Please," *Atlanta Journal and Constitution*, March 13, 1986; Russ DeVault, "Luther Vandross' Performance Postponed Because of Accident," *Atlanta Journal and Constitution*, January 15, 1986; Russ DeVault, "Luther Vandross' Performance Postponed," *Atlanta Journal and Constitution*, January 16, 1986; Russ DeVault, "Night Beat: Despite False Starts, Satellites Flying High with Ambition, Hope," *Atlanta Journal and Constitution*, January 24, 1986; Michael Fleming, Karen Freifeld, and Susan Mulcahy, "Inside New York," *Newsday*, December 19, 1986; Ben Fong-Torres, "Gregory Hines: Heels Up in All Departments: Film, Dance Star Leads an Open Life," *San Francisco Chronicle*, April 13, 1986; Merle Ginsberg, "Sweet Inspiration: Her Mother Sang Backups for Elvis and Aretha and Cousin Dionne Knows What Friends Are For: No wonder Whitney Houston Dominates the Pop and Soul Charts," *Newsday*, June 15, 1986; Patrick Goldstein, "Labeling the Hits and Misses of 1985," *Los Angeles Times*, January 5, 1986; Patrick Goldstein, "Pop Eye," *Los Angeles Times*, December 21, 1986; Gary Graff, "Arts at Large. Vandross Aiming at Crossover," *Chicago Tribune*, October 17, 1986; Gary Graff, "Vandross Charts a Course to the Top," *The Record*, October 16, 1986; Paul Grein, "Vandross: 'Tis the 'Reason,'" *Los Angeles Times*, October 12, 1986; "Grammy Nominee to Be Charged," *Houston Chronicle*, January 22, 1986; Richard Harrington, "Bringing Back the Ballad: Anita Baker and Her Washington 'Rapture,'" *Washington Post*, August 15, 1986; Richard Harrington, "Comedowns: Rocking the Industry: Springsteen, Righteousness & Revivals," *Washington Post*, December 28, 1986; Richard Harrington, "Little by Little, Luther Is Making It Big," *Chicago Sun-Times*, August 10, 1986; Richard Harrington, "Luther Vandross, Soul & Body: The Pudgy Jingle Singer Emerges as a Svelte Pop Star," *Washington Post*,

April 6, 1986; Richard Harrington, "Natalie Cole and the Second Reprise Back Again from Drug Problems, She's Hitting Her Musical Stride," *Washington Post*, April 30, 1986; Richard Harrington, "On the Beat Solidifying the Scene Musicians Group Tries to Build a Local Network," *Washington Post*, January 8, 1986; "Here's What Rock Stars' Children Are Listening to," *Chicago Tribune*, January 12, 1986; Robert Hilburn, "Compact Discs: Excellent Good Fair Poor," *Los Angeles Times*, January 28, 1986; Robert Hilburn, "Hilburn's Best LP's of '85," *Los Angeles Times*, January 19, 1986; Robert Hilburn, "Robert Hilburn in New Video Offers Rare 'Live' Twist of Lennon," *Los Angeles Times*, February 8, 1986; Robert Hilburn, "Vandross, LaBelle: The Spirits Soar," *Los Angeles Times*, July 21, 1986; Geoffrey Himes, "Luther Vandross, in Top Form," *Washington Post*, April 5, 1986; Geoffrey Himes, "Whitney Houston, in Top Voice," *Washington Post*, July 28, 1986; Connie Johnson, "Mr. Osborne Carves Out a Soulful Niche," *Los Angeles Times*, June 1, 1986; Connie Johnson, "Starpoint Takes the Ballad Path," *Los Angeles Times*, May 26, 1986; Steve Kelley, "Bullets' Tall Rookie Needs Culture Shock Absorber," *Seattle Times*, February 16, 1986; Jan Klunder, "Singer Pleads No Contest in Crash Death," *Los Angeles Times*, December 10, 1986; Jan Klunder, "Vandross Trial Jury Selection Starts," *Los Angeles Times*, December 9, 1986; David Kronke, "Movies Keep Hines on His Toes," *The Record*, August 17, 1986; Joe Logan, "Doing or Dying at the Apollo," *The Record*, February 21, 1986; "Manslaughter Charge Dropped Against Singer," *Toronto Star*, December 11, 1986; "Luther Vandross (5), Starpoint (8)," *Variety*, May 28, 1986; Peter Marks, "Mourning a Brother and Partner," *Newsday*, January 21, 1986; Peter Marks, "Brookhaven Almanac," *Newsday*, February 20, 1986; Don McLeese, "Earl's Pub Finds Right Musical Mix," *Chicago Sun-Times*, February 17, 1986; Larry McShane, "Isley-Jasper-Isley Are a Team That's Very Focused," *Chicago Sun-Times*, March 25, 1986; David Nathan, "Whitney Houston Is Ready for More: Despite Grammy, She Has No Plans to 'Get Left Behind," *Chicago Sun-Times*, March 9, 1986; David Nathan, "Luther Vandross: The Complete Soul Man!," *Blues & Soul*, December 2–15, 1986; "National Briefs," *Houston Chronicle*, February 13, 1986; "National Briefs," *Houston Chronicle*, January 23, 1986; "Night Beat," *Atlanta Journal and Constitution*, January 17, 1986; "Passenger Dies in Car Crash Driven by R&B Singer Vandross," *Los Angeles Times*, January 13, 1986; Sandra Peddie, "Singer Charged in Fatal Crash," *Newsday*, January 23, 1986; "People in the News," *Associated Press*, January 18, 1986; "People in the News," *Associated Press*, January 20, 1986; "People," *Dallas Morning News*, January 13, 1986; Shirley E. Perlman, "Sorrow in Home of a Rising Star," *Suffolk*, January 16, 1986; "Personal Mention," *Houston Chronicle*, December 11, 1986; "Police Seek Charge Against Vandross," *Seattle Times*, January 13, 1986; Steve Pond,

"Gospel Gets Some Special Attention," *Los Angeles Times*, November 1, 1986; Tom Popson, "Vocal Variety Makes Isley Spinoff Distinctive," *Chicago Tribune*, March 28, 1986; "Probe of Vandross' Fatal Crash Continues D. A. Reject Charging Singer," *Los Angeles Times*, January 14, 1986; "Prosecutors Reject Initial Police Request for Manslaughter Charge," *Associated Press*, January 13, 1986; James Quinn, "Singer Luther Vandross Hurt in Crash; Rider Dies," *Los Angeles Times*, January 13, 1986; "The Region," *Los Angeles Times*, January 15, 1986; "The Region," *Los Angeles Times*, January 22, 1986; "The Region: No Charges Over Fatality," *Los Angeles Times*, January 14, 1986; "Reviews: Pop," review of "Give Me the Reason," *Toronto Star*, November 28, 1986; Lennox Samuels, "Young Woodentops Carve Neat Niche for Themselves," *Dallas Morning News*, November 2, 1986; "Sentenced to Sing?," *Omaha World-Herald*, December 12, 1986; "Singer Hurt in Crash," *Newsday*, January 13, 1986; "Singer Hurt, Brother Dead in Crash," *Nassau and Suffolk*, January 15, 1986; "Singer in Car Accident that Kills Friend," *Seattle Times*, January 14, 1986; "Singer Luther Vandross Charged in Fatal Car Accident," *Associated Press*, January 22, 1986; "Singer Vandross Faces Charges in Fatal Crash," *Chicago Tribune*, January 23, 1986; "Singer Vandross to Be Charged in Fatal Crash," *Los Angeles Times*, January 22, 1986; Patricia Smith, "Vandross Gets Down to Business," *Chicago Sun-Times*, March 31, 1986; Michael Sneed and Kathy O'Malley, "Dateline: New Orleans . . ." *Chicago Tribune*, January 13, 1986; Michael Sneed and Kathy O'Malley, "Sports Shorts . . ." *Chicago Tribune*, January 14, 1986; Michael Sneed and Kathy O'Malley, "The Big Scooooooop! . . ." *Chicago Tribune*, February 20, 1986; Michael Sneed and Kathy O'Malley, "A Police Bulletin," *Chicago Tribune*, January 22, 1986; Michael Sneed and Kathy O'Malley, "The Big Probe . . ." *Chicago Tribune*, January 17, 1986; Eric Snider, "Patti LaBelle, Audience: A Musical Love Affair Series: Music Review," *St. Petersburg Times*, August 11, 1986; Eric Snider, David Okamoto, Peter Smith, and Michael Fleming, "Records That Were Made to Be Rated Series: Records," *St. Petersburg Times*, December 21, 1986; Eric Snider, David Okamoto, Peter Smith, and Michael Fleming, "Vandross Hits the Spot Spree: Records," *St. Petersburg Times*, November 9, 1986; "Soul Singer Charged in Fatal Crash," *San Francisco Chronicle*, January 23, 1986; "Soul Singer Luther Vandross Hurt in Car Wreck," *San Francisco Chronicle*, January 13, 1986; "Soul Singer to Do Benefit in Pal's Traffic Death," *San Francisco Chronicle*, December 10, 1986; "Special Rendition of 'We Shall Overcome' to Be Introduced in Recognition of Black History Month," *PR Newswire*, February 19, 1986; "Stars Tinkle on Top 40 Shopping List," *Los Angeles Times*, December 21, 1986; Keith L. Thomas, "Clips More Popular—and Better—Than Ever," *Atlanta Journal and Constitution*, August 3, 1986; "Vandross Agreement," *Newsday*, December 10, 1986;

"Vandross Agrees to Plea Bargain Series: People," *St. Petersburg Times*, December 10, 1986; "Vandross Facing Charges," *Globe and Mail*, January 14, 1986; "Vandross Hoping to Cross Over on 5th Try," *Chicago Tribune*, October 16, 1986; "Vandross Hospitalized in Crash," *Chicago Sun-Times*, January 14, 1986; "Vandross to Headline July's Kool Festival," *Atlanta Journal and Constitution*, May 9, 1986; Lynn Van Matre, "Dire Straits Band, Leader Put Britain High on Grammy Chart," *Chicago Tribune*, January 10, 1986; Stephen Williams, "Vandross Formula Has 'Em Swooning," *Newsday*, May 3, 1986; Jennifer Wolff, "Vandross Sets New Year's Show," *Chicago Sun-Times*, December 12, 1986; Clarence Waldron, "Luther Vandross Tells What Inspires Him as Songwriter and Entertainer," *Jet*, 1986.

1987

Articles include: "Ballads in B&W," *Los Angeles Times*, August 16, 1987; Lynden Barber, "Good, Bad and Ugly of Black Pop," *Sydney Morning Herald*, July 6, 1987; Gary Binford, "Garden Giving Dr. J Headache Cure," *Newsday*, April 5, 1987; "Black Radio," *Los Angeles Times*, November 29, 1987; Lori Boyer, "Singers at 16th Atlanta Kool Festival Receive a Warm Response," *Atlanta Journal and Constitution*, July 19, 1987; Jon Bream, " '87 Isn't Music to Diana Ross' Ears," *Star-Tribune Newspaper of the Twin Cities*, June 5, 1987; Jon Bream, "Balladeer Jackson Is Top-Notch Contender as a Romantic Idol," *Star-Tribune Newspaper of the Twin Cities*, May 29, 1987; Jon Bream, "Popular Music," *Star-Tribune Newspaper of the Twin Cities*, May 22, 1987; Jon Bream, "Rookie Class Goes on Record with New Sounds," *Star-Tribune Newspaper of the Twin Cities*, October 4, 1987; "Briefly," *USA Today*, June 1, 1987; Bruce Britt, "Bowie Back-Up Alomar Sees Reason for Elation in Letdown," *Chicago Tribune*, August 20, 1987; Joe Brown, "Chairwomen of the Boards," *Washington Post*, May 1, 1987; Joe Brown, "Whitney Houston," *Washington Post*, July 13, 1987; Angela Bryant, "Luther Vandross: Soul-Searching Ends at Reunion," *Dallas Morning News*, April 17, 1987; "Caine Won't Be Host for Oscar Program Series: Headliners," *St. Petersburg Times*, March 2, 1987; "Concert Held," *Baton Rouge Morning Advocate*, June 2, 1987; J. D. Considine, "Records," *Houston Chronicle*, July 26, 1987; Richard Cromelin, "Baker Plays It Loose and Lively at the Greek," *Los Angeles Times*, September 5, 1987; Richard Cromelin, "In 3 Sold Out Universal Shows Surprises and Control from Freddie Jackson," *Los Angeles Times*, March 16, 1987; Richard Cromelin, "Pop Music Review: Vandross Just Doesn't Go That Extra Distance," *Los Angeles Times*, April 17, 1987; Sandy Cullen, "Whitney Houston Showcases Her Talents Before 20,000," *Harrisburg Patriot*, August 14, 1987; Russ DeVault, "Night Beat: Cameo, Luther Vandross Headline Kool Festival," *Atlanta Journal and Constitution*, July 17, 1987;

Bill Douglas, "Show Business: Wednesday Night Live Amateurs at the Apollo," *Newsday*, November 29, 1987; "Dross Attack," *Los Angeles Times*, May 2, 1987; "Drummer for Luther Vandross in Apparent Suicide," *Associated Press*, June 8, 1987; "Drummer for Luther Vandross Leaps to Death," *San Francisco Chronicle*, June 9, 1987; Chris Farley, "Hype Aside, Ava Cherry (And Her Name) Is for Real," *Chicago Tribune*, August 21, 1987; Michael Fleming, "Inside New York," *Newsday*, August 17, 1987; Michael Fleming, Karen Freifeld, and Susan Mulcahy, *Newsday*, February 13, 1987; Ben Fong-Torres, "KBLX: The Station Quietly Goes Upscale," *San Francisco Chronicle*, April 26, 1987; Betty Goodwin, "Fabrice Has a Good Bead on What's Hot," *Los Angeles Times*, March 6, 1987; Edna Gundersen, "Superfest Swings from Slow to Sizzling," *USA Today*, June 17, 1987; Richard Harrington, "Classy Soul Train Awards; Janet Jackson, Run-DMC Among Winners," *Washington Post*, March 24, 1987; Richard Harrington, "Starlight, Stars Bright," *Washington Post*, June 5, 1987; Lee Hildebrand, "The Whispers / Still on Top After 20 Years," *San Francisco Chronicle*, June 21, 1987; Steve Hochman, "Alomar Generates a Little Fame on His Own Hook," *Los Angeles Times*, August 6, 1987; Stephen Holden, "Popularity of Balladeers Shows That Rappers Aren't Ruling Black Pop," *Chicago Tribune*, January 1, 1987; Anne V. Hull, "Simon's Amazing 'Graceland' Wins Top Grammy Award," *St. Petersburg Times*, February 25, 1987; "In Brief: Drummer Jumps to Death," *Newsday*, June 9, 1987; Barbara Jaeger, "Anita Baker in Top Form," *The Record*, October 16, 1987; Barbara Jaeger, "For Musical Knockout," *The Record*, August 10, 1987; Barbara Jaeger, "Freddie Jackson: A Hype-Powered Performance," *The Record*, February 27, 1987; Connie Johnson, "Pop Ballads: What's Race Got to Do with It?" *Los Angeles Times*, August 2, 1987; Connie Johnson, "Pop Weekend a Subdued LaBelle Set at Superfest," *Los Angeles Times*, June 22, 1987; Connie Johnson and Don Snowden, "Black Music Fans Say They Can't Always Get What They Want," *Los Angeles Times*, November 22, 1987; Connie Johnson and Don Snowden, "Radio's Blackout: Why Are So Many Acclaimed Black Artists Ignored by Black Stations?," *Los Angeles Times*, November 22, 1987; Jae-Ha Kim, "Dreams Generate Music," *Chicago Sun-Times*, August 21, 1987; Jae-Ha Kim, "Tiffany (Only 15 Years Old) Grows into Pop Star Role," *Chicago Sun-Times*, July 31, 1987; Ann Kolson, "Cissy Houston Shines on in the Background," *Chicago Tribune*, August 20, 1987; Ann Kolson, "Cissy Houston, Long-Burning Star," *The Record*, August 12, 1987; "L.A. Black Radio," *Los Angeles Times*, November 22, 1987; "Last Ode for a Shining Star," *The Record*, June 18, 1987; Randy Lewis, "Stadium Shows Make a Comeback," *Los Angeles Times*, June 5, 1987; "Local News in Brief City Settles in Car Crash," *Los Angeles Times*, December 10, 1987; "Luther Vandross (The Forum, L.A.)," *Variety*, April 22, 1987; Patrick Mac-

Donald, "Freddie Was Ready for Soul-Music Fame," *Seattle Times*, March 27, 1987; Eve Markowitz, "Teaneck Drummer's Suicide Stuns His Friends," *The Record*, June 9, 1987; James McBride, "Marcus Miller's Talent for the Top; The Versatile Bass Player & His Modern Day Mastery of Soul," *Washington Post*, October 11, 1987; James McBride, "Modern Soul Master Marcus Miller's Talent for the Top," *Houston Chronicle*, November 22, 1987; Don McLeese, "'Higher Love' Gets Highest Honors / Winwood and Simon Take Top Two Grammy Awards," *Chicago Sun-Times*, February 25, 1987; Margo Miller, "120-Acre Purchase Will Give BSO Twice the Room at Tanglewood," *Boston Globe*, January 4, 1987; John Milward, "Popular," *USA Today*, June 17, 1987; Steve Morse, "Anita Baker Holds a Love-In at Wang Center," *Boston Globe*, October 23, 1987; Steve Morse, "Standoff at the Grammys: Something for Everyone at This Year's Awards," *Boston Globe*, February 25, 1987; Lawrence O'Toole, "NY Clips: Northerners Prefer Blue Velvet over Hannah on 10-best List Canadian and U.S. Critics at Odds in Poll," *Globe and Mail*, February 20, 1987; John Pareles, "The Color of Money Often Decides the Color of Successful Music," *St. Petersburg Times*, May 31, 1987; Tony Perry, "Warwick Stays Popular Despite Lack of Solo Chart Topper," *Sunday Patriot-News Harrisburg*, March 29, 1987; "Personal Mention," *Houston Chronicle*, June 10, 1987; "Pop/Rock," *Los Angeles Times*, June 1, 1987; "Pop/Rock," *Los Angeles Times*, June 4, 1987; "'Quiet Storm' Radio Format Weathers Well with 'Beautiful Music,'" *Chicago Tribune*, March 5, 1987; Greg Quills, "Diana Ross on Long Slow Roll," *Toronto Star*, June 26, 1987; Wayne Robins, "Asbestos—Work Delay Cancels Garden Concert," *Newsday*, June 3, 1987; Wayne Robins, "Roberta Flack's Passionate Pop," *Newsday*, March 14, 1987; Wayne Robins, "Romantic Sounds from a Soulful Past," *Newsday*, June 13, 1987; Ruth Ryon, "New York Singer Buys Beverly Hills Gated Estate," *Los Angeles Times*, January 18, 1987; Joel Selvin, "Vandross Leaves 'Em Fantasizing," *San Francisco Chronicle*, April 20, 1987; Tom Shales, "Mysticism à la MacLaine; Plus 4 Others in a Weekend Smorgasbord," *Washington Post*, January 17, 1987; Richard Simon, "Council Committee Backs $50,000 Settlement to Family of Traffic Collision Victims," *Los Angeles Times*, December 2, 1987; Patricia Smith, "Vandross's Pipes Spring a Leak," *Chicago Sun-Times*, September 4, 1987; Eric Snider, "Death Rumors Exaggerated," *St. Petersburg Times*, June 10, 1987; Eric Snider, "Soul Singer Freddie Jackson's Audience Grows," *St. Petersburg Times*, July 17, 1987; Eric Snider, "Vandross' Vocal Light Shines Brightly, but Briefly," *St. Petersburg Times*, April 4, 1987; Sable St. Regis, "Travel in Style. Comings and Goings," *Chicago Tribune*, February 4, 1987; "Vandross Cancels Phoenix Concerts to Protest Ariz. Snubbing of King Holiday," *Jet*, June 15, 1987; "Vandross Drummer Dies in Jump From 17th Floor," *Toronto Star*, June 9, 1987; Lynn Voedisch, "Vandross to Perform at the Arie Crown," *Chicago Sun-Times*, June 26, 1987; John Voland, "Limo Work: Mostly Drive, Drive, Drive," *Los Angeles Times*, February 25, 1987; John Voland, "Soul Train Awards Show Debuts," *Los Angeles Times*, March 25, 1987; Alona Wartofsky, "Alexander O'Neal," *Washington Post*, August 3, 1987; Maurice Weaver, " 'Soul Train' Awards Are a 1st for Black Music," *Chicago Tribune*, March 23, 1987; Harriet Wesley, "Marcus Miller Made 'Tutu' a Tour de Force," *Sunday Patriot-News Harrisburg*, May 17, 1987; Bruce Westbrook, "Crouch, Houston's Holliday Join Simon for Gospel Session," *Houston Chronicle*, January 1, 1987; Stephen Williams, "Anita Baker, Pursuing Perfection," *Newsday*, July 26, 1987; Jennifer Wolff, "Peter, Paul, Mary Tickets on Sale," *Chicago Sun-Times*, July 24, 1987; Tracey Wong Briggs, "Idle Idol," *USA Today*, June 4, 1987; Todd Allan Yasui and Alona Wartofsky, "Eddie Money," *Washington Post*, June 17, 1987.

1988

Articles include: Randy Alexander, "Aretha Franklin Reaches a Turning Point," *Chicago Sun-Times*, December 23, 1988; "Baker and Vandross Are Feuding Backstage," *San Francisco Chronicle*, December 17, 1988; Marilyn Beck, "Danny DeVito, Michael Douglas to Team Up for Movie in March," *Orange County Register*, October 3, 1988; Marilyn Beck, "Producer develops 7th 'Police Academy' movie," *Orange County Register*, December 2, 1988; Donna Britt, "Gregory Hines Takes His Talents to the Limits," *USA Today*, March 22, 1988; Joe Brown, "Ballads Make a Better Bryson," *Washington Post*, March 25, 1988; Joe Brown, "Luther Vandross: Light and Lively," *Washington Post*, September 30, 1988; Joe Brown, "Records; Streisand's Latest, Loved and Lost; Missing the Magic in a Self-Conscious Set," *Washington Post*, November 23, 1988; Bruce Butterfield, "WZOU-FM Union Seeks Support," *Boston Globe*, December 14, 1988; Mary Campbell, "A Tapping Actor Who Happens to Also Sing," *Associated Press*, July 14, 1988; Mary Campbell, "Gregory Hines Taps New Singing Talent," *Dallas Morning News*, July 20, 1988; Mary Campbell, "Versatile Gregory Hines Taps into Singing Career with Release of 1st Album," *Chicago Sun-Times*, July 20, 1988; Mary Campbell, "Versatile Gregory Hines Taps into Singing Career," *Chicago Sun-Times*, July 22, 1988; John Carman, " 'Remember My Name'/ TV Film on AIDS Quilt Tour," *San Francisco Chronicle*, October 8, 1988; Louis Chunovic, "Jackson's Party Man," *Los Angeles Times*, May 14, 1988; Chrisena Coleman, "A Show Goes on at the Apollo," *The Record*, October 7, 1988; Paul D. Colford, "AM/FM Vaughn Harper's 'Quiet Storm,' " *Newsday*, March 9, 1988; Lydia J. Davis, "Black Achievement," *Chicago Tribune*, January 25, 1988; Russ DeVault, "Night Beat 'Best-Known Unknown'

Is Making a Name for Herself," *Atlanta Journal and Constitution*, July 22, 1988; Russ DeVault, "Night Beat Malone, Phillips to Give It a Go as Twosome?" *Atlanta Journal and Constitution*, September 30, 1988; Robert Feder, "WBMX Disappears; New 'V-103' Emerges," *Chicago Sun-Times*, October 19, 1988; Nelson George, " 'Never Too Much' Recognition for Reigning Vocal King: Vandross Deserves 'Superstar' Status," *Billboard*, October 22, 1988; Jefferson Graham, "Hines and Davis, Tops in Taps," *USA Today*, June 1, 1988; Paul Grein, "Baker, Vandross: The Billing, No Cooing," *Los Angeles Times*, December 11, 1988; Paul Grein, "Pop Music Review: Anita Baker Steals the Show from Headliner Vandross," *Los Angeles Times*, December 3, 1988; Paul Grein, "Pop Weekend: It Was Jackson's Concert but Day Who Stole Show," *Los Angeles Times*, August 15, 1988; Edna Gundersen, " '80s Pop Gold Diggers Recover Hits of Yesteryear," *USA Today*, October 18, 1988; Richard Harrington, "Singing 'Cissy's' Praise," *Washington Post*, February 8, 1988; Karen Harris, "Soulful 'Heat' from a Winning Pair: Vandross and Baker Are Both in Fine Voice for Reunion Show," *Dallas Morning News*, October 18, 1988; Thomas B. Harrison, "Not Tapped Out/The Dance Floor Has Been Kind to Hines Series: Cover Story," *St. Petersburg Times*, July 29, 1988; Geoffrey Himes, "Second-Generation Sweet Soul Music," *Washington Post*, July 15, 1988; Carla Hinton, "Baker, Vandross Concert Good," *Daily Oklahoman*, November 23, 1988; Carla Hinton, "Baker, Vandross Ready to Take on Oklahoma," *Daily Oklahoman*, November 17, 1988; Paul Hirshson, "A Time to Give, a Time to Sing," *Boston Globe*, December 12, 1988; Stephen Holden, "Gregory Hines' Voice Dances Up the Charts," *Chicago Tribune*, July 14, 1988; Dennis Hunt, "Luther Vandross on Tour with Sizable Shadow," *Los Angeles Times*, December 1, 1988; Dennis Hunt, "Macho Alexander O'Neal Grabs an Audience with 'Hearsay,' " *The Record*, February 21, 1988; Dennis Hunt, "O'Neal's Instant Success Is 'Hearsay,' " *Los Angeles Times*, February 21, 1988; Dennis Hunt, "Song-and-Dance Man," *Los Angeles Times*, July 9, 1988; Dennis Hunt, "Walden—A Pop Hit Machine," *Los Angeles Times*, March 13, 1988; Dennis Hunt, "Weight Gain Almost Stopped Singer's Tour," *St. Petersburg Times*, December 6, 1988; Maudlyne Ihejirika, "Fans Agree: Luther and Anita No. 1," *Chicago Sun-Times*, December 28, 1988; Connie Johnson, "Luscious, Lonely Luther," *Los Angeles Times*, October 2, 1988; Connie Johnson, "Pop Music: Britain Turns on the Black Power," *Los Angeles Times*, March 13, 1988; James T. Jones IV, "Anita Baker, a Christmas Bride?," *USA Today*, December 29, 1988; James T. Jones IV, "Like Hot Music? This Superfest's for You," *USA Today*, July 13, 1988; James T. Jones IV, "Sax Tunes Are Horning in on Pop," *USA Today*, March 22, 1988; James T. Jones IV, "Soul's Sweet Revival; New Voices Are Gliding into the Groove; The Sound Is Gospel-True and Red-Hot," *USA Today*, May 18, 1988; James T. Jones IV, "They're Setting Soul on Fire; Vandross-Baker Tour Opener Generates 'Heat'; Giving Fans Their Best Love Songs," *USA Today*, September 30, 1988; Lewis Lazare, "Urban (Radio) Warfare," *Crains Chicago Business*, October 24, 1988; "Luther Vandross," *Ebony*, March 1988; "The Marvelettes' Old Motown Magic," *St. Petersburg Times*, September 30, 1988; "Luther Vandross, Anita Baker, Sinbad (Sports Arena, L.A.)," *Variety*, December 7–13, 1988; Nathan McCall, "Jackson Holds Birthday Bash with a Political Flavor Ex-Atlanta Mayor, 50, Casts Eye on City Hall," *Atlanta Journal*, March 24, 1988; Don McLeese, "Chaka Khan Makes a Strong Comeback," *Chicago Sun-Times*, December 16, 1988; John Milward, "A Soulful Talent/Luther Vandross Outshines Many of His Peers but Gets Less Recognition," *Houston Chronicle*, October 9, 1988; John Milward, "Crossover Can Mean Success, Concession," *Seattle Times*, September 29, 1988; John Milward, "Pop, Soul and Sex: From Elvis to Teddy," *Chicago Tribune*, April 28, 1988; Steve Morse, "AIDS Benefit a Garden Party," *Boston Globe*, December 14, 1988; Steve Morse, "An AIDS Concert with a Difference," *Boston Globe*, October 8, 1988; Steve Morse, "Not Just Whitney's Mother: PBS Tells Cissy Houston's Oft-Overlooked Story," *Boston Globe*, February 10, 1988; Steve Morse, "Pop Concert Season Was Super-Crammed," *Boston Globe*, December 25, 1988; Steve Morse, "Regina Belle Rings Loud and Clear," *Boston Globe*, May 10, 1988; Steve Morse, "Vandross, Baker Score with Singles," *Boston Globe*, November 13, 1988; "Motown Returns to the Apollo 50th Anniversary for the Musical Celebration of the Century," *PR Newswire*, October 24, 1988; David Nathan, "Luther: The Heat Is On!," *Blues & Soul*, October 25–November 7, 1988; Ken Perkins, "Anita Baker: Luther Vandross Other Half of Show's Dynamic Duo," *Dallas Morning News*, October 14, 1988; Greg Quill, "Patti Howls Back from 9 Years of Domestic Bliss," *Toronto Star*, July 29, 1988; Marty Racine, "Baker opens for Vandross . . . and May Have Closed as Well," *Houston Chronicle*, October 14, 1988; Wayne Robins, "Double Garden Party, Madison Style," *Newsday*, October 7, 1988; Lennox Samuels, "New LP Proves Rockers Grow Old Gracefully," *Dallas Morning News*, December 18, 1988; David Silverman, "Anita Baker's a Top Seller with Chicago Concert Fans," *Chicago Tribune*, December 16, 1988; David Silverman, "Beauty and the Beast: Vandross Outshines Baker in Horizon Twin Bill," *Chicago Tribune*, December 29, 1988; David Silverman, "Tour De Force: Anita Baker Hits the Road—And Is Determined Not to Miss a Beat," *Chicago Tribune*, December 25, 1988; Eric Snider, "Savor the Subtlety of Luther Vandross/'It's All About Love' as Only He Can Tell It Series: Recording," *St. Petersburg Times*, November 13, 1988; Michael Snyder, "Julie Brown of 'Club MTV'/British Hostess Is the Life of the

U.S. Dance Party," *San Francisco Chronicle*, April 3, 1988; "Stanley Jordan and Kirk Whalum to Perform at Roy Thomson Hall," *Canada News-Wire*, June 22, 1988; Zan Stewart, "Television Reviews: An Incomplete Portrait of Cissy Houston," *Los Angeles Times*, February 12, 1988; Bob Strauss, "Gregory Hines heads 'Off Limits'/Dancer-Actor Sweats the Details in Vietnam War Thriller," *Chicago Sun-Times*, March 27, 1988; Jim Sullivan, "Citi Benefit Lacks Luster But Gets Job Done," *Boston Globe*, December 15, 1988; Lynn Voedisch, "Anita Baker's Upbeat Mode Sparkles at Horizon," *Chicago Sun-Times*, December 28, 1988; "Warwick Finds Out What Friends Are For," *USA Today*, June 13, 1988; Jim Washburn, "Sly and Robbie Leave Studio Work and Go on the Road to Keep 'Fresh,'" *Los Angeles Times*, October 22, 1988; Hedy Weiss, "Stephanie Mills Faces the Music in 'Harlem Suite,'" *Chicago Sun-Times*, October 16, 1988; Steve Zipay, "Jazz Festival Hall of Famers Miles Davis at Avery Fisher," *Newsday*, June 27, 1988.

1989

Articles include: Michael Arkush, "Canoga Park Club Shuts Down; Heavy Metal Format Fails to Fly," *Los Angeles Times*, October 15, 1989; Lynden Barber, "Chuck Out the Chaka," *Sydney Morning Herald*, February 14, 1989; David Bauder, "Grammys Camouflage Music Industry's Racial Problems," *Associated Press*, February 15, 1989; David Bauder, "Music Industry's Disharmony Series: Commentary," *St. Petersburg Times*, February 22, 1989; Hugh Boulware, "Gospel Truths New Lyrics Restate an Old-Fashioned Faith for BeBe and CeCe Winans," *Chicago Tribune*, July 23, 1989; Hugh Boulware, "This Is What Friends Are For," *Chicago Tribune*, July 2, 1989; Joe Brown, "Alston's Sweet, Manhattans-less Suite," *Washington Post*, March 10, 1989; David Browne, "Barking Replaces Applause When a Show Is 'Top Dog,'" *Austin American-Statesman*, January 4, 1989; Terry Byrne, "How to Properly Feed and Care for Your Rolling Stone 'You Know How Those Brits Like to Clog Up Their Arteries,'" *Globe and Mail*, December 2, 1989; Cary Darling, "Wistfully, the Temptations and O'Jays Forge Ahead," *Orange County Register*, February 3, 1989; Angela Fox Dunn, "Arsenio Hall Realizes a Tonight on TV," *Chicago Sun-Times*, January 3, 1989; James Endrst, "24-hour Music Channel Singing Different Tune with Success," *Austin American-Statesman*, April 15, 1989; James Endrst, "Cable's VH-1 Has Found Its Place and Time Series: Television," *St. Petersburg Times*, March 6, 1989; Robert Feder, "WGN Builds Its Lead Over WGCI-FM While 'V-103' Moves Up Fast," *Chicago Sun-Times*, April 19, 1989; Michael Fleming, Karen Freifeld, and Susan Mulcahy, "Inside New York," *Newsday*, April 12, 1989; Gary Graff, "Greatest Hits Packages Used to Be Just That—Now They've Got More," *Dallas Morning News*, November 26, 1989; Jefferson Graham, "Music Is Still This Isley's Thing," *USA*

Today, September 7, 1989; Paul Grein, "McCartney: Low-Key with New Album," *Los Angeles Times*, May 28, 1989; Edna Gundersen, "Dude Is Back on the Block," *USA Today*, December 7, 1989; Richard Harrington, "Rap & Metal, Hitting the Mainstream," *Washington Post*, January 1, 1989; Lee Hildebrand, "Mixed Blessing/Blues Queen Denied Her Radio Throne/Etta James Soars but Not on the Air," *San Francisco Chronicle*, May 14, 1989; Edward Hill, "Really, Aretha. Act Your Age," *Plain Dealer*, May 13, 1989; Geoffrey Himes, "New Soul Men's Rhythm and Ruse," *Washington Post*, September 8, 1989; Geoffrey Himes, "On the Way to 'Heaven,'" *Washington Post*, April 21, 1989; Ann Hodges, "Murphy Says Hall 'Born to Be a TV Talk Host,'" *Houston Chronicle*, January 5, 1989; Dennis Hunt, "Black Rocker Bares His Soul," *Los Angeles Times*, June 11, 1989; Dennis Hunt, "Producer Perry Finds Rhythm Is Better with Warner Records," *Los Angeles Times*, May 27, 1989; Dennis Hunt, "Where Are the Great R&B Singers of Today? As Tastes, Tempo and Technology Change the Genre, Gone Are Solid Vocalists Who Could Dazzle Without Flash," *Los Angeles Times*, July 2, 1989; Barbara Jaeger, "Bowie: The One and the Many," *The Record*, September 28, 1989; Barbara Jaeger, "Crossover: Black, White, and Heard All Over," *The Record*, April 14, 1989; James T. Jones IV, "He Masterminds a Little 'Night' Music," *USA Today*, January 4, 1989; James T. Jones IV, "Jazz and R&B; A Cruel Blow for Brown," *USA Today*, February 22, 1989; James T. Jones IV, "White, a Soulful 'Superwoman,'" *USA Today*, April 25, 1989; Marvin Kitman, "The Marvin Kitman Show: Arsenio Hall: A Letterman Wakeup Call?" *Newsday*, January 5, 1989; Rick Kogan, "Arsenio Hall's New Show Struts onto Airwaves," *Chicago Tribune*, January 5, 1989; "Kup on Sunday," *Chicago Sun-Times*, June 25, 1989; Art Levine, "Rhythm and Blues, on the Upbeat Performers from the '50s and '60s Are Playing to Packed Halls—and Claiming Some Long Unpaid Debts," *U.S. News & World Report*, January 16, 1989; Laurie Levy, "Clothes Circuit Taking the High (Fashion) Road to Milan with Chicago Buyers Joy and 'Jeem,'" *Chicago Tribune*, August 20, 1989; Steven Long, "Ridin' . . . Ropin' . . . Rodeo! / Weekend Captures Flavor of the Event," *Houston Chronicle*, February 17, 1989; "Luther: The Leader of the Pack," *Blues & Soul*, April 4–17, 1989; "Luther Vandross Breaks U.K. Record," *PR Newswire*, April 11, 1989; Aleene MacMinn, "Pop/Rock," *Los Angeles Times*, April 14, 1989; "Monday's People," *The Record*, May 15, 1989; Dalton Narine, "'Blue-Eyed Soul': Are Whites Taking Over Rhythm & Blues?," *Ebony*, July 1989; "Newsmakers," *Houston Chronicle*, September 2, 1989; Lynn Norment, "Luther Vandross' $8.5 Million Hideaway," *Ebony*, June 1989; "Patti Austin Gets 'Real' with Oldies," *USA Today*, January 25, 1989; "People," *Dallas Morning News*, November 11, 1989; Claudia Puig, "Waltz Ends at KFAC as New Crew Gears Up for Rock Format,"

Los Angeles Times, September 20, 1989; Claudia Puig and Aleene MacMinn, "TV & Video," *Los Angeles Times*, May 15, 1989; Greg Quill, "Emmylou's Bluebird Flies but Fails to Soar," *Toronto Star*, January 20, 1989; Marty Racine, " 'Lu, Lu!' of a Concert Given by Vandross," *Houston Chronicle*, March 1, 1989; Marty Racine, "Rodeo Brings Out the Best in Artists," *Houston Chronicle*, March 6, 1989; Marty Racine, "Vandross Luuuu-sens Up Livestock Show Crowd," *Houston Chronicle*, March 1, 1989; Wayne Robins, "Collection from a Ch-Ch-Changing Bowie," *Newsday*, October 1, 1989; "Rockers Tune in to Investments," *Los Angeles Daily News*, September 2, 1989; Howard Rosenberg, "Grammy's '89: A Show Short on Talk and Long on Song," *Los Angeles Times*, February 23, 1989; Chuck Ross, "Watch Out, Johnny/Arsenio Hall All Set to Talk," *San Francisco Chronicle*, January 2, 1989; Matt Roush, "If You're Lonesome for 'Dove,' It Will Be Back," *USA Today*, March 7, 1989; David Silverman, "Soulful Anita Baker's 'Best' a Sound That Satisfies Millions," *Austin American-Statesman*, January 2, 1989; Eric Snider, "Notes from the Cutting Edge/New York's New Music Seminar Is a Walk on the Wild Side," *St. Petersburg Times*, July 30, 1989; Eric Snider, "Silky Tunes for Loving: Series: Audio Files," *St. Petersburg Times*, December 1, 1989; David Patrick Stearns, "The Listening Room," *USA Today*, August 15, 1989; Irwin Stambler, "Luther Vandross," *Encyclopedia of Pop, Rock, & Soul*, revised ed. (New York: St. Martin's Press); Jeannine Stein, "Into the Night," *Los Angeles Times*, January 13, 1989; Robyn Taylor, "Black Radio's Frequency," *Los Angeles Times*, March 26, 1989; "VH-1 Comes of Age," *Hartford Courant*, April 2, 1989; John Voorhees, "Johnny's Newest Challenger Adds Zest to Late-Night Talk Derby," *Seattle Times*, January 5, 1989; Irving Wallace, David Wallechinsky, and Amy Wallace, "Some Famous Fatties and Their Diets," *San Francisco Chronicle*, August 23, 1989; Don Waller, "Pop Music Review: Original Dells Reprise '50s Sound," *Los Angeles Times*, May 20, 1989; Barry Walters, "D'Arby LP Marred by Pretension," *San Francisco Examiner*, December 1, 1989; Ellis Widner, "Jazz Star Whalum Still Learning to Play," *Tulsa Tribune*, August 8, 1989; Jeffrey Yorke, "WMMJ, Making it Motown," *Washington Post*, February 28, 1989; Steve Zipay, "A Rhythmic Showcase," *Newsday*, February 18, 1989.

1990

Articles include: "Barry White: The Voice Is Purrrrfect," *The Record*, June 16, 1990; Marilyn Beck, "Film 'Phantom' Still Up in the Air," *Los Angeles Daily*, January 30, 1990; Marilyn Beck, "Time to Put the Bass in Action," *The Record*, May 6, 1990; Mike Boehm, "Pop Music Review: Seductive Singing by Vandross," *Los Angeles Times*, June 16, 1990; Mike Boehm, "Pop Music Review: Vandross Gently Turns Up the Heat," *Los Angeles Times*, June 16, 1990; Greg

Braxton, "Rap Under Siege Pop Music: The Furor Over Legal Moves Against 2 Live Crew Has Sparked Intense Debate in the Local African-American Community," *Los Angeles Times*, June 14, 1990; Jon Bream, "Luther Puts New Gloss on the Word 'Showman,'" *Star-Tribune*, September 21, 1990; Jon Bream, "Music," *Star-Tribune*, September 14, 1990; G. Brown, "Weather Spoils Vandross Performance at Red Rocks," *Denver Post*, September 19, 1990; Joe Brown, "Belle Epoque: Rise of Regina," *Washington Post*, March 9, 1990; Joe Brown, "Two Trios, One Goal," *Washington Post*, June 29, 1990; Gail Campbell, "Ooh Baby . . . The Return of Barry White," *Washington Times*, June 8, 1990; Bill Carbine, "Atlanta Today," *Atlanta Journal, Atlanta Constitution*, August 21, 1990; Thor Christensen, "Playing the Big Gig's Big Room: Marcus Amphitheater Balances Its Lineup," *Milwaukee Journal*, June 24, 1990; Thor Christensen, "Summerfest Vandross to Perform at Marcus Amphitheater," *Milwaukee Journal*, May 8, 1990; "Claiborne Plans a Birthday Bash," *Los Angeles Daily News*, August 30, 1990; Chrisena A. Coleman, "Here Comes 'Amen' Bride," *The Record*, February 3, 1990; J. D. Considine, "Whitney Houston's Latest Release Never Quite Ignites," *Sun Pop Music Critic*, November 6, 1990; Cary Darling, "Houston and Sure! Bring Back Ballads," *Orange County Register*, November 9, 1990; Cary Darling, "Vandross Wows Crowd with Ballads," *Orange County Register*, June 15, 1990; "Di, Charles Visit Spanish Royalty," *Atlanta Journal, Atlanta Constitution*, August 13, 1990; Robin Farmer, "A Day Late, Vandross Set Was Well Worth the Wait," *Richmond Times-Dispatch*, July 30, 1990; Leonard Feather, "Nat Adderley: The Other Brother Arrives Jazz," *Los Angeles Times*, August 16, 1990; "For Celebrities: Another Day in the Fishbowl," *Baton Rouge Morning Advocate*, January 26, 1990; Paul Freeman, "She Can Go 'Home' Again/Stephanie Mills," *San Francisco Chronicle*, March 11, 1990; "Get Luther Vandross Refunds by Friday," *Richmond News Leader*, August 1, 1990; Tom Gilatto, "Lifeline," *USA Today*, January 31, 1990; Calvin Gilbert, "Generic Production Nearly Claims Another Victim," *Baton Rouge Morning Advocate*, November 23, 1990; Gary Graff, "Vandross Looks at Career of Sex Appeal and Greatest Hits," *Los Angeles Daily News*, October 1, 1990; Gary Graves, "Isley Brothers Have Mellower Shout Now," *Washington Times*, September 13, 1990; Richard Harrington, "The Flip Side of Johnny Gill; The New Edition Star Takes a Solo Turn," *Washington Post*, July 1, 1990; Karen Harris, "Preview," *Dallas Morning News*, March 9, 1990; Chris Helm, "Class Act Luther Vandross at Star Plaza," *Chicago Tribune*, August 31, 1990; Robert Hilburn, "Lisa with an 'S'-for Soul England's Lisa Stansfield Gets Annoyed When People Make a Big Deal Over Her Being a White Soul Singer," *Los Angeles Times*, May 20, 1990; Edward Hill, "En Vogue Can Wail with Best Girl Groups," *Plain Dealer*, May 4, 1990; Edward Hill, "Vandross Captivates

Crowd," *Plain Dealer*, June 22, 1990; Geoffrey Himes, "Jamaica Boys Stay Within the Groove," *Washington Post*, August 10, 1990; Diane Holloway, "Awards Show 'By the People' Attracts Big Names," *Austin American-Statesman*, March 11, 1990; Dennis Hunt, "Marcus Miller Is Flying High as the 'Superman of Soul,'" *Los Angeles Times*, May 20, 1990; Barbara Jaeger, "Kids' Stuff a Gentleman and a Star," *The Record*, July 20, 1990; Barbara Jaeger, "Soulful Punch Over Pop," *The Record*, November 8, 1990; Robert E. Johnson, "Luther Vandross Tells How and Why He Lost 100 Pounds," *Jet*, June 11, 1990; James T. Jones IV, "Baker Takes to Jazz; She turns a New Leaf of Composure," *USA Today*, July 5, 1990; James T. Jones IV, "Johnny Gill, Rubbing Listeners the Right Way," *USA Today*, May 23, 1990; James T. Jones IV, "Old Lions of Jazz Still Have the Roar," *USA Today*, August 29, 1990; James T. Jones IV, "Pop Success Eludes Black Soul Singers," *USA Today*, April 17, 1990; James T. Jones IV, "Smokey Is Fired Up; Motown Legend Has Momentum; Robinson's Parade of Hits," *USA Today*, February 16, 1990; Steve Jones, "Music Doesn't Make Up for Muddled Logistics," *USA Today*, July 2, 1990; Mike Joyce, "Budweiser Superfest," *Washington Post*, July 2, 1990; Drew Jubera, "Apollo South from the Offbeat to the Off-Key, Stargazers Find Venue in Atlanta," *Atlanta Journal, Atlanta Constitution*, August 16, 1990; Dan Kening, "Luther Vandross Proves There Is Never Too Much of 'The Voice,'" *Chicago Tribune*, September 4, 1990; Jae-Ha Kim, "Right Here Waiting for the Respect That He Deserves," *Chicago Sun-Times*, January 28, 1990; Jae-Ha Kim, "Singer Dionne Warwick Looks for Young Viewers in Wee Hours," *Chicago Sun-Times*, January 25, 1990; Dave Luhrssen, "Vandross Knows What Pleases," *Milwaukee Journal*, July 3, 1990; Patrick MacDonald, "Recordings," *Seattle Times*, May 17, 1990; Patrick MacDonald, "Vandross Tour Ends on High Note," *Seattle Times*, October 1, 1990; Patrick MacDonald, "Vandross: Master of the R&B Form," *Seattle Times*, September 28, 1990; Dennis McDougal, "Mom and Dad Huxtable Do Vegas a Showroom Act by Bill Cosby and Phylicia Rashad Is Part of the Gaming Resort's Wooing of Families," *Los Angeles Times*, March 4, 1990; Cathy Milam, "Rock Star Heartthrob Craves Peers' Respect," *Tulsa World*, March 2, 1990; John Milward, "Neil Diamond Top Artist for Putting Couples in the Mood for Love," *Austin American-Statesman*, February 14, 1990; John Milward, "Tunes to Turn on By," *Toronto Star*, February 10, 1990; Rick Mitchell, "'80s Top Pop: Bruce, Prince, and Michael," *Houston Chronicle*, January 1, 1990; Kharen Monsho, "Keyboardist in Accord with Local Music," *Austin American-Statesman*, June 23, 1990; Steve Morse, "A July 4 Surfin' Safari at Otis Air Force Base," *Boston Globe*, June 8, 1990; Steve Morse, "A New Lady of Soul Quickly Takes Charge," *Boston Globe*, May 15, 1990; Steve Morse, "Silky Soul Stages a Sweet Return," *Boston Globe*, April 29, 1990; Steve Morse, "Starr's

Newest Kids 'Magic Man' of Teen Pop Turns More Acts to Gold," *Boston Globe*, May 10, 1990; Bonnie Newman, "New Voices on R&B Scene Dazzle Mosque Audience," *Richmond News Leader*, April 18, 1990; Bonnie Newman, "Pianist Alex Bugnon's Star Is Rising on a Grand Scale," *Richmond News Leader*, November 1, 1990; Bonnie Newman-Stanley, "Vandross Better Late Than Never? Not Really," *Richmond News Leader*, July 30, 1990; "Newsmakers," *Houston Chronicle*, July 1, 1990; Barry Patton, "Vandross' Concert Is a Real Smoothy," *Milwaukee Sentinel*, July 3, 1990; "People in the News," *Associated Press*, September 8, 1990; Chuck Philips, "Widening the Scope of Soul, Via Cable Donnie Simpson, Host of 'Video Soul,' Gives Viewers a Larger Glimpse of What Black Artists Are Really Like," *Los Angeles Times*, May 6, 1990; Patrick Pierce, "Weather and Crowd Cooled as 'Stars' Rose," *Richmond Times-Dispatch*, June 9, 1990; Mitch Potter, "Caribana: Hip-Hopping into the Present," *Toronto Star*, August 3, 1990; Tom Powell, "Yet-to-Be-Named Russian Show Dazzles Arena Officials," *Amusement Business*, June 11, 1990; Claudia Puig, "Successor Changes Formats Again Radio: KKBT Scrapped Classical Music for Rock, but Now It Has Switched to 'Urban Contemporary,'" *Los Angeles Times*, February 7, 1990; Claudia Puig, "Urban Contemporary Radio Is Catching On," *St. Petersburg Times*, March 18, 1990; David Ritz, [no title], *Rolling Stone*, September 6, 1990; Wayne Robins, "A Steamy Night with Vandross," *Newsday*, July 20, 1990; Jube Shiver, Jr., "Charting the Rise of 'Urban Contemporary' Radio: KKBT's New Format Has Launched It into Southern California's Top 10," *Los Angeles Times*, August 8, 1990; Fred Shuster, "Out on the Town: Ritenour, Tuning Up for Tour, Joins Notable Jazz Lineup," *Los Angeles Daily News*, May 25, 1990; Patricia Smith, "Wilson Spreads the Joy of Gospel," *Chicago Sun-Times*, March 30, 1990; "Some Other Visits to the Chapel of Love," *USA Today*, February 2, 1990; Brett Thomas, "Margaret Urlich," *Sun Herald*, March 25, 1990; Keith L. Thomas, "Bum Rap? Beyond Inner-City Roots, a Propulsive Lyric Force Enraptures and Enrages," *Atlanta Journal, Atlanta Constitution*, April 11, 1990; Dave Tianen, "Rock, Reggae, R&B at Big Gig's Big Top," *Milwaukee Sentinel*, June 22, 1990; Dave Tianen, "Summerfest Lineup Less Than Lustrous," *Milwaukee Sentinel*, May 11, 1990; Dave Tianen, "Vandross, Cray Are Added to Lineup," *Milwaukee Sentinel*, May 9, 1990; "Vandross Cancels, Adds Shows," *Richmond Times-Dispatch*, July 29, 1990; "Vandross Postpones Song Date at Front Row," *Plain Dealer*, January 23, 1990; "Vandross Refund Deadline Is Friday," *Richmond Times-Dispatch*, August 1, 1990; "Vandross Tired of Weighty Talk," *Houston Chronicle*, August 29, 1990; "Vandross, Barr Top Red Rocks 'Summer of Stars,'" *Denver Post*, April 20, 1990; Chris Verner, "Newsmakers Chuck Berry Faces Accusers After Raid," *Atlanta Journal, Atlanta Constitution*, June 29, 1990; Jeannie Williams, "Tom Hanks Lands Lead in 'Vanities,'" *USA Today*, January 11, 1990.

1991

Articles include: Patricia Bates, "Black Music Promoters Are Facing Same Problems as Others: Economy," *Amusement Business*, September 16, 1991; Patricia Bates, "Vandross' Tour," *Amusement Business*, September 9, 1991; Susan Bickelhaupt, "Rise of Urban Music Takes Its Toll on WILD," *Boston Globe*, June 14, 1991; Michael Blowen, "The Emmys Remember Landon," *Boston Globe*, August 19, 1991; Bruce Britt, "Vandross Tunes Vocals to Perfection," *Los Angeles Daily News*, October 31, 1991; Joe Brown, "'Power': Play from Vandross," *Washington Post*, September 13, 1991; Roger Brown, "Singer Shows Why He's Called King of Rhythm and Blues," *Plain Dealer*, December 2, 1991; Molly Carpenter, "Vandross Takes Darts with Humor," *Richmond Times-Dispatch*, September 11, 1991; Roger Catlin, "To Luther Vandross Fans, He's Always in Fine Shape to Vandross Fans, He's Off the Scale of Superstardom," *Hartford Courant*, September 27, 1991; J. D. Considine, "Luther Vandross Getting in Touch with Musical Feelings," *Baltimore Sun*, September 13, 1991; J. D. Considine, "Luther Vandross," *Portland Oregonian*, October 1, 1991; J. D. Considine, "New Album Displays Vandross' 'Power,'" *Baltimore Sun*, May 3, 1991; J. D. Considine, "Special Effects Can't Mask Vandross' Bravura Singing," *Baltimore Evening Sun*, December 16, 1991; J. D. Considine, "Vandross Puts His Heart in His Songs," *Chicago Sun-Times*, September 16, 1991; Mark Cooper, "Battle of the Bulge," *Q*, August 1991; Cary Darling, "Freddie Jackson Drives 'Em Wild," *Orange County Register*, April 27, 1991; Robyn L. Davis, "Marx Release Is OK, Again," *Richmond News Leader*, November 19, 1991; John Doyle, "Radio Nocturnes: Flip the Dial Most Evenings and Be Seduced into Slumber or Awakened to the Magic and Music of the Night," *Globe and Mail*, June 29, 1991; Julie Fingersh, "Miller-Sponsored Vandross Tour to Benefit Thurgood Marshall Fund," *Amusement Business*, July 1, 1991; Gary Graff, "'Mr. Love' Luther Vandross Leaves Political Themes to Other Singers," *Las Vegas Review-Journal*, November 7, 1991; Gary Graff, "Singer Still Plans to Stop for Love Luther Vandross Is Aware of Other Subjects, He Just Doesn't Care to Sing Songs About Them," *Kansas City Star*, October 18, 1991; Ernest Hardy, "Getting Emotional with Luther Vandross: R&B's Getting a Bad Rap," *Chicago Sun-Times*, October 15, 1991; Samuel Harps, "Love Ballads Keep the Listeners Swooning," *The Record*, October 6, 1991; Randolph Heaster, "The Voice Bewitches 10,000 Fans Luther Vandross Brings Silk and Power to a Rapt Kemper Crowd," *Kansas City Star*, October 22, 1991; Geoffrey Himes, "The Ballad of Luther Vandross," *Washington Post*, September 19, 1991; David Hinckley, "Corporate Sponsorship of Musicians Draws Heated Debate from Critics," *New York Daily News*, October 11, 1991; Dave Hoekstra, "Fans Soak Up Love Sponge Vandross' Stylish Soul," *Chicago Sun-Times*, October 17, 1991; Rob

Hoerburger, "Mr. Love's Lament: Luther Vandross, Master of the Romantic Ballad, Has a Stack of Platinum Albums. So Why Does He Feel So Unappreciated?," *New York Times Magazine*, September 22, 1991; Stephen Holden, "The Pop Life," *New York Times*; Marty Hughley, "Luther Vandross," *Portland Oregonian*, October 25, 1991; Marty Hughley, "No Doubt About It: They Love Luther," *Portland Oregonian*, October 29, 1991; Dennis Hunt, "Pop Music Downing Lacks Range, Emotion at the Strand," *Los Angeles Times*, June 24, 1991; Dennis Hunt, "Vandross: The Sheik of Shriek," *Los Angeles Times*, October 31, 1991; Esther Iverem, "Will Downing's 'Dream Fulfilled': Standing at Success' Door," *Newsday*, July 9, 1991; Connie Johnson, "Tasteful but Tame from Vandross," *Los Angeles Times*, June 9, 1991; Dean Johnson, "Vandross Fills Centrum with Romance," *Boston Herald*, December 21, 1991; Mary A. Johnson, "Few Blacks Find Room at the Top," *Chicago Sun-Times*, March 1, 1991; James T. Jones IV, "Albums in Tune with Tenderness," *USA Today*, May 30, 1991; James T. Jones IV, "Vandross Has the 'Power'; Album Moves Up Pop Chart," *USA Today*, June 19, 1991; James T. Jones IV, "Vandross' Silky, Sultry Power," *USA Today*, September 13, 1991; Dan Kening, "Marx's Spot a Unique Promo Tour Gives the Singer a Chance for Quick Hits," *Chicago Tribune*, November 8, 1991; Milton Kent, "Vandross Offers Uneven Evening of Love Songs," *Baltimore Evening Sun*, September 18, 1991; Tom Kessler, "Ringo Starr Classic Reappears on CD, Complete with Bonus Cuts," *Dallas Morning News*, April 28, 1991; Greg Kot, "Rhythm, Audience Returning to R&B—So Are Teenagers," *Chicago Tribune*, January 21, 1991; Greg Kot, "Vandross Uses Master's Touch to Weave Spell," *Chicago Tribune*, October 16, 1991; Peter Landsdowne, "Vandross Builds Power/'Love' Tour May Help Him Cross Over in Popular Music," *Sunday Telegram*, September 29, 1991; Cheryl Lavin, "Fast Track. Runners," *Chicago Tribune*, February 3, 1991; J. Leland, "At Play in the Fields of Love," *Newsweek*, June 24, 1991; Rhonda Chriss Lokeman, " 'Magic' Is More Heroic Than Fans Had Imagined Los Angeles Basketball Star Has, by His Announcement, Already a Long Way Toward Educating Blacks About AIDS," *Kansas City Star*, November 12, 1991; "Luther Vandross Gets Serious," *Dallas Morning News*, May 19, 1991; "Luther Vandross' New Single; Catch Sting on the Radio," *USA Today*, April 9, 1991; Patrick MacDonald, "Sweet-Sounding Luther Vandross Is Still Riding the Power of Love," *Seattle Times*, October 25, 1991; William R. Macklin, "Color Blind White Rockers Making Inroads with Black Fans," *Chicago Tribune*, June 27, 1991; Jimmy Mass, "Singer Takes Center Stage," *Austin American-Statesman*, December 12, 1991; Harriet McLeod, "Pop 1990: Classic to Controversial," *Richmond News Leader*, January 2, 1991; Larry McShane, "Quincy Jones Wins Six Grammys at 33rd Annual Grammy Awards," *Associated Press*, February 20, 1991; Larry Mc-

Shane, "The Best Stuff Never Gets on Television," *Associated Press*, February 21, 1991; Rick Mitchell, "Love Still Moves Balladeer Vandross," Houston Chronicle, May 26, 1991; Rick Mitchell, "Smooth Vandross Can Drop Gimmicks," *Houston Chronicle*, November 14, 1991; Steve Morse, "Pop Music Aims for the Funny Bone on Latest Releases," *Boston Globe*, May 12, 1991; David Nathan, "Vandross Gains Multiformat 'Power,'" *Billboard*, June 22, 1991; Alan Niester, "Power of Love: Luther Vandross," *Globe and Mail*, July 22, 1991; Alan Niester, "Soul Singer in the Classic Mold," *Globe and Mail*, December 13, 1991; Lynn Norment, "Love Power!: Luther Vandross Talks About the Ups and Downs of Love and Dieting and the Strains of Stardom," *Ebony*, December 1991; Ashley Norred, "A Good Song Still Plays in Harlem," *Insight Magazine*, March 25, 1991; Ashley Norred, "Apollo's Amateur Night Isn't for the Faint of Heart," *Washington Times*, March 18, 1991; Ken Parish Perkins, "Luther Vandross' 'Power of Love,'" *Dallas Morning News*, November 12, 1991; Tom Phalen, "For Vandross Fans, It Was a Smooth Night," *Seattle Times*, October 28, 1991; Steve Pond, "Luther Hears a Whoo!" *US*, September 1991; Howard Reich, "Queen of Soul Gets Ultimate Pop-Culture Honor: A Postal Stamp," *Las Vegas Review-Journal*, May 10, 1991; Wayne Robins, "Luther Vandross on the Buttons," *Newsday*, October 4, 1991; Wayne Robins, "No Future? Rap, High Gloss Pop, and Dance Music Have Come on Strong. The Rock Veterans Seem Played Out and the Young Guns Fire Blanks. The Audience Spreads Out, and Wonders Whether Rock Matters Any More," *Newsday*, February 17, 1991; Steven Rosen, "Soul Singers Becoming a Diminishing Resource," *Denver Post*, June 9, 1991; Patricia Smith, "Luther Vandross' Love Songs: On His First New Album in Three Years, He's Still Got What He Calls the 'Emotional Dynamic,'" *Boston Globe*, May 26, 1991; Patricia Smith, "Mo' Better Music from Lee?," *Boston Globe*, June 7, 1991; Patricia Smith, "Moved by the Passion of a Song," *The Record*, June 5, 1991; Patricia Smith, "Queen of Soul Is Cooking Again," *Toronto Star*, June 22, 1991; Patricia Smith, "Vandross: Too Dazzling for His Own Good?" *Boston Globe*, September 30, 1991; Eric Snider, "A Career Built on Love's Power," *St. Petersburg Times*, November 15, 1991; Eric Snider, "Love Notes Series: Pop Music," *St. Petersburg Times*, February 13, 1991; Eric Snider, "The Master of Love Songs," *St. Petersburg Times*, June 7, 1991; Eric Snider, "To Be Precise, 'Billboard' Changes," *St. Petersburg Times*, June 11, 1991; Eric Snider, "Vandross Sweeps Crowd Off Its Feet," *St. Petersburg Times*, November 22, 1991; William H. Sokolic, "Romantic Soul Singers Coming Back," *Tulsa World*, September 22, 1991; William H. Sokolic, "The Men of Soul Reach for Heart," *Orlando Sentinel*, October 5, 1991; Michael Specter, "Make or Break at the Apollo's Amateur Night," *San Francisco Chronicle*, January 4, 1991; Deborah Starr Seibel, "Williams Bridges the Generations with 'Soul of VH-1,'" *Chicago Tribune*, August 18, 1991; Otis Stokes, "Rap/Dance Trend Imperils Talent Pool: Real Artistry Is No Longer Required in Today's Music Industry," *Billboard*, August 3, 1991; Lenny Stoute, "Vandross in Full Control but at Expense of Passion," *Toronto Star*, December 13, 1991; "Vandross Out of Tune Romantically," *Chicago Sun-Times*, August 16, 1991; "Vandross Says Music Hurts Private Life," *Tulsa Tribune*, August 16, 1991; "Vandross' Love Life Light on Power," *Seattle Post-Intelligencer*, August 16, 1991; Barry Walters, "'Godfather of Rap' Opens at Kimball's East," *San Francisco Examiner*, February 8, 1991; Barry Walters, "With Vandross, Time Is in Suspense," *San Francisco Examiner*, October 25, 1991; Peter Watrous, "Look Out, New Jack, the Love Man's Back," *New York Times*; Peter Watrous, "The Sensuous Life, Lived to the Full," *New York Times*; Mike Weatherford, "Almost-Too-Laid-Back Vandross Gave Fans What They Came For," *Las Vegas Review-Journal*, November 9, 1991.

1992

Articles include: Vince Aletti, "Lexicon of Love: Luther Vandross, Babyface, Daryl Hall," *Village Voice*, November 9, 1993; Sylvia P. Flanagan, "Luther Vandross' Revealing Interview About His Expanding Entertainment Career," *Jet*, June 28, 1993; James T. Jones IV, "Luther Vandross, a First-Class Act," *USA Today*, September 7, 1993; Melissa Key, Rosemarie Lennon, and Dave La Fontaine, "Whitney's Wedding Wish: Give Me a Baby Now!" *Star*, August 4, 1992; Greg Kot, "Luther! Others Just Sing; He Seduces an Audience," *Chicago Tribune*, October 3, 1993; "Luther Vandross' Concert Fans Helped Him to Success While Some Superstars Flopped," *Jet*, December 30, 1991–January 6, 1992; Michael Musto, "La Dolce Musto," *Village Voice*, November 9, 1993.

1994

Articles include: Alan Black, Review of *Luther Vandross: Songs, Alternatives*, November 1994; Herb Boyd, "If Luther's Music Be the Food of Life . . ." *Class*, October/November 1994; Sylvia P. Flanagan, "Luther Vandross: Tells Why He Recorded Remakes on New Album," *Jet*, October 24, 1994; Stephen Holden, "Great Voices and Gilded Cages," *New York Times*, September 25, 1994; Steve Holsey, "The Crooner Just Can't Win," *Michigan Chronicle*, November 1, 1994; Gary Jackson, "Songs . . . In the Key of Luther"; "Luther Vandross: In a Class by Himself," *Ebony Man*, December 1994; Charles E. Rogers, "Luther Vandross: The Man, the Music, the Controversy," *Black Elegance*, November/December 1994.

1995

Articles include: Michael Eric Dyson, Review of *Anita Baker: Rhythm of Love*, *Rolling Stone*, February 23, 1995; David Hannah, "Luther Vandross Delights Crowd in Camden," *Philadelphia Tribune*, June 23, 1995; Dianne Williams Hayes, "Luther: Always & Forever," *Upscale*, February 1995; J. R. Reynolds, "Versatile Vandross Will Get Major Epic Push," *Billboard*, September 14, 1996.

1996

Rose Baker, "Luther Vandross: 'What a Show,'" *New York Beacon*, March 20, 1996.

1997

Peter Watrous, "In Vandross, Excellence as a Form of Rebellion," *New York Times*, October 10, 1997.

1998

Articles include: Anita M. Samuels, "Luther Vandross Keeps the Music Interesting on His 14th Set, 'I Know'; Bad Boy Gets . . ." *Billboard*; Shawnee Smith, "Virgin Is 'Know' Place for Vandross: Label Debut Sees Veteran R&B Crooner Diversifying," *Billboard*, July 11, 1998; "Luther Vandross Says That He's Ready for a Romantic Relationship," *Jet*.

1999

Florence Anthony, "Go with the Flo: Soul Train Awards Are Hottest Show in Town," *New York Amsterdam News*, April 1, 1999.

2001

Articles include: Jim Abbott, "Vandross' Smooth Voice Conquers Production That's a Bit Too Slick," *Orlando Sentinel*, July 13, 2001; Steve Appleford, "Mellow Romance from Vandross," *Los Angeles Times*, November 26, 2001; Dan Aquilante, "At the Top of the Voice; Luther Vandross' Self-Titled Disc Has Already Gone Gold," *New York Post*, June 29, 2001; Dan Aquilante, "Love, Luther," *New York Post*, February 13, 2003; Fred Bronson, "Vandross Makes It in with 'Out,'" *Billboard*, July 21, 2001; David Browne, "Oh Happy J; After a Lifetime in the Music Business, Clive Davis Was About to Get the Hook. But the Hitmaker Is Taking His Career—and J Records—Out for Another Spin," *Entertainment Weekly*, August 10, 2001; Simon Button, "I Know There Is Nothing Better Than Love," *The Express*, October 19, 2001; Cloe Cabrera, "Prime Time for Luther Vandross," *Richmond Times-Dispatch*, November 8, 2001; Cloe Cabrera, "R&B Crooner Vandross Is Chasing Pop Stardom," *Tampa Tribune*,

November 2, 2001; Cloe Cabrera, "Vandross Heats Up the Stage with His Slow-Burn Ballads," *Tampa Tribune*, November 6, 2001; Jessica Callan, Eva Simpson, Polly Graham, "3 AM—It's Luther Van-loss," *Mirror*, October 3, 2001; Roger Catlin, "He's Not Heavy, He's Got Soul: Luther Vandross' Weight Fluctuates, but Not His Talent," *Hartford Courant*, November 28, 2000; Ed Condran, "Making Necessary Changes; Vandross Shifts Weight, Music," *The Record*, October 26, 2001; "Cover Story: Luther Vandross," *Jet*, July 16, 2001; James Davis, "Cobbler to the Stars: Andre Rostomyan Knows That George Clooney Has Hairy Toes and Barbra Streisand Has Bunions," *National Post*, January 20, 2001; Sheila Edmundson, "Vandross Draws Big Crowd to the Civic Center," *Commercial Appeal*, November 5, 2001; Gary Eskow, "Ray Bardani and Luther Vandross," *Mix*, September 1, 2001; David John Farinella, "Marcus Miller," *Mix*, December 1, 2001; Mitchell Fink and Lauren Rubin, "Magazine's a Hit with 'Producers,'" *New York Daily News*, May 7, 2001; Mitchell Fink and Lauren Rubin, "Denise Out of Sight, but Not Out of Action," *New York Daily News*, February 22, 2001; Timothy Finn, "Vandross' Smooth Showmanship Backs a 'Fount of Liquid Soul,'" *Kansas City Star*, November 19, 2001; Michael A. Gonzales, "Staying Power," *Savoy*, November 2001; Renee Graham, "Vandross Stays True to Himself," *Boston Globe*, July 3, 2001; Isaac Guzman, "It's Vandross, More or Less: A Slimmed-Down Luther Plays Westbury with His Updated Style," *New York Daily News*, May 23, 2001; Rafer Guzman, "Vandross Likes it Hot," *Newsday*, March 2, 2003; Sean Hamilton, "MOBO Blow as Luther Pulls Out," *Daily Star*, October 3, 2001; Richard Harrington, "In the Age of Crass, Luther Vandross Maintains an Air of Romantic Class," *Washington Post*, June 7, 2002; Richard Harrington, "Never Too Much Luther," *Washington Post*, November 9, 2001; Leon Harris, "Recording Industry Executive Clive Davis Discusses His Career in Music," *CNN Morning News*, January 8, 2001; "Hotly Anticipated New Luther Vandross Album Out June 19th; Luther Vandross to Honor Whitney Houston on June 19th at BET Awards," *Business Wire*, June 15, 2001; "Hotly Anticipated New Luther Vandross Album Out Today June 19th; Luther Vandross to Honor Whitney Houston on June 19th at BET Awards," *Business Wire*, June 19, 2001; Ashante Infantry, "Vandross Wants to Go Pop—Popular Crooner Is Tired of Being Pigeonholed," *Toronto Star*, October 22, 2001; "Interview: Luther Vandross Is Finally Tackling His Weight Problem," *ABC News: World News Now*, July 11, 2001; Kevin C. Johnson, "Vandross' Performance Is Fine and Familiar," *St. Louis Post-Dispatch*, December 19, 2001; Ivor Key and Nigel Pauley, "Bitter End for Jennifer and Puff Lopez Dumps Puff on Valentine's Day," *Daily Star*, February 15, 2001; Michael Klein, "Sharing a Real-Life Temple Fairy Tale," *Philadelphia Inquirer*, November 4, 2001; Robert Lenzner,

"Steel Wrapped in Velvet When Bruce Springsteen, Bob Dylan or the Rolling Stones Have a Date in Court, They Call on Peter Parcher," *Forbes*, April 30, 2001; Jay Lustig, "Cool Passion—Concert of R&B Hits Displays a Vandross Smoothly Under Control," *Star-Ledger*, October 27, 2001; "Luther Produces Vintage R&B 'Vandross' Sound," *Patriot-News*, July 19, 2001; "Luther Vandross Arrives at #6 on Billboard's Album Chart with Critically Hailed New Album on J Records," *Business Wire*, June 27, 2001; "Luther Vandross Plans Book on Obesity," *AP Online*, July 19, 2001; Paul MacArthur, "Reappearing Act," *Down Beat*, August 1, 2001; Patrick MacDonald, "Luther Vandross, Lean and Versatile," *Seattle Times*, December 1, 2001; Patrick MacDonald, "Versatile Luther Vandross reaches beyond R&B," *Seattle Times*, November 23, 2001; Tracy Mack, "Sing for Your Supper? Vandross Can Help Jump-Start Your R&B Career at Wide-Ranging WGCI Seminar on Music Industry," *Chicago Tribune*, May 16, 2001; Ron Maxey, "Civic Center Hits Right Note with Latest Musical Acts," *Commercial Appeal Memphis*, November 11, 2001; Malcolm Mayhew, "Love Power; Veteran Balladeer Luther Vandross and New Soul crooner Maxwell; Bring Sounds of Sweet Nothings and Long-Lasting Romance," *Fort Worth Star-Telegram*, December 7, 2001; Brian McCollum, "Here & Now: After a 3-Year Break, R&B Legend Luther Vandross Is Back with a New Album, a New Label and a Reinvigorated Attitude," *Detroit Free Press*, August 31, 2001; Tara McKelvey, "The Lighter Side of: Ten Stupid Questions," Nia Ngina Meeks, "Under Vandross' Spell, Chrysler Crowd Slides Along Silky Smooth," *Virginian-Pilot and the Ledger-Star*, October 31, 2001; Nia Ngina Meeks, "Vandross Concert May Provide Needed Salve for Many," *Virginian-Pilot and the Ledger-Star*, October 26, 2001; Gail Mitchell, "Coming Back, Vandross Taps Young Writers, Producers," *Billboard*, June 11, 2001; Gail Mitchell, "The Rhythm the Rap and the Blues," *Billboard*, April 23, 2001; Gail Mitchell, "Veterans Luther Vandross, Miki Howard Are Back on the Scene," *Billboard*, April 28, 2001; Nakesa Mumbi Moody, "Svelte Sounds a Slimmer Vandross: Returns with Renewed Hopes for Crossover Success," *Grand Rapids Press*, August 30, 2001; Nakesa Mumbi Moody, "Luther Vandross Still Making 'Em Swoon," *Cincinnati Post*, December 27, 2001; Nakesa Mumbi Moody, "Back in Top Form—Slimmed-Down Vandross Looks to Regain His Platinum-Selling Ways," *Star-Ledger*, July 24, 2001; Nakesa Mumbi Moody, "After Long Break, Vandross Release Puts Him Back on Top of the Charts," *Commercial Appeal*, July 13, 2001; Nakesa Mumbi Moody, "Vandross Returns with a Youthful Sound," *AP Online*, July 12, 2001; Steve Morse, "Luther Vandross Is Still Doing Justice by His Brand of Soul," *Boston Globe*, October 21, 2001; Steve Morse, "Vandross Fills Wang with His Silky Soul," *Boston Globe*, October 23, 2001; "Multi-Platinum Music Icon Luther Vandross to Host Lady of Soul

Awards and Perform New Single 'Can Heaven Wait,'" *Business Wire*, August 20, 2001; Sonia Murray, "R&B King Vandross Aiming for Pop Crown," *Atlanta Journal-Constitution*, June 17, 2001; Sonia Murray, "Vandross Covets a 'Pop' Moment," *Atlanta Journal-Constitution*, June 19, 2001; Sonia Murray, "Vandross Maintains His Style; Sisqo Remains Radio-Friendly," *Atlanta Journal-Constitution*, June 19, 2001; Sonia Murray, "Music Industry Trumpets Clive Davis' Achievements," *Chicago Tribune*, January 10, 2001; Alan Niester, "Gone From the Spotlight, but Not Forgotten," *Globe and Mail,* October 27, 2001; Anastasia Pantsios, "Luther Vandross Drops Names and Carries a Tune," *The Plain Dealer*, October 26, 2001; Minal Patel, "The Rhythm Section," *Billboard*, May 12, 2001; Franklin Paul, "Don't Call Luther Vandross 'The Love Doctor,'" *Chicago Tribune*, November 29, 1996; "R&B Luminary Luther Vandross Hosts Intimate Press Brunch in Los Angeles," *Business Wire*, April 29, 2001; Guy Rickards, "Obituary—Robert Starer—The Most Prolific American Composer of His Generation," *The Guardian* May 5, 2001; Sarah Rodman, "Vandross Knows Sweet Success," *Boston Herald*, October 21, 2001; Melissa Ruggieri, "The Velvet Sounds of Vandross," *Richmond Times-Dispatch*, November 9, 2001; Hector Saldana, "An Evening of Romance; Vandross' Smooth Sound Comes to S. A.," *San Antonio Express-News*, December 7, 2001; David Segal, "The Man with the Golden Ear; at 67, Music Mogul Clive Davis Still Moves at the Speed of Pop and Can Spot a Hit a Mile Off," *Washington Post*, March 16, 2001; Pat Seremet, "Java," *The Hartford Courant*, January 8, 2001; Craig Seymour, "Soul Man," *Buffalo News*, October 19, 2001; Craig Seymour, "Vandross Is 'So Amazing,'" *Buffalo News*, October 23, 2001; David Sinclair, "Ladies' Man Going Solo—Arts—Music—Pop—Interview—Luther Vandross," *The Times*, December 4, 2001; Donnie Snow, "Settle in for Soulful Bliss with Osborne, Vandross in Tunica," *The Commercial Appeal*, January 12, 2001; Donnie Snow, "Vandross Puts Audience 'In the Mood,'" *The Commercial Appeal*, January 13, 2001; "Soul's Alive and Well," *The Malay Mail*, November 2, 2001; "Superstar Luther Vandross Visits Los Angeles in Preparation for Hot Debut with Clive Davis' J Records," *Business Wire*, April 26, 2001; Laurin Sydney, "Pre-Grammy Party Hottest Ticket in Town," *CNN: Today*, February 20, 2001; Jonathan Takiff, "Vandross, Still King of Romantic Soul: He's Got a New Album and a New Tour," *The Philadelphia Daily News*, October 25, 2001; Bell Tush, Mark Scheerer, Sherri Sylvester, Lori Blackman, Dennis Michael, "Life Imitates Art in 'State and Main'; Popular TV Shows Age-Defying Face Lifts," *CNN: Showbiz Weekend*, January 6, 2001; Simon Wheeler, "Luther Plays Cupid," *Daily Star*, February 9, 2001; Bill White, "Vandross Delivers Solid Night of Soul," *Seattle Post-Intelligencer*, November 30, 2001; Jeannie Williams, "Puffy Gives J. Lo musical Valentine," *USA Today*, February 8,

2001; David Yeats, "What's On—Music—Soul survivor," *Evening Mail*, March 30, 2001.

2002
Articles include: Dan Aquilante, "It's Thanks a Lot, Jacko!—Waves Off Performing at Awards Show," *New York Post*, January 10, 2002; Jon Bream, "Pop Music; Luther Vandross," *Star-Tribune Newspaper,* January 20, 2002; Jon Bream, "Sultry R&B style of Vandross Still Speaks Volumes," *Star-Tribune*, January 25, 2002; L. Z. Granderson, "Luther Vandross; Grand Rapids Concert Caterer Has Inside Scoop on Singer's Touring Life," *The Grand Rapids Press*, February 3, 2002; Keith Harris, "Love Will Prevail–At a Vandross Show," *St. Paul Pioneer*, January 25, 2002; Lamont Jones, "Brilliant Luther Vandross Give His All, Much to Benedum Audience's Delight," *Pittsburgh Post-Gazette*, January 15, 2002; "Jaguar of Troy Presents an Evening with Luther Vandross; Due to Overwhelming Demand, a Second Show Has Just Been Added on February 9," *PR Newswire*, January 15, 2002; Michael Miller, "Luther! When Loother Croons, Lovers Swoon (And Sometimes Squeal)," *The State*, January 25, 2002; Craig Seymour, "Vandross Serves Up Sophisticated Soul," January 28, 2002; Donna Isbell Walker, "Luther Vandross' Presence Glitz, Voice Smooth," *Greenville News*, January 21, 2002.

2003
Articles include: Tom Sinclair, "Lost Soul," *Entertainment Weekly*, October 17, 2003; Jill Smolowe, "Luther Sings Again," *People*, October 20, 2003.

2004
Articles include: Jamie Foster Brown, "Luther Vandross's Grammy Watch," *Sister 2 Sister*, March 2004; Lynne Duke, "The Rhythms of Two Lives; For Luther Vandross, the Songs Carry Him Back from a Devastating Illness," *Washington Post*, February 7, 2004.